CW01583374

LIFE IN THE NORTHERN DALES
Stories from a Farming Family

Frank Sanderson

ISBN-13: 978-1502865670

Printed by CreateSpace, an Amazon.com company

Also by the author:

Life and Times in Victorian Weardale: The Letters of Francis Vickers (2014)

Cuba 2015: Before the Americans Change it (2016)

CONTENTS

1. INTRODUCTION 1

2. WEARDALE, COUNTY DURHAM 7

The People of Weardale 8

The influence of the Church 9

The dialect 10

The Weardale Sandersons 11

3. THE SANDERSONS OF BISHOPLEY 13

John Sanderson of Low Bishopley (1725-1775) 13

John Sanderson of Milnhouses (1752-1835) 15

John Sanderson of Bishopley (1782-1865) 16
- Moving to Wolsingham Parish 17
- Sanderson Wandlis 18
- John's Marriage to Margaret Vickers from Pease Myers 18
- The Village of Hamsterley 19
- The Rev JG Milner and the Hamsterley Vestry Men 21
- Death of the Perpetual Curate 22

John and Margaret's children 23
- From High Shipley to Low Harperley 25
- The Stephenson Lasses 26
- Times of Great Change 30

4. A TRUE SON OF THE NORTHERN DALES 33

John Sanderson of Broomley (1821-1897) 34
- Marriage to Sarah Kipling 35
- Bradley to Broomley 38

5. THE FAMILY OF JOHN SANDERSON OF BROOMLEY 41

The Trials of Janey 42
- Avoiding a Scandal 43

The Trials of Ruth 50
- A Fracas and a Horse-whipping in Weardale 51

Frank Sanderson of Nafferton 53
- A Keen Horseman 56
- A Bit of a Swankpot 56
- William Sanderson 57
- Thomas Sanderson of Broomley 58
- Hannah Richardson Sanderson and Tom White 60

6. THE PLOUGHMEN 63

Accidentally burnt to death in school 63
- A Village in Mourning 64
- A Common Victorian Tragedy 65
- The Enduring Impact on the Family 67

The Samplers 69
The Victorian Era 72
The Double Wedding in 1855 73
Life on the Farm 73
Harvest Time 74
Speed the Plough 76
Ransomes' Ploughs 78
Plough Wars 80
Ralph Stothard in the Spotlight 82
Champion Ploughman marries Lizzie Sanderson 86
Infant Mortality 88
A School Board for Wolsingham 89
Back to Hamsterley 94
The Five Franks 95
7. THE PRODIGAL SON 97
John Sanderson of Burnigill 97
Marriage to Mary Eleanor Raine 97
Crook's Altar Farm 98
Highs and Lows 99
John's Annuity 100
Back to Ravensford 102
The Surviving Twin and the Maiden Aunt 102
Nellie and the Browning Birthday Book 104
Another Frank 106
John Sanderson 107
A Good Sort 107
The Decorated Policeman 108
A Very Sad Accident 109
The Inquest 111
Great Shock for Walter Dalton 112
8. A CANNY OLD FELLA 113
The Life and Death of William Henry 113
Frank's early ill-health 117
Bournemouth: the healthiest resort in all the land 117
Bishop Lightfoot's Example 120
Courtship and Marriage 123

Honeymoon at Whitley Bay ... 126
FJS and Ella ... 127
Having some fine times of it: holidays and leisure time ... 128
An Encounter with a Murderer ... 131
Chalk and Cheese ... 134
The recollections of Freda Ellis ... 134
Arthur Henderson's visit to Hamsterley ... 137
Nowadays, no-one gives a damn if you die or you don't ... 140
Edith's poor health ... 141
The Wearmouth Sisters ... 143
The end of an Era ... 145
The Surrogate Mother ... 146
A grand old gentleman ... 150
9. THE STEPHENSONS OF BEDBURN ... 153
Melancholy Deaths at Bedburn ... 154
Joseph Stephenson Junior's emigration ... 157
A Nice Old Boy ... 158
Death of Joseph Stephenson of Bedburn ... 160
George Stephenson ... 161
Rose Ellen Douglas ... 162
Thomas Stephenson ... 162
Death on Redford Bank ... 164
Matt Dodds, Jack Marquis, and Mary Jane Fatkin ... 167
Robberies with Violence ... 169
Mary Jane's Terrifying Accident ... 170
PC James Thompson ... 171
Tragic Death of Jack Marquis ... 173
Mary Jane's Second Marriage ... 174
Mary Jane's Puzzling Death ... 174
Matt Dodds Charged with Murder ... 175
The Sensational Trial ... 175
Verdict of "Guilty" ... 178
Execution after Appeal Fails ... 179
Postscript ... 181
10. THE SIMPSONS OF PENNINGTON ... 183
Highway Robbery ... 184

Clippings Days at Pennyton 185

The Teesdale Bard returns to Pennington 189
A Hard Life and an Agonising Death 191
Weardale's Salute to the Teesdale Bard 194

William Simpson and Mary Hankey 195

11. AYHOPE SHIELD AND THE MEETING OF THE GRAINS 197

"Ape Shield – it's where the Hankeys come from" 198

The Canons of the Third Prebend 199

The Letter from Richard Glass 203
The Captain and his Lady 206
The Newcastle-Edinburgh Steamboat 207

The Joannah Simpson Letter 208

Picnics at the Meeting of the Grains 213
Visits to Ayhope Shield and the Meeting of the Grains 213

12. AN ENGLISHMAN THROUGH AND THROUGH 219
The Impractical Lady Eleanor 219
Warming the bedclothes 220
Head-first in the watter! 221
The biggest dunce that ever went to school 222
The Old Man from Bedburn Lane 223

The Story of Little Titch 225
The Unpopular Farm Manager (Baron von Scheissen) 226
Little Titch and Peggy 226
The Rest of the Cast 227

Mischief at Hamsterley St James 230

A strict upbringing 230

The broken knee-cap 231

Afternoon tea at Kinninvie 232

The Cowley family 233

Buying and selling 233

An Englishman and proud of it 234

Brough Hill Fair 235
The Miners' Dispute 235
The Greatest Horse and Cattle Fair 235
Brough Hill Rascality 236
Rough Justice for Highwaymen 237
Kicking Jinny 238
The Pony with One Ear 238
A Sadder and Wiser Man 238
Horse-Dealer Disappears with Farmers' Cash 239
Violent Robbery 239

In Quest of Clydesdales 240
Seven in a Two-Seater Car 241
Visitors and friends 242
FJS's love of singing 244
Leaving the North-East 246
INDEX 249

ACKNOWLEDGEMENTS

This book has been 40 years in the making, ever since my father Henry Sanderson's death in 1974 triggered my curiosity about the Sanderson family. Many people have helped me over the years with personal memories, family photographs, and other memorabilia, and all of them became not only sources of information but also friends to whom I will always be grateful. Inevitably, many are now departed but I trust that through this book they and their life stories will be appreciated by a twenty-first century audience.

I am deeply grateful to the following individuals, many of whom are referenced in the text, who have helped me in a variety of ways: Francis Terrence Atkinson, Joey Brown Humes, my mother Elizabeth Sanderson née Chapman, Moses Chapman, Jackie Cousins, June Crosby, Walter Dalton, Frank Davey of Ontario, John Denby, Freda Ellis née Gibson, Valerie Glass, John Graham, Eileen Perkins née Hankey, Sheila Potter née Harrison, Henry and Connie Hewitson, Tom Hutchinson, Joan Keith of Canberra, John Perkins, Jon Preston, John Rueben Ross, my brothers Christopher Anthony Sanderson and Richard Chapman Sanderson, Nancy Sanderson née Reed, Nancy Sanderson née Rogerson, John Taylor Sanderson, Jack Sanderson of Stocksfield, Jenny Thompson née Sanderson, Jill Barber née Sanderson, Francis William and Thomas Sanderson, Margaret Monk, Mavis McLean née Sanderson, Elsie Tipler née Sanderson, Robyn Roper née Siddle, Marjory Cooper née Stephenson, Ena Gowland née Stephenson, Ken Stephenson, John Stothard of Pickering, Bill Swinbank of Carabooda, WA, Canon JSG Turnbull, Harry Vickers, Minnie Farage née Vickers, Joy Walker of Crook, Angela Watson of Carlisle, Essie Jewitt/Sanderson, née Wearmouth, Geoff Wearmouth, Mary Weir née Adkins, Mary Kathleen Douglas née White, Francis Vickers White, John White, and Fred Whitfield.

The internet has been a massive help to my research over the past 20 years, but I have also had invaluable assistance from staff at *inter alia*, Liverpool John Moores University Library, Durham County Records Office, Weardale Museum, Crown Street Library, Darlington, the Public Records Office, The London Probate Department, The Family Records Centre, London, and Durham University Library.

The inspiration for the book is my father's brother Francis Joseph Sanderson (FJS) of Hamsterley (1904-1993) whose reminiscences I tape-recorded in April 1980 at Vesey Farm, Great Holland, Essex. Over the course of three days, my uncle provided me with the bulk of the material for the book, recounting stories not only from his early life but also retelling family stories about events as long ago as 1834. Without him the book would not have been written and I accordingly express my deep gratitude to FJS and dedicate the book to his memory.

My wife Patricia has been a great help to this project in many ways. At the outset she was instrumental in the visit to Vesey Farm taking place at all. In April 1980, she was attending a three-day conference at the University of Cambridge and it provided an opportunity for me to drive her to Cambridge and continue on to Great Holland, and afterwards collect her for the return journey to Liverpool. Since then, Patricia has always been interested in and supportive of my project, not least over the past 18 months when I have often been preoccupied with completing the book. When you also include a frequent preoccupation with golf, you can understand my deep appreciation of Patricia's loyal forbearance.

Note: This book, originally published in November 2014, has now been updated and improved. A few corrections have been made and photographs together with about 10,000 words of new information have been added, much of which came to light as a consequence of correspondence with a number of people pleasantly surprised to read about the lives of their ancestors in the Northern Dales.

Frank Sanderson,
30th June 2016
Liverpool

1. INTRODUCTION

When I first became interested in family history in the 1970s, I acquired a slim paperback book on "how to trace your ancestors". On the first page I noted the following:-

> The art of tracing a family tree, genealogy, covers a much vaster hunting ground than may be apparent. The aim is not glory, fortune or the discovery of royal blood, but the fun and the absorbing interest of tracing 'one's own', with perhaps a little notoriety thrown in for good measure and certainly a few surprises – some not particularly welcome.[1]

Tracing one's own certainly opens up a vast hunting ground, well beyond the creation of a family tree full of names with dates of births, marriages and deaths. Once I began the research, I became increasingly interested in local history, the social, economic and cultural context within which our ancestors lived their lives. The history books and school history syllabuses have tended to focus on national and international history, on the rise and fall of great empires and on the wars and battles that have shaped our world. In recent times, local history has become more mainstream, not least because of the dramatic rise in the popularity of genealogy and the production of a wealth of information about the sometimes extraordinary lives of ordinary people. As I have written elsewhere:-

> Alongside the great events of history, there was a parallel universe occupied by the vast majority of English people, the vast majority of our ancestors. This universe until recent times conducted most of its business in small tightly knit rural communities and, although the history of these communities appears less glamorous and less important than the momentous events described in history books, there is nevertheless a great fascination for many people today in discovering more about the lives of their unsung ancestors. Indeed, researching family history soon uncovers countless people of extraordinary talents and provides the family historian with the opportunity to collate and record information about them for posterity.[2]

I first became interested in family history after my father Henry Sanderson died in 1974 at the age of 53. There was no Will, and I was appointed the Administrator of the Estate. Among his few personal possessions was a dog-eared bundle of postcards that had been collected by his mother, Edith Sanderson née Stephenson. They had been sent to Edith at Hamsterley between 1902 and 1918, from shortly before she was married in 1904 until 4 years before her death from pneumonia in 1922. After Edith died, the postcards were carefully preserved by her husband Frank Sanderson of Hamsterley until his death in 1955. At the time of his death, Frank was living with his son Henry, and Henry Sanderson in turn inherited the postcards. Typically, ephemera such as postcards which have little intrinsic worth are thrown out when the owner dies – I therefore have not only my father but my grandfather to thank for preserving this legacy of a bygone age, a legacy which served to awaken my interest in local and family history.

---

[1] Meda Mander (1977) *How to trace your ancestors*. St Albans, Mayflower Books

[2] Frank Sanderson (2012) *Life and Times in Victorian Weardale: The Letters of Francis Vickers* (Amazon) p.1

In 1977, I began reading books on family history, and thereafter, began visiting family history archives such as the County Records Office in Durham, and the Public Records Office and Somerset House[3] in London. I also visited churchyards at Stanhope, Wolsingham and Hamsterley in search of relevant monumental inscriptions. I also began talking to older members of the family and visiting previously unknown cousins in the NE of England.

1-1 Francis Joseph Sanderson (FJS) in 1978, aged 74

The most fruitful meeting with an older relative was with Francis Joseph Sanderson (FJS) in April, 1980 at Vesey Farm, Great Holland, Essex. Born in 1904 in Bedburn, near Hamsterley in County Durham, he had an amazing memory, a strong streak of romanticism, a yearning for immortality, and was loquacious enough to provide me with over 4 hours of taped interviews without any difficulty. He'd also had a particularly interesting life. The interviews provide a significant part of the narrative of this family history, and I believe that he knew I was going to write about family history before I did.

I also made contact at that time with Jack Sanderson of Stocksfield in Tynedale, my third cousin, thereby re-establishing contact with a part of the family with which there had been no links for over 50 years. I also met and corresponded with Essie Sanderson née Wearmouth of Toft Hill, the widow of my cousin Frank Sanderson, and with Minnie Farrage née Vickers of Durham, my third cousin, once removed. They both gave me valuable information about the Sanderson and Vickers families and a large number of priceless photographs - although unfortunately I have no photographs of my g.g. grandparents, Minnie Farrage gave me photos of g.g. grandmother Margaret Vickers' nephew, Frank (1822-1903) – pictured on the previous page with his wife, Mary Bowman, and Margaret's brother and my g.g. Uncle Joseph (1790-1885). I thus acquired a vivid connection with my Weardale kin from the eighteenth century. Although people generally have contact with first cousins, contact between succeeding generations is usually limited or non-existent, despite the shared heritage which often extends to shared Christian names down through the generations. In our family, the names Francis and John are recurrent names: I have, for example, a g.g.g.g.g. grandfather Frank Little, a g.g.g. grandfather Frank Vickers, a g.grandfather Frank Sanderson, a grandfather Frank Sanderson, an uncle Frank Sanderson, and first, second and third cousins called Frank Sanderson.

My second cousin John Taylor Sanderson of Benton, Newcastle, has a g.g.g.g. grandfather, a g.g.g. grandfather, a g.g. grandfather, a grandfather, an uncle, and first, second and third cousins all called John Sanderson.

Additionally, there are many other members of the family through female lines that have Frank as a Christian name as a consequence of marriage to family members, e.g., Francis

[3] Probate Records were kept at Somerset House at that time.

Terrence Atkinson, recently of Colchester[4], and Francis Sanderson Stothard[5], recently of Driffield in Yorkshire.

Shortly after the interviews with FJS, the family history research was put to one side for a dozen years. It was only when I was asked to give the address at FJS's funeral in Great Holland, Essex in 1993, thereby requiring me to listen to the tapes of FJS's reminiscences, that my interest in family history was rekindled.

FJS had a younger sister, Ella, and a much younger brother, Henry (my father). Sadly, both Auntie Ella and my father died before my interest developed in family history, and so their accounts can only be pieced together from second-hand sources. Another regret is that although FJS had helped me assemble much priceless information about the family, and had made the following observations in one letter in February 1978, "How very pleased I was to receive all these papers about the history of Hamsterley and our forefathers. It is all so very interesting", he did not live to see a written version of the family history. I'm sure he would have been more than pleased, particularly as he contributed so much to its creation.

Having researched the historical context in which several generations of the family have lived their lives it has struck me just how typical a North Country tenant farming family they have been. They can be traced from the early eighteenth century as hill-farmer/miners on the bleak Bollihope Burn near Stanhope. The Britain of the early 1700s was predominantly agricultural and covered in woodland, with a population of circa 8 million.[6] By the end of the eighteenth century, through a mixture of ability, hard work and good fortune, the Sandersons had become well established and successful tenant farmers and key players in their communities:-

1-2 Joseph Vickers of Howl John (1790-1885) and his son, Francis Vickers (1821-1903) with Mary (Bowman) of Belle Vue Farm, near Stanhope.

---

[4] Son of Richard Thomas Atkinson and Eleanor Eliza Sanderson

[5] Son of Francis Sanderson Stothard and grandson of Ralph Stothard and Elizabeth Eleanor Sanderson.

[6] By 1914, the population had reached 45 million.

> Paying rent to the landowners and providing employment for a huge population of landless agricultural labourers, the farmer's position in rural society was central. Furthermore..., by forming an important clientele for village shopkeepers and tradesmen, farmers contributed more widely to the whole fabric of rural society.[7]

Over time, some of the family moved down the Wear Valley to the Hamsterley area, then branching out to Tynedale and beyond. In the nineteenth century, their fortunes largely reflected the prevailing economic conditions for North Country farmers, with more or less tough times after about 1815 followed by an unprecedented period of prosperity in the third quarter of the century, a prosperity which sustained many of them until well into the twentieth century. This meant that the economic difficulties which beset many farmers from the late 1870s did not fully impact on the family until after the First World War - with the exception of John Sanderson (1862-1939) who had the misfortune not only of beginning his farming career during the agricultural depression of the late 1870s but also of having a damaging attraction to drinking and gambling

A number of kinfolk from Weardale migrated to Australia in the mid-Victorian period, including my great grandfather's cousins Joseph Vickers and Jane Siddle née Vickers in the 1850s, my grandfather's cousin, John Stephenson in the 1870s, and my grandmother Edie's half-brother Joseph Stephenson in the 1880s. Two other cousins of my great grandfather, George and Thomas Vickers, migrated to Ontario in the mid-nineteenth century,[8] and two of John Sanderson of Broomley's grandchildren, John George and Mary Hannah Sanderson, immigrated to Saskatchewan in the early years of the twentieth century. Today, there are numerous descendants of these migrants in Australia, New Zealand, Canada and America.

From the 19th Century many struggling Scottish and North Country farmers migrated to Essex where farms could be rented very cheaply. Unlike their southern counterparts who had abandoned the land in large numbers, they were able to succeed through their sheer efficiency, hard work and ability to "cut their cloth". Francis Joseph Sanderson (FJS, 1904-1993) joined this migration in the 1930s, linking up with the Race family who had left Teesdale along with many others earlier in the century. He was joined in the 1940s by his elderly father Frank, his sister Ella Atkinson, and brother Henry.

> **Essex (is) a county said to have suffered depression much worse than any other in the kingdom. Essex farms that were heaviest in character went very generally out of cultivation early in the eighties and the fact that they were going a-begging became so notorious that a large number of Scotch dairy farmers came down and took them.**[9]

Like many successful tenant farmers, they have invariably been members of the Church of England, with several being Church Wardens in the last 200 years. As Methodism took a firm hold on the labouring class of the Durham Dales, farmers such as the Sandersons

---

[7] Eveleigh, D.J. (1996) *The Victorian Farmer*, p 3. Princes Risborough, Bucks., Shire Publications.

[8] Joseph Vickers and Jane Siddle (Australia) and George and Thomas Vickers (Canada), all originally from Stanhope, feature prominently in my book, *Life and Times in Victorian Weardale: The Letters of Francis Vickers*, published in 2012.

[9] *Bristol Mercury*, March 29, 1894.

experienced a growing gulf between them and their farm workers, a gulf accentuated by the influence of Methodism on the growth of the labour movement. And being farmers, they were most often staunchly conservative in politics. Grandmother Edith Sanderson was Secretary to the Conservative and Unionist Party in Hamsterley before the First World War at a time when there were growing concerns about the developing labour movement. During one election campaign, Edith had the dubious distinction of chasing Arthur Henderson (MP for Barnard Castle and future Nobel Peace Prize winner) out of the village by throwing sods at him. Edith and her kind were accustomed to employing farm workers who did what they were told and they certainly did not relish the prospect of the labouring class becoming organised.

Despite their relative prosperity and the relatively better sanitary conditions in rural communities throughout the nineteenth century (as compared with the burgeoning towns and cities), the Sanderson family seems to have had more than its fair share of premature deaths. Great great grandparents John and Margaret Sanderson were pre-deceased by four of their five daughters, including Jane who was burnt to death at Hamsterley School in 1834 aged eight years. And great grandparents Frank and Eleanor Sanderson lost five of their eight children during infancy, including four-year-old William Henry who died of croup in his sister Lizzie's arms in 1875. Although medical treatment was at best rudimentary during the nineteenth century, the misfortune of my great grandparents seems to have been at least partly attributed by the family to the dangerous impracticality of Eleanor.

In contrast, a number of the family lived to a ripe old age. John and Margaret were 83 and 84 when they died in the 1860s, Frank and Eleanor, 87 and 78, and grandfather Frank Sanderson 87 when he died in 1955. His cousin, Frank Sanderson of Nafferton died in 1934 aged 82 and was described in his obituary as coming from "a long-lived family".

One of the greatest achievements of nineteenth century Britain was the coming of the railways. John and Margaret Sanderson were in their early forties when George Stephenson's *Locomotion* first travelled from Stockton to nearby Darlington in 1825 and they no doubt experienced the wonder and convenience of this new form of travel. But it would have been their children and grandchildren who most benefited from the ability to travel on relatively long excursions and return within the day, to transport livestock quickly and cheaply, and to travel to the seaside and spa towns for holidays and recuperation with great convenience. There are no records to confirm it but it is likely that members of the family travelled to London in 1851 to see the Great Exhibition at Hyde Park; inexpensive excursions to the exhibition from all parts of the country were extremely popular, and six million people attended. There are however postcard records of family trips to Saltburn-by-the-Sea, Whitley Bay, Redcar and Whitby, as well as to Harrogate and Knaresborough in the early years of the twentieth century.

The first half of the twentieth century saw a continued exodus from the land and increased difficulty for many tenant farmers in making a decent living. Those that would succeed, such as Francis Joseph Sanderson and John George Sanderson, migrated to pastures new, whereas many other family members began to embrace a variety of careers unrelated to farming. So a family who for generations had worked the soil and been governed by the rhythm and vagaries of the seasons took on new directions and new challenges after the Second World War. Their stories remain to be told.

For this book, the reminiscences of Francis Joseph Sanderson are central to the narrative. The material in Chapters 1-4 provides some historical context about the Sanderson of Weardale, and FJS would have been entirely unaware of the detail. His contribution is evident from Chapter 5 onwards where I have used historical records to elaborate on and supplement the information contained in the taped interviews.

Many of FJS's stories, together with local stories I have extracted from Victorian newspapers, are laden with tragedy, with very few "good news stories". Thus, alongside one idyllic story about picnics at the Meeting of the Grains at Ayhope Shield (See p.213), there are accounts of tragic deaths of children resulting from, for example, croup, clothes catching fire, and accidental gun-shot wounds, and untimely deaths of adults from disease, suicide, murder, drowning – and accidental gun-shot wounds. This is not altogether surprising, given that family tragedies tend to stay vividly in the memory, and that newspapers then, as now, saw tragic and sensational stories as particularly newsworthy.

In summary, the book has evolved from the hours of tape-recorded interviews with my Uncle Frank Sanderson in 1980. He ranged far and wide in his reminiscences, touching on stories he'd been told of events which had occurred long before he was born and stories focusing on his life in Hamsterley before he moved to Essex in 1929. He made frequent reference to childhood friends, cousins, uncles and aunts, farmers and village characters, in the process providing me with ample material to organize, contextualize and supplement for this book. The result is a mixture of family and local history which should appeal not only to family historians but also to anyone interested in the history of the Northern Dales, of lives and times long departed.

2. WEARDALE, COUNTY DURHAM

Weardale is situated in County Durham – a county of England, lying on the German Ocean, and bounded by Northumberland, Cumberland, Westmorland, and Yorkshire. It is about 40 miles in length and 30 in breadth, and contains 1 city, 8 market towns, and 113 parishes. It is hilly, and some points are nearly 2000 feet high. There are wide moors amongst the hills and other tracts completely uncultivated. There are some islands on the coast, Holy Island being the largest. The coast is cliffy in some parts; other parts are shelving sands. The principal rivers are the Wear, the Tees, the Tyne, and the Derwent. Coal, iron, lead, mill-stone grit, limestone, &c.;, are found here abundantly. The east and south parts of the county are fruitful in corn and pasture, and have a milder air than the other parts. It sends to other parts of the United Kingdom, and to foreign countries, both its native productions, and the goods it manufactures, such as coarse woollen goods, sail-cloth, steel, glass, iron, &c.; &c.; This county was formerly under the special jurisdiction of the bishop of Durham as a Prince Palatine, but in 1836 the palatinate was vested in the crown. Population, 342,284.[10]

From at least the late sixteenth century, the Sanderson family has been located in Weardale and the surrounding region. During the seventeenth century, the direct family was centred on Stanhope and settlements to the south-west, then moved down the Wear valley to Wolsingham and Hamsterley in the eighteenth century, and then branched out to Teesdale, Tynedale and well beyond during the nineteenth and twentieth centuries. Though now widely dispersed, the family retains strong links with south-west Durham and Tynedale.

2-1 Old drovers' road in Upper Weardale

An ancient poem describes towns and villages which have been very familiar territory to the family for 300 years:-

Hamsterley hunger town, stands on a hill
Witton-le-Wear lies in a gill
Wolsingham is full of pride, and that's a donnet,
Frosterley is hungered but has a good stomach,
Shittlehope side stands in a raw,
But Stanhope's the bonniest town of them a'.

Weardale is the upper valley of the Wear, extending as far down as the eastern outskirts of Wolsingham, the earliest 'capital' of the Dale. It is an area of considerable mineral wealth - lead, ironstone, a little silver, and limestone, and this has been exploited since

[10] From *Barclays Complete and Universal English Dictionary*, 1842

Roman times, but mainly after the Norman Conquest. By the late sixteenth century, stock farming became a major activity, and many of the dale's farmers supplemented their precarious income by working in the quarries or becoming miners for the London Lead Company, founded in 1692, whose headquarters was in Stanhope.

The People of Weardale

A mid-nineteenth-century writer said of the people of Weardale,

> There is a strong good feeling and a deep sincerity to be found among them. The occupation of mining naturally leads to reflection... they are marked by a firm spirit of independence; and many of them evince considerable intellectual activity and acquirements.

More recently, June Crosby has written:-

> Undoubtedly, the isolation of the Dale, the dangers of mining, the hazards of quarrying and the unpredictable fortunes of farming have helped create an independent, caring and versatile community and one with a wonderful sense of place. Life for many was hard until after the last war, yet resilience and creativity emerged, backed by the Methodist ethos.[11]

Life has been hard over the centuries in the Durham Dales. Before global warming, winters were long and the weather was often harsh. Very cold weather, blizzards, and deep snow, less common recently, made winters especially difficult for the farmer, who was unlikely to have had the convenience of running water and electricity until after WW2.

2-2 Front Street, Stanhope in winter (courtesy of June Crosby).

[11] From *Weardale in Old Photographs*, June Crosby, Stroud, Alan Sutton Publishing, 1989.

The influence of the Church

Weardale was part of the remote western estates of the Bishops of Durham and the activities of hunting, stock rearing and mining were controlled by ecclesiastical officers "of varying quality and integrity". The involvement of the established church, the predominant (absentee) landowners, in the affairs of Weardale over the centuries continued to have an impact until well into the twentieth century. There was a strong non-conformist ethos in the dale fuelled by resentment and hostility to the Anglican Church which was viewed as exploitative and responsible for many of the area's problems. This helps to explain the behaviour of Joseph Walton (Jos) Coatsworth, a Hamsterley man who was known to shout abuse at the Rev John Holliday in the early years of the twentieth century, a story recounted on page 223. Alcohol undoubtedly played its part but the fact that it was the vicar in particular who was the recipient of the abuse is telling.

There was a keen rivalry between the Anglicans and the Dissenters:-

> Although some families (labelled 'devil dodgers') attended both Church and Chapel, and thereby had a foot in each of the competing religious camps, in many cases rivalry between the two groups was bitter. Nonconformists resented the privileged position of the Church and called for its disestablishment, while Anglican clerics regarded their Nonconformist counterparts as members of an inferior breed.[12]

Whereas the typical Victorian tenant farmer was a smallholder, farming less than 50 acres, the Sandersons were working much bigger farms. Frank's father John farmed 140 acres in the 1850s, Frank himself farmed 350 acres, and his brother John of Broomley eventually farmed 800 acres. They, like the typical landlord, were Church of England rather than the usual Weardale chapel goers. Souden quotes an observer:-

> In the chapel gather "ungenteel" farmers, usually the smaller tenants, artisans, and shopkeepers, with a sprinkling of 'free' labourers and farm servants. The congregation taken in the bulk is worth much less money than in the parish church, and the dissenting parson is in many ways the same as his hearers. "Oh, we don't mind the minister, he is just like one of ourselves," the cottager will say.[13]

Better off tenant farmers and the yeomanry tended to have a strong sense of social responsibility which led many to take an active part in parish life. John Sanderson and his grandson, Frank Sanderson of Hamsterley, were Churchwardens at St James Hamsterley for many years, and appear to have aligned themselves with the landowning 'gentleman farmers'. With their important place in village life, providing work not only for agricultural labourers but also for many village craftsmen, they appear to have had a well-developed sense of their status in the village. FJS observed that his father and grandfather would certainly have expected the ordinary villager to touch his cap in greeting. His grandfather in particular was a proud man who expected deference from his workers and due respect from landlords or perhaps more precisely, landlords' agents.

---

[12] Pamela Horn (1976) *Labouring Life in the Victorian Countryside*. (p.165)

[13] Souden, David (1991) *The Victorian Village.* Collins & Brown

Their Vickers kin in the heart of Weardale were equally successful farmers but notably more radical and liberal in their conduct and politics. The Sandersons were Tories and supporters of the established Church, eager to preserve the status quo and fearful of the labouring classes becoming restless. On the other hand, the Vickers family in general terms, were radical democrats, dissenters, Liberals, intent on promoting social reform, although no doubt enjoying the powerful position they held and the respect they were accorded in their community.

The dialect

The South-West Durham dialect has many variations but the words and sounds can be placed on a continuum which extends from Tyneside to North Yorkshire. It is also constantly changing and will be noticeably different today from what it was, say fifty years ago, particularly in the use of dialect words.

There is reference in this history to the local pronunciation of common English words such as 'water' being pronounced 'watter' to rhyme with 'matter' (by FJS, who had not lived in the North-East for 50 years when he used the expression), and to the use of the northern dialect word 'canny' to mean 'nice' rather than the usual Scottish use meaning 'shrewd' (farmworker Jackie Cousins liked my grandfather and described him as 'a canny old fella', although I am sure he was also 'canny' in the Scottish sense). John Taylor Sanderson describes how his Aunt Lizzie used the word 'ket', a north-country dialect word meaning 'rubbish', to describe bought cakes. The local variation in dialect usage is evidenced by this word with which I was entirely unfamiliar, even though Hamsterley where Aunt Lizzie lived was only 4 miles from St Helens Auckland where I grew up.

The Wear Valley dialects which I remember from my youth were quite distinct from the Geordie dialect, despite the fact that people from outside the region tend to classify all Durham and Northumberland residents as Geordie. This was exemplified by a television drama about West Auckland FC winning the 'World Cup', *The Sir Thomas Lipton Trophy*, by beating Juventus in 1909. All the characters had Geordie accents, thereby ruining the authenticity for any viewers from that part of County Durham.

It was not only the words used and the pronunciation of the words which was distinctive about the dialect. It was also the way in which words were used in phrases and sayings, some examples of which can be gleaned from the postcards preserved by Edith Sanderson née Stephenson.

In 1908, Edith's friend Eva Lowson wrote that she would walk over to see her "if it be fine on Tuesday". Similarly, Nellie from Hunwick told Edith that she would be up to Hamsterley the next day "if the day be fine".[14]

In 1908, Frank Sanderson of Nafferton described FJS as "a fine little chappie", having been sent a photo of him. There are many examples of the use of Scottish words and phrases in the North-East, and this appears to be an example. Another comes from Rose Ellen Douglas who had moved to Newcastle in 1909 when young Frank and Ella would have been 5 and 2 years old respectively. In a postcard to Edith in 1911, she sent her love

---

[14] Frank Davey of Ontario observes, "The friends of your grandmother Edith were writing a very correct form of English, the subjunctive mood, and one that is more precise than the forms that have replaced it for most people today. Fascinating how once very correct usage can begin to sound quaint."

to "the bairnies", who she guessed would "have grown out of all knowing" (possibly another Irish idiom).

In 1910, Eliza Stephenson née Beadle was on holiday in Redcar and wrote to her grandson FJS, "… I hope you will gather a lot of brambles again I come home." Here the phrase "again I come home" means "by the time I come home again".

In 1905, Edith wrote to her cousin Emma Swinbank[15], "…we are having some fine times of it", which sounds Irish in origin, quite probable given the large influx of Irish immigrants to County Durham throughout the nineteenth century.

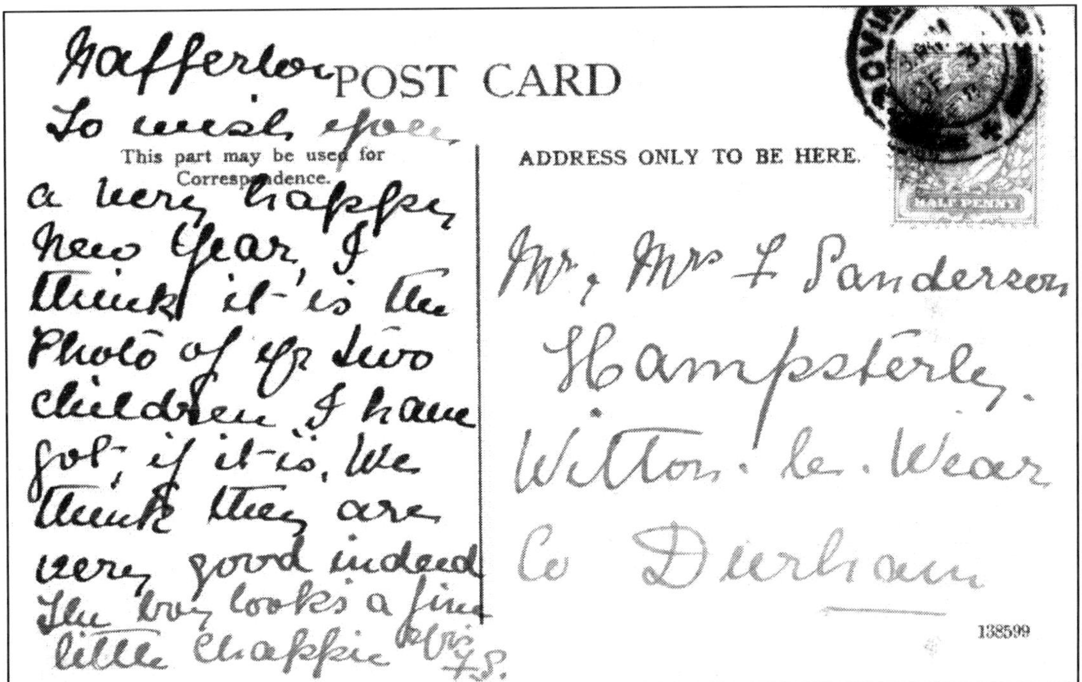

2-3 Postcard from 1908 from Frank Sanderson of Nafferton to his cousin Frank Sanderson of Hamsterley. The "fine little chappie" is FJS (See p.54).

The Weardale Sandersons

The Sandersons of Weardale probably originated in Normandy rather than, as might have been expected, in Scotland. "Sanderson" is a Scottish name with Scandinavian connections, deriving from "Ale**xander's son**".

It is possible that the family name did derive from "the son of Alexander", but the Alexander in question was Alexander de Biddick[16], a nobleman of Norman descent. Alexander had lands between Chester-le-Street and Sunderland, with the family seat being at Biddick Hall, situated about a mile east of Lambton Castle. As the de Biddick family became more and more anglicised during the fourteenth century, Alexander decided to bestow an English name on his son James. James de Biddick, Alexander's son thus became James Sanderson.

[15] Emma Swinbank was the daughter of Joseph Swinbank and Elizabeth (Simpson) who 'eloped' in 1871 (See p.184). Elizabeth was the half-sister of Edith's mother Eliza (Simpson)

[16] de Biddick was variously spelt 'de Beddick' and 'de Bydick'

There are records of the Sanderson family from over 400 years ago in the Wear Valley. For example Agnes Sanderson was married to Raphe Wilburn on Monday, August 1, 1597, and Steven Sanderson to Alyce Follansby on Saturday, 23 May, 1609, both marriages taking place at St James' Church, Hamsterley. On 10 November, 1605, Allison, the daughter of John Sanderson of "Hamsterley by Bishop Auckland" was christened. Whereas it is possible that they and the de Biddick Sandersons are direct ancestors, it has proved difficult to verify the connections with the eighteenth century Sandersons of Weardale.

There are several branches of the Sanderson family of Weardale and many are not recorded here – I have tended to focus on verifiable descendants of the eighteenth century Bollihope Burn Sandersons and then mainly on my direct ancestry. Thus for example, I do not include much information about the Sandersons of Thimbleby Hill[17], of Aller Gill, of Low Doctor Pasture or of Newlandside. One distinctive Sanderson Christian name from the Bollihope Burn in the eighteenth century is 'Lancelot' but I have not investigated his line. The name recurs across several generations locally and is recorded elsewhere in England and also in Australia.

2-4 Map of County Durham showing many of the places mentioned in the book. A more detailed map of Hamsterley and district is on p.197

[17] In his Will of 1756, Thomas Sanderson's dwelling at Thimbleby Hill is described as "Thimellbohill", providing an indication of local pronunciation in those days.

3. THE SANDERSONS OF BISHOPLEY

John Sanderson of Low Bishopley (1725-1775)

Great great great great grandfather John Sanderson was born at Low Bishopley, a hamlet 2½ miles south-east of Stanhope and a mile south of Frosterley, in 1725. This was during the reign of King George I and was the year in which Peter the Great of Russia died and in which The Black Watch Regiment was founded.

It was also the year in which the Joseph Butler became Rector of Stanhope:-

> Stanhope's most famous incumbent was the saintly Joseph Butler (Rector 1725-40) who held that office together with the bishopric of Bristol which was then worth only £400 per annum. Butler was elected Bishop of Durham in 1750 but survived less than two years in the post. He had however written *Analogy of Religion* (1736), seeking 'the Way of the Truth', and a classic of Anglican theology.... His ill-health may have made him pessimistic, but he may also have been despondent to observe how the enthusiasm of the frequent visits of the evangelistic John Wesley from the 1740s onwards had captured the imagination of the county.[18]

3-1 St Thomas's Church, Stanhope, where John Sanderson of Bishopley was baptised and where he married Elizabeth Emerson in 1744

John had forebears called John and the name "John" has appeared in every generation of the Sanderson family up to the present day.

John Sanderson spent his early life in Low Bishopley and, no doubt like his father before him, became a tenant farmer, probably with periodic employment in the local limestone quarries. There is a family legend that he was conscripted to fight against Bonnie Prince Charlie in the Jacobite Rebellion of 1745, but paid someone to go in his place.

[18] Pocock, D & Norris, R (1990) *A History of County Durham*. Guildford, Phillimore. p.44

John Sanderson married Elizabeth Emerson in 1744 in Stanhope, five days after the death of Alexander Pope. They lived successively at Broadwood, Bishopley, and Milnhouses[19]. They had several children, including John at Milnhouses, born in early 1752.

The Stanhope Parish records reveal that there were several Sanderson households on the Bollihope Burn in the 18th Century. In addition to John, other contemporary Sandersons, possibly brothers, included Ralph, James and Nicholas of Whelpshillend (now known as Hillend), Lancelot of Bollihope, and Thomas Sanderson of Bishopley.

In 1773, John Sanderson of Low Bishopley made his Last Will and Testament.

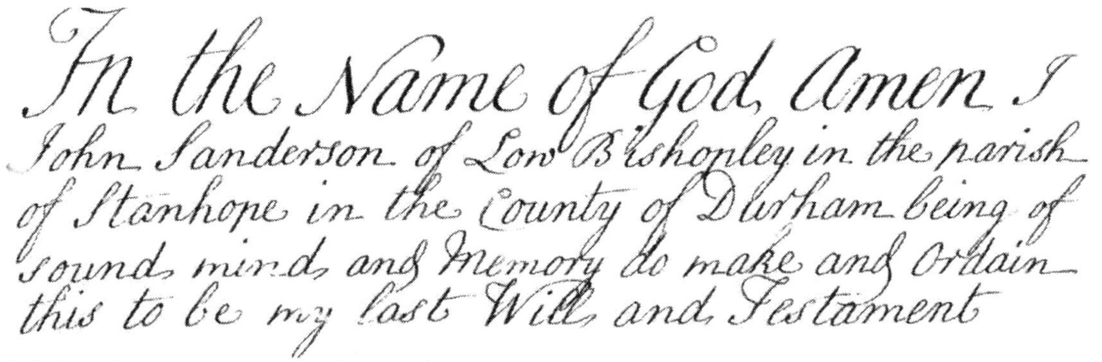
In the Name of God, Amen I John Sanderson of Low Bishopley in the parish of Stanhope in the County of Durham being of sound mind and Memory do make and Ordain this to be my last Will and Testament

3-2 Opening statement of John Sanderson's Last Will and Testament, February 20, 1773

John was literate, as evidenced by his signature on the Will (See below). The Will, drawn up by Benezer Powell[20], a Gentleman from Shield Ash, declared that John's wife Elizabeth née Emerson, was to receive £40, "together with all of the household furniture which she brought with her". His daughters, Ann Watson, Mary Moralee, and unmarried Elizabeth[21] each received £20, and the residue of the estate was given to his son and sole executor John Sanderson of Milnhouses. The witnesses of the Will were Ralph Sanderson of Whelpshillend and Benezer Powell.

3-3 Unlike many of his contemporaries, John had learned to read and write.

[19] Broadwood, Bishopley and Milnhouses are small adjacent settlements on the Bollihope Burn, a tributary of the River Wear

[20] Benezer Powell, the local "scribe", was married to an Emerson and so may have been related through marriage to John Sanderson.

[21] Elizabeth, with her newly acquired dowry of £20 (purchasing power in 2013 of > £2,200), married Joseph Stobbs at Stanhope St Thomas in June 1775.

John Sanderson died at the age of 50 and was buried on 14th March, 1775, just as the American War of Independence was beginning.

3-4 Lower Weardale. The Sandersons lived on Bollihope Burn in the 18th Century before migrating down the Wear valley to Hamsterley and beyond.

John Sanderson of Milnhouses (1752-1835)

In 1752, we were at war with France. It was also the year of the last sitting of the Cornish (Stannary) Parliament and the year in which the British Parliament approved a switch from the Julian to the Gregorian calendar. John Sanderson of Low Bishopley's son John, my g.g.g. grandfather, was born on Monday, 14 February, 1752 at Milnhouses, Low Bishopley. Like his father, he was a tenant farmer. In his early life, he will have had some schooling and thereafter worked on the family farmstead, perhaps supplemented by periodic work as a lead miner or limestone quarryman.

In 1771 when John was 19 years old Weardale witnessed the Great Floods following a prolonged period of torrential rain. The flooding was extensive with many of the bridges crossing the Wear throughout its course being totally destroyed, and only one left undamaged. Milnhouses is on higher ground about half a mile from the Wear but is on the banks of one of its tributaries, Bollihope Burn. The burn, a raging torrent at the time, no doubt caused damage and disruption to the small settlement at Milnhouses.

In 1778, the year in which philosophers Voltaire and Rousseau died, William Sanderson, described in the Stanhope Church Register as "the bastard son of John Sanderson", was baptised. In the Eighteenth Century, when a child was born to an unmarried woman, it was often the case that the mother but not the father was named in the parish register. It was also not uncommon for marriage to follow the birth of a first child, so it is possible that

Hannah Grey, who married John Sanderson the following year at Hamsterley St James, was the mother of William. They married in May 1779 in the presence of John's brother-in-law Thomas Moralee and John Grey, either Hannah's father or brother.

Meanwhile, the War of American Independence was in progress and the Industrial Revolution was gaining momentum. Spain declared war against Britain and Samuel Crompton invented the spinning mule. Further afield, Captain Cook was murdered by natives in the Sandwich Islands.

John Sanderson of Bishopley (1782-1865)

In 1782, Britain acknowledged that it had lost the 13 American colonies following the surrender of the British Army under Lord Cornwallis to George Washington at Yorktown the previous October. A jubilant Thomas Jefferson noted of the British Empire, "The sun of her glory is fast descending the horizon", although another 160 years would pass before his words were really appropriate. Elsewhere, there were continuing skirmishes with France and Spain who had been allied against Britain in the American War of Independence; on 12 April, the British and French fought a naval battle in the Saints Passage, West Indies, and in September the British fortress at Gibraltar repelled an attack by the French and Spanish fleets. At home, a Bill sponsored by the Duke of Montrose repealed the Act of 1747 which had forbidden the wearing of Scottish kilts.

In 1782 at Bishopley, g.g. grandfather John was born in 1782 to John and Hannah Sanderson.

3-5 Low Bishopley Farm, home to my Sanderson ancestors in the 18th Century (Detail from photograph taken by John Graham of White Kirkley).

Moving to Wolsingham Parish

Soon after John was born, the family moved 5 miles across Pikestone Fell from Low Bishopley to West Moorhill near Hamsterley, then to Ruddy Carr, a sheep farm 900 feet above sea-level on the edge of Pikestone Fell, and finally to nearby Rushy Lea. John Sanderson of Milnhouses died in 1835 at Rushy Lea[22] and was buried at Wolsingham. His wife Hannah died at Rushy Lea in 1839 aged 85 years, the cause of death being "Decay of Nature", i.e., old age.

It is likely that one of John's children, perhaps my g.g. grandfather, John, inherited the tenancy of Ruddy Carr. Ruddy Carr was certainly farmed by Thomas Sanderson of Broomley, my grandfather's cousin. Thomas was born to John Sanderson, the son of John of Bishopley, in 1853, and he farmed Ruddy Carr along with farms at Ayhope Shield and Broomley in Northumberland. FJS was familiar with these farms, as described later (See p.59).

3-6 A postcard to Edie Sanderson from 'Barbara' depicting Wolsingham Parish Church. Barbara was probably Barbara Angus from High Shipley, whose sister Alice Ann married John Joseph Hankey and began her married life at Ayhope Shield (See p.197 ff).

The Sandersons were successful tenant farmers and would have employed agricultural labourers and house servants at this time. Almost 90 percent of farmers were tenants during the 19th Century, the majority farming 100-300 acres. Tenants rarely purchased their holdings, not least because it would divert scarce resources from working operations. As Mingay (1990) noted:-

[22] Described as Rashilee in the Burial Register

> Most farmers were content to be tenants, seeing their capital producing a good return, and feeling perfectly secure under a good landlord. There was little or no tendency towards the purchase of land by farmers… (p.50)[23]

Sanderson Wandlis

It would also be the case that female house servants would often come into over-familiar contact with the sons or master of the household – sometimes quite deliberately so but more often by seduction. Permanent liaisons were more than frowned upon, as social relations were extremely hierarchical and a maidservant from the labouring class would normally not be considered as a suitable marriage partner for a farmer's son. However, casual liaisons may have been tolerated and in some instances, encouraged as a means of a young man gaining experience by "sowing his wild oats". One consequence of this behaviour was the 'base born' or 'bastard child', a common enough phenomenon in the 18th and 19th centuries.

An intriguing example is the illegitimate birth of Sanderson Wandlis on October 31, 1810 in Wolsingham. His mother was Hannah Wandlis and originally from Fulwell, Sunderland, but his father is unnamed. A possible explanation of the name 'Sanderson' as a Christian name is that Hannah was working locally as a servant and had a relationship with a farmer named Sanderson. The father, perhaps John Sanderson of Bishopley who was single at the time, refused to acknowledge his involvement with Hannah because it would be damaging socially and financially – and it may have put at risk his prospects of marriage to a suitable partner. Hannah, distressed at the father's refusal to admit his involvement, chose an effective way to expose him, by giving her son the father's surname as his Christian name. Perhaps this action would also strengthen the chances of the father having a Bastardy Bond awarded against him.[24]

John's Marriage to Margaret Vickers from Pease Myers

The major European news in 1812 was of Napoleon's devastating retreat from Moscow and the destruction of his Grand Army. At home, but certainly not in the Durham Dales, gas lighting was first used as street lighting. In that year, John married Margaret Vickers of Pease Myers Farm on Saturday, 18 July at Stanhope St Thomas, in the presence of Joseph Brown, Margaret's brother-in-law, and her cousin Esther Vickers.

The Vickers family were prominent farmers in the Stanhope area, being particularly associated with farms at Pease Myers, Greenhead, Snowfield, Howl John and Guy's Close. Although John Sanderson was resident in Wolsingham Parish, he had been born near Frosterley in the parish of Stanhope and the family would have retained many connections with the farming community there. The two parishes are adjacent and John and Margaret are likely to have had many opportunities to meet, perhaps at local agricultural fairs and markets. Another reason for them to have known each other is that James Vickers, Margaret's uncle, was married to Jane Sanderson[25], which meant that the Vickers and

[23] Mingay, G.E. (1976) *Rural Life in Victorian England.* Bridgend, Sutton

[24] On 6th July 1817 Henry Emerson & Hannah Wandlass both of the Parish of Hamsterley, were married in the presence of Cuthbert Vasey and John Dixon.

[25] James Vickers married Jane Sanderson at Stanhope St Thomas on 31 July 1783 in the presence of Thomas Sanderson and Francis Vickers (James' brother).

Sanderson families were already connected. Jane was Margaret Vickers' aunt and a cousin of John Sanderson.

Margaret was the daughter of Francis Vickers (1749-1822) and Mary Raine (1753-1833) from Pease Myers, a farm about 2 miles north-west of Stanhope.

In May the previous year, John's brother William married Ann Watson at St James Church, Hamsterley, with the witnesses being Catherine Vasey, John Sanderson and George Gibson. A month earlier, itinerant sailor Neil Swinney who had been wounded at the Battle of Trafalgar almost 6 years previously, finally succumbed at the age of 37 in Hamsterley and was buried in the churchyard.

William and Ann first lived at High Moor Hill Farm, near Hamsterley and had a daughter, Dinah[26], in 1817. They eventually farmed at Jolby Farm, near Croft in North Yorkshire. Ann died at Jolby Farm in 1835 and William died at nearby Hurworth in 1859. The cause of death was "Dropsy", and the death was reported by the Parish Clerk, Thomas Alderson – which suggests that William died without the presence of family members. His age is given as 84 years when the date of his baptism would suggest that he was 80 years old. There may have been a simple error in recording his age, or it could indicate that he was 3 or 4 years old when baptised in 1778, perhaps as a consequence of his illegitimacy.

The Village of Hamsterley

After their marriage, John and Margaret Sanderson moved to Ravensford, a 65-acre farm on the outskirts of Hamsterley, and members of the family were to stay in that locality up to the present day. Indeed, members of the family were at Ravensford Farm up to the 1960s, although the tenancy was not continuous from 1812.

A newspaper report from 1981 touches on the history of Hamsterley:-

> It is an historic farming village, and despite the changes through the years which have developed it into a satellite of Bishop Auckland, it has kept the spirit of a farming community.
>
> And the history is still there to be discovered. The past has meant that the parish church [27]of St James stands away from the main village itself. Dating from 1300, it was surrounded in those days by strips of land cultivated by the villagers who were obliged to give some of their produce each harvest to the church.
>
> And believe it or not, some still remain today, rented by the villagers, but they certainly pay more than one shilling a year now.
>
> Many people passing through Hamsterley spot the large stone by the bus shelter at the corner of the main street with the road down to Bedburn. This is all that remains of the village Blacksmith's workshop, which was demolished nearly 100 years ago. The last blacksmith was called John Henderson and his son still lives in the area today.
>
> It is not that long since there were water pumps and wells all the way down the main street on each side. Not until after World War II did the village get a proper running water system to each home, and electricity only arrived then too. Residents had to haul, buckets of water to their homes and each home had a tub or tank to store any water and collect the rain. [28]

---

[26]Dinah was a Watson family name, Ann's mother and sister both being called Dinah.

[27] Robert Sanderson, yeoman, was living at Ravensford whe n he made his Will in 1696.

[28] *Teesdale Mercury*, January 15, 1981

3-7 Roslyn Terrace, Hamsterley. The Workmen's Club on the right was formerly *The Spinning Wheel*, where Lizzie Gibson née Pallister was born (See p.136).

Whellan's History describes Hamsterley Parish:-

> This parish, which comprises the townships of Hamsterley and South Bedburn, formed part of the parish of St. Andrew's Auckland, and is bounded on the north by the parish of Wolsingham, on the west by Middleton-in-Teesdale, on the south by the chapelry of Lynesack, on the south-east by Evenwood, on the north-east by Witton-le-Wear, and on the east by Etherley.
>
> Hamsterley Township contains an area of 4003 acres, and the value of property assessed to the county rate in 1892 was £2684. There are two corn-mills in the township: the one called Beckside Mill is situated south of the village, on the Lynburn, which, though fordable at most times, becomes very much swollen by heavy rains, and is crossed by a foot bridge at the high road.
>
> Hamsterley Village is situated pleasantly on the brow of a hill, seven miles west by north of Bishop Auckland, and two miles and a half south-west from Witton-le-Wear. It retains its rural aspect, and some of the houses are still thatched, whilst others are falling into ruins. The annual feast, or hopping, was considered one of the most noted in the county, the sports consisting of cricket, wrestling, dog-trailing, quoiting, foot races, donkey races, &c. &c.
>
> South Bedburn Township is very extensive, though a thinly populated district. Its area is 6765 acres, and the property was assessed to the county rate, in 1892, at £2693. The township occupies the north-western portion of the chapelry; the scenery is bold and picturesque; and the tools, spades, &c., was carried on. It has now become a stocking

factory and saw-mill, which is driven by water, and is the principal industry of the township.[29]

3-8 Several of the Sanderson family are buried at St James Church, Hamsterley

St James Church in Hamsterley is completely isolated from the village, being fully half a mile north. It is dedicated to St. James, and is a cruciform edifice of very ancient foundation, comprising nave, chancel, and north and south transepts. The earliest portion is the entrance doorway on the south, of simple Norman architecture, the remainder being of the Early Decorated style, dating from about the close of the thirteenth century.

The Rev JG Milner and the Hamsterley Vestry Men

After a few short years at Ravensford Farm, John Sanderson and family moved to High Shipley and farmed there for 25 years. By the 1830s, John had been elected as one of the 12 Vestry Men at Hamsterley St James. He was present at Hamsterley Church Vestry meetings on Tuesday, 9 April 1833, and on Friday, 17th October, 1834. The October meeting was particularly bad tempered with the Vestry Men in open conflict with the resident curate, the Reverend James George Milner.[30] The 2nd Resolution stated:-

> That this meeting cannot separate without protesting against the vexatious and illegal interference of the Rev J.G. Milner, Curate, in endeavouring to break through the immemorial custom of this Chapelry in choosing their own churchwardens and sexton, by appointing - in the face of our appointment, of a churchwarden in 1833, for which he subsequently apologised and is now endeavouring, persevering in his

[29] Whellan's *History, Topography, and Directory of Durham*, 1894.

[30] The Vestry Men were parish rate-payers, some of whom may have been dissenters disposed to conflict with the curate.

> interference by himself appointing a sexton in opposition to the man of our appointment.
> Moved by Mr Thomas Hodgson, seconded by Mr Joseph Atkinson of Kays Lea and carried unanimously.

It seems that there were limits to the respect and deference enjoyed even by Anglican clergymen. It is quite reassuring to see that in times noted for hierarchy and class division, the clergy, or at least some of the clergy, could not count on automatic deference from parishioners but had to earn respect just like their modern day counterparts. It is also interesting to see farmers and tradesmen, the representatives of the parishioners, acting collectively against 'authority' in a way which the labouring class had not yet imagined was possible against their paymasters.

The 4th resolution stated that:-

> As the flue of the stove interferes with the vestry chimney and renders it useless, the churchwardens shall put it and the fireplace into the same state as they were before the alteration.

Moved by George Bell and seconded by John Sanderson[31], the resolution was carried unanimously. Cockfield-born George Bell farmed at Lunton Hill near Woodland, and would have been a friend and associate of John Sanderson of Bishopley. Coincidentally, John Sanderson's son Frank and an unrelated George Bell were involved in a double wedding in 1855 to Eleanor and Ann Alderson respectively (See p.73).

Death of the Perpetual Curate

The Rev James George Milner had been installed as the first resident "Perpetual Curate of Hamsterley" in 1825. He was to remain as curate of St James Church for a total of 60 years, his incumbency ending with his death in 1885 at the remarkable age of 89,[32] prompting the Rev Dr Robert Hooppell from Byers Green who conducted the funeral service to observe:-

> The deceased has been taken from us at a ripe old age. It is permitted to few to live the time of life that the late Vicar has attained. Seventy years is the allotted span of life; eighty years is an extreme age, yet the late Vicar was close upon ninety.

If he had not quite earned local respect in 1833, he had certainly done so by the time of his death. It was reported that on the day of his funeral, nearly every villager wore an emblem of mourning:-

> From what had been witnessed in that quiet and secluded parish that day it was evident the parishioners revered and loved their late Vicar. It was a few days over sixty years since he took charge of that parish… and there was still living in the village a parishioner who heard the deceased clergyman preach his first sermon at Hamsterley, where for many years the Vicar had to labour single-handed. Admirable harmony prevailed in the parish.

The "quiet and secluded parish" was anything but quiet on the day of the funeral. A severe north-westerly gale affecting all parts of the North-East was at its height during the

[31] Three weeks after this meeting, John Sanderson's daughter Jane died in a school fire (See p.63).
[32] The Rev Milner's daughter Anne died at Hamsterley in 1922 at the age of 97.

funeral, and the Church of St James in its exposed position "on the crest of a lofty hill" was at the mercy of the elements:-

> ...the gale raged with such terrific violence that a considerable part of the service was inaudible. The rafters vibrated visibly, and part of the service which should have been read at the grave-side had to be read inside the church.[33]

The Perpetual Curate had been absent from his Hamsterley Parish for many years. In the 1850s, he moved to Bellerby, near Leyburn and his son William Kirkbank Milner took his place in Hamsterley in 1858. William moved to the parish of Knarsdale, Northumberland in 1867, and was replaced by the Rev George Metcalfe. In the early 1870s, the Rev James G Milner, then about 75 years old, moved back to his Hamsterley Parish to see out his years.

John and Margaret's children

Margaret Sanderson, their first child, was born in 1813 at Ravensford. In 1844, she married Joseph Hall, a farmer from nearby Monkfield. On the day of the 1851 Census, they had a visitor from Stanhope, William Sanderson, aged 72, Margaret's uncle. As mentioned earlier, William was born in 1778, the illegitimate son of John Sanderson of Milnhouses.

3-9 Margaret Sanderson (1813-1893)

There is no doubt that Margaret was a great favourite of her parents - not only was she the first-born, but she was the only surviving daughter of five at the time John Sanderson made his Will in 1857.

[33] *Northern Echo,* March 21, 1885

Joseph Hall died on Sunday September 3rd 1871 aged 63 years. His gravestone, adjacent to Sanderson gravestones in Hamsterley churchyard, bears a typical Victorian inscription, “In the midst of life we are in death”.

His Will of less than £100 was administered by the sole surviving trustee, Frank Sanderson of Low Harperley, his brother-in-law.

In 1879 in Sunderland, his widow Margaret married 71 year old widower Thomas Toward, and they lived in Hamsterley where the retired colliery agent tended a small farm until his death in 1883.

How they would be cared for in old age was a major concern for Victorians, and so it is no surprise that Margaret moved to Witton-le-Wear, a few doors away from Richard Pattison and his wife Mary, one of the Stephenson Lasses, and next door to close family friends George and Mary Langstaff.

Margaret died in 1893, having lived out her days in Witton-le-Wear, cared for by a house servant, and with her niece Mary Pattison née Stephenson living close by (See p.27).

Mary Sanderson, John and Margaret’s second daughter, was born in 1815. A story handed down suggests that in the late 1830s, the family employed John Stephenson of Brancepeth as a groom, and Mary “ran off with him”. This does not appear to have been an elopement as Mary and John were married on Sunday, August 9th, 1840 at Hamsterley Church, the marriage being witnessed by John and Margaret Sanderson - perhaps her brother and sister if her parents, also John and Margaret, were not happy about the union. It may be that the reference to Mary “running off with him” was the way in which John Stephenson indicated to his children that there was an initial, and apparently fleeting, opposition to the relationship within the Sanderson family. Another source of family tension might have been the fact that Mary was 4 months pregnant when she married.

Mary and John Stephenson had four daughters and two sons: Ann, Margaret, Mary, Elizabeth Jane, John and Francis, the latter taking the name of Mary’s brother Frank Sanderson. Mary Stephenson died in 1856, the year after her brother Frank was married.

John and Margaret’s third daughter Hannah was born in 1818 at High Shipley and died aged 20 in 1839.

Eldest son John Sanderson was born early in 1821 at High Shipley and baptised on Saturday, 5th May, the same day that Napoleon died at St Helena. John Jnr married Sarah Kipling in 1846 and had ten children, establishing a prominent branch of the Sanderson family (See p.41ff).

Elizabeth Sanderson was next, born in 1824, followed by Jane in 1826, the year that the Menai suspension bridge was opened. Poor Jane died in a school fire in 1834, "accidentally burnt to death", aged 8 years (See p.63).

Finally, Frank Sanderson, my g.grandfather, was born on July 3rd, 1828 at High Shipley (See p.63ff).

In 1841, John and Margaret Sanderson were still at High Shipley. Although over 2 miles from High Shipley by road, Hamsterley was only just over a mile away by footpath: down past North Carr Wood to Carrwood Hill, over a footbridge at Bedburn Beck, and straight up the hill through Adder Wood to Hamsterley. Also present were children Margaret 27, John 20, Elizabeth 16 and Frank, aged 12, together with their daughter Mary aged 25, her husband John Stephenson and their first child John aged 5 months.

3-10 High Shipley Farm where John Sanderson of Bishopley farmed from 1820 to the early 1840s. The farm consisted of 130 acres of arable, meadow and pasture ground.

From High Shipley to Low Harperley

The Sanderson family together with John Stephenson and his family moved from High Shipley to Harperley Farm in the early 1840s when John Sanderson was nearing retirement and his eldest son John was ready to take more responsibility for managing the farm. By 1851, John Jnr had married and moved away from Harperley (See p.35), leaving the way clear for 23 year-old Frank to run the farm. The Stephenson family were still with them and by that time, had five children. Six labourers were employed on the 160-acre farm, and over the country as a whole there were over a million of such agricultural labourers. They were the single largest occupational group in the country and worked in much the same way as their predecessors had for centuries – much carrying, lifting, digging, trenching, hedging, sawing, felling, reaping, mowing, picking, sifting and threshing, in all weathers, day in and day out through sheer muscular effort.

Less than a month after the death of Abraham Lincoln, John Sanderson died of old age at Harperley on Wednesday, 3rd May, 1865, aged 82. His son Frank was present at his death. John Sanderson of Bishopley had a fulfilling and successful life by any measure – a God-fearing man, he served as a Vestry Man and Church Warden at Hamsterley for many years, was an excellent tenant farmer, enjoyed a good marriage with his "dear wife", and raised able children, including two sons who were making a success of farming by the 1860s. The major sadness of his life must have been that four of his five daughters pre-deceased him and Margaret. Although not a wealthy man, he was able to pass on a useful inheritance to his surviving children. He is buried in the churchyard of Hamsterley St James.

In John's Last Will and Testament, witnessed on 8 December, 1857, it was stated:-

> I give and bequeath unto my son, Francis Sanderson all my farming stock, crop, implements of husbandry and dairy utensils and all else upon Harperley Estate which I now occupy (excepting the household furniture hereafter named). Subject to the payment of my just debts, funeral and testamentry expenses, I give and bequeath unto my son John Sanderson and my said son Francis Sanderson all my money which I have secured to me upon Bonds, Notes or otherwise equally between them share and share alike.

John also made provision for his wife Margaret: the disbursement of all his money to his sons was:-

> ..subject nevertheless to the payment of an Annuity or yearly sum of Fifteen pounds unto my dear wife Margaret Sanderson for and during the term of her life to be paid to her by half yearly instalments.

The Stephenson Lasses

The four daughters of John and Mary Stephenson were collectively and affectionately known as "The Lasses" and were favourites of their grandparents. They were mentioned prominently in the Will of John Sanderson, as was his daughter Margaret Hall:-

> And upon the death of my said Wife I give and bequeath unto my daughter Margaret, wife of Joseph Hall, an annuity or yearly sum of ten pounds by half yearly instalments for and during the term of her life to be paid by my aforesaid sons John Sanderson and Francis Sanderson equally between them. I give and bequeath all my Household Furniture unto my said wife Margaret Sanderson during her life. And after the death of my said Wife as follows I give unto my granddaughter Ann Stephenson all the Furniture standing in the best room. I give to my Granddaughter Margaret[34] Stephenson all the Furniture in the Parlor (sic), also the Clock, Dresser and Shelf, standing in the fore Kitchen I give to my Granddaughters Mary Stephenson and Elizabeth Jane Stephenson each a Bedstead and Bedding thereunto belonging standing in the Lasses Room. I also give unto my said Granddaughters Ann, Margaret, Mary and Elizabeth Jane Stephenson all my Bed Linen that is the remainder over and above required for each Bedstead, also all my Table Linen to be equally divided among them.

Unlike their sisters, neither John nor Frank Stephenson was mentioned in their grandfather's will. The Stephensons were however close to the Sandersons and it is likely that John Sanderson will have helped his grandsons become established with farm tenancies during his lifetime.

Margaret Sanderson lived another 4 years. Son-in-law John Stephenson was present at her death from bronchitis on Sunday, March 21, 1869 at Marshall Green, Witton-le-Wear, signing the Death Certificate with his mark. John Stephenson was by then a widower, his wife Mary having died in 1856, pre-deceasing her mother Margaret by over 12 years. Margaret's eldest son John had farmed at Marshall Green from the late 1840s before moving to Black Hall Lodge in 1853. It appears that John Stephenson took over the tenancy

---

[34] Margaret was known as "Meggie" throughout her life

of Marshall Green, a farm of 180 acres, in the early 1860s and that after his father-in-law died, John assumed responsibility for looking after his mother-in-law in her old age.

At the 1871 Census, 60 year-old John Stephenson was still at Marshall Green farming 165 acres and employing two men. Also present were his children, Frank, 23, Mary, 20, and Elizabeth Jane, aged 16. John Stephenson Jnr had by this time left home, having married Mary Moore in 1866. He then farmed at Helme Park near Harperley, raising a family and perpetuating the names of "The Stephenson Lasses", Elizabeth, Mary, Jane, and Margaret.

John Stephenson Snr died in October 1876 at Marshall Green and exactly two years later, John Stephenson Jnr, like many North Country farmers before him, headed for pastures new. He arrived in Queensland aboard the *Scottish Admiral* in October 1878 with his wife Mary and four children – the second generation of "Stephenson Lasses". The family settled in Cairns where John worked as a carpenter. He died in 1918.

3-11 John Stephenson Jnr and Family emigrated to Australia on *Scottish Admiral*

The Stephenson family had an inauspicious start to their journey to Brisbane. The *Scottish Admiral* left Gravesend with 309 passengers on July 11th 1878 but within hours, it was reported that the vessel was "high and dry" on Maplin Sands, Shoeburyness. The stricken ship was towed off the sands by two tugs and returned to Gravesend in tow. It was quickly established that no damage had been done, and she finally sailed from Gravesend on 19th July with 343 passengers on board[35].

QUEENSLAND EMIGRATION
SAILINGS FROM GREAT BRITAIN
The Fine Ships, *Rodell Bay,* **from Glasgow to Brisbane, 5th June**
Caroline, **from London to Maryboro', 12th June**
Scottish Bard, **London to Rockhampton, 3rd July**
Scottish Admiral, **from London and Plymouth to Brisbane, 10th July**
Female Domestic Servants and Farm Labourers have Free Passage.
Apply to:
THE AGENT GENERAL FOR QUEENSLAND,
32, CHARING CROSS, LONDON, S.W.

3-12 Newspaper advertisement from 1878

The *Scottish Admiral* carried emigrants to Australia for many years but by 1893, was anchored in the Medway without employment. On the afternoon of Saturday, February 10, 1894, the newly-commissioned battleship *Edinburgh* was steaming down the Medway when its steering gear suddenly malfunctioned and, despite the best efforts of the pilot and the ship's officers, it rammed into the *Scottish Admiral* and caused extensive damage to the starboard bow below the water line. Taking on water fast, an attempt was made to tow the vessel onto the mud to prevent her sinking, but she filled so rapidly with water that "she went down on her beam ends" in deep water.[36]

Several months later it was reported that the Admiralty had decided to blow up the wreck of the *Scottish Admiral*.[37]

3-13 John Stephenson Jnr (1840-1918) and Mary Moore migrated to Queensland in 1878.

[35] *Morning Post,* July 23, 1878
[36] *Birmingham Daily Post,* Fenruary 12, 1894
[37] *Aberdeen Weekly Journal,* August 15, 1894

John's mother Mary Stephenson née Sanderson was the closest in age to her sister Margaret and the family bonds remained strong. Margaret had many nieces and nephews but in her will of 1893, she only acknowledged members of her first husband Joseph Hall's family and members of Mary's family, i.e., the three surviving Stephenson Lasses together with the daughters of the deceased Ann Stephenson – Mary Eleanor Sanderson née Raine and Annie Eliza Raine.

> I give and bequeath unto my nephew Joseph Hall, Farmer of Hamsterley, my Weather Glass and to my niece Hannah Proud,[38] wife of Charles Proud of (Low) Shipley, my Oak Cupboard, and I give and bequeath all the remainder of my Household Furniture and personal estate belonging to me, or which may be due to me at my decease unto my nieces and great nieces as follows: one fourth part to my niece Margaret (Meggie) Ayton, wife of Joseph Ayton of Thornley, one fourth part to my niece Mary Pattison, wife of Richard Pattison of Witton-le-Wear, and one fourth part to my niece Elizabeth Jane Seavers, wife of John Seavers of Thirsk, and the remaining one fourth part to be equally divided between my great nieces Mary Eleanor Sanderson, wife of John Sanderson of Burnigill, Sunderland Bridge, and Annie Eliza Raine, now in service to Mr (George) Manners of Westerton in the County of Durham. ....I appoint my brother John Sanderson of Broomley, Stocksfield on Tyne, Farmer, the executor.

Meggie's husband Joseph Ayton was a school master and a noted angler:-

The *Fishing Gazette* in 1879 refers to Joseph Ayton as one of the best anglers in Weardale. He was a schoolmaster at Thornley School and a prominent member of the Church there, so he will have been very embarrassed when he was fined by Wolsingham Magistrates for fishing without a license and fishing with salmon roe (which had been banned in 1861) on 4th June 1889.[39]

3-14 Elizabeth Jane Seavers née Stephenson, one of the "Stephenson Lasses".

[38] Joseph Hall and Hannah Proud née Hall, were the son and daughter of John Hall of Monkfield, who was the brother of Joseph Hall (1808-1871).
[39] Email communication from angling historian John Austin, 25 January, 2015.

Joseph Ayton (b. 1840) was the son of stone mason William, and Charlotte and the family lived in Thornley, a small village near Harperley and Helme Park. Joseph became a teacher, first a pupil teacher in the late 1850s and thereafter Schoolmaster at Thornley School until his retirement. During his long career, his pupils would have included my great uncle John Sanderson of Burnigill and my grandfather Frank Sanderson of Hamsterley – the latter known to have travelled every day to Thornley School from Harperley on a donkey.

As a young man, Joseph Ayton, along with his brothers John, Thomas and William, was a member of Helme Park Cricket Club, as evident from the photograph below.

Helme Park Cricket Club, August 7th 1860

Back : John Ayton, Joseph Parkin, Thomas Ayton, Edward Glenton, William Ayton, Benjamin Messenger, and Robert Hall
Front : John Thompson, Robert Potts, Joseph Ayton and George Hall

3-15 This remarkable photograph was taken at Newcastle-upon-Tyne. All but one of the team were residents of Thornley (courtesy of Jon Preston).

Times of Great Change

John Sanderson of Bishopley and his children and grandchildren were witness to profound changes in country life. The growth of the railway network in the mid-1800's when Frank was a young man was the first major change, followed by motorcars towards the end of his life and the gradual mechanisation of agriculture during the lifetimes of his children. Laurie Lee, born in 1914, describes the changes in rural life which he experienced, albeit much later than was the case in more industrialised Weardale where the railways had made such an impact:-

> I belonged to that generation which saw, by chance, the end of a thousand years' life. The change came late to our Cotswold valley, didn't really show itself till the late 1920s; I was twelve by then, but during that handful of years I witnessed the whole thing happen.
> Myself, my family, my generation, were born in a world of silence; a world of hard work and necessary patience, of backs bent to the ground, hands massaging the crops, of waiting on weather and growth; of villages like ships in the empty landscapes and the long walking distances between them; of white narrow roads, rutted by hooves and cart-wheels, innocent of oil and petrol... the horse was king, and almost everything grew round him: fodder, smithies, stables, paddocks, distances and the rhythm of our days. His eight miles an hour was the limit of our movements, as it had been since the days of the Romans... This was what we were born to, and all we knew at first. Then, to the scream of the horse, the change began. The brass-lamped motor car came coughing up the road, followed by the clamorous charabanc.[40]

The first railway in the world designed for steam locomotives was established in the North-East in September 1825. There were "wild scenes of enthusiasm" at the opening of George Stephenson's Stockton to Darlington line.

By 1830, there was 100 miles of track in Britain, and by 1852, 6,600 miles. And by the death of Queen Victoria the figure had risen to 19,000 miles.[41] This phenomenal growth spanned the lifetime of John Sanderson of Broomley and had a truly revolutionary effect on British society:-

> It was only yesterday but what a gulf between now and then. Then was the old world. stage coaches, more or less swift riding horses, packhorses, highwaymen... But your railroad starts a new era... We who lived before the railways and survive out of the ancient world, are like Father Noah and his family out of the Ark.[42]

The arrival of the railways had a stunning impact on people – in the 1850s they were mesmerised by the sight of the huge steam engine:-

> The men at work in the fields and quarries stood like statues...and women in their best gowns and bonnets fled the villages and congregated at the corner of every intersecting lane...Every horse was on the alert, viewing the huge moving body as it approached, with a mixture of fear and surprise.[43]

This development in the middle of the nineteenth century completely transformed communications and transport, thereby widening the horizons of people who had lived their lives in enclosed communities, not least in Weardale and Teesdale. Dennis Coggins writes:-

---

[40] Lee, Laurie (1959) *Cider with Rosie,* Hogarth Press
[41] Freeman, M, (1999) *Railways and the Victorian Imagination*, YUP, pp. 1 and 4
[42] Quoted in Asa Briggs (1963) *Victorian Cities*, p 14.
[43] Quoted in Souden (1991), p.120

> A farmer's diary of 1872 shows that it was possible for him to leave home at Holwick, (just over two miles up the Tees from Middleton), travel to Penrith and return with some sheep, something quite impossible by public transport today. [44]

On the other hand, as Mingay, (1998) points out that "with the passing of the coaches an element of colour went out of country life, and a living proof of a connection with great cities and distant events was broken" (p.4).

There were great compensations for those who took advantage of the railways. For example, Frank Sanderson of Hamsterley was able to travel to Bournemouth quickly and easily on the train for treatment for a chest complaint (See p.117). But for those who stayed at home, the village became a duller place.

3-16 Opening of the Stockton-Darlington Railway, 1825

[44] Coggins, D. (1989) *Teesdale in Old Photographs*. Stroud, Alan Sutton Publishing.

4. A TRUE SON OF THE NORTHERN DALES

O ye whose cheek the tear of pity stains,
Draw near with pious rev'rence, and attend!
Here lie the loving husband's dear remains,
The tender father, and the gen'rous friend;
The pitying heart that felt for human woe,
The dauntless heart that fear'd no human pride;
The friend of man - to vice alone a foe;
"For ev'n his failings lean'd to Virtue's side."[45]

Born in Weardale

Married in Teesdale

Buried in Tynedale

4-1 John Sanderson of Broomley (Courtesy of John Ross, John's great grandson).

[45] Epitaph written by Robert Burns *On my Ever Honoured Father.* 1784. An extract was included in John Sanderson's Obituary in 1897.

John Sanderson of Broomley (1821-1897)

The eldest son of John and Margaret Sanderson, John was a true son of the Northern Dales: born in Weardale, married in Teesdale, and buried in Tynedale. Living at a momentous period of history, he was a contemporary of Queen Victoria, and enjoyed the good fortune of being the eldest son of a successful tenant farmer. From early childhood through to old age, he witnessed the birth and massive development of the railways, a development that fundamentally transformed British society. Moreover, he began farming in his own right in the late 1840s at the very onset of the Victorian Golden Age of agriculture. During this quarter-century period of unparalleled prosperity, John farmed with notable success at various locations in Weardale, all within about 2 miles of his birthplace.

John was born in 1821 at High Shipley Farm, just over a mile north of Hamsterley, midway between the latter and Harperley (See p.25 for photograph of High Shipley Farm). During that year, George IV was crowned King and Queen Caroline died, as did John Keats, the latter of tuberculosis in Rome. Nearer home, the *Manchester Guardian* was founded.

John's lifetime encompassed massive transformation in English country life. When he was born, the nation was overwhelmingly rural, with three quarters of the population living in the countryside. By 1851, half the population lived in towns, and by his death in 1897, only one quarter of the population remained in the countryside[46].

As GE Mingay explains:-

> There is a tendency for us to think of country life as essentially stable, conservative and unchanging. In fact, this is far from the truth, and especially so in the hundred years after 1815.... This was a hundred years which saw fundamental and dramatic changes in the nature of the country, and many of these changes had an indelible impact on life in the countryside. There occurred at this time the rapid growth of a new industrial system based on steam power, machinery, railways and steam shipping. As one result of these developments the typical Englishman ceased to be a countryman and became a town-dweller. A large part of the food he ate now came in from overseas, and the clothes he wore, and the articles he used in his home and work, were mass-produced in factories and workshops. It was an age of movement: the attractions of town life drew many of the poorly paid and under-employed from the countryside, and numerous villages saw their growth level off and their numbers stagnate or decline as the nineteenth century advanced (p.vii)[47]

He will have experienced the typical childhood of a farmer's son at that time – helping out on the farm from an early age and attending Hamsterley School to learn to read and write. When he was 13 years old, he had to cope with the horrific death of his 8 year-old sister Jane in the fire at Hamsterley School (See p.63) – in much the same way that his namesake and nephew John Sanderson at the age of 13 had to endure the death of his 4 year-old brother William Henry in 1875 (See p.113).

---

[46] In 1851, more than 20 percent of the population was employed in agriculture, which produced about the same percentage of the national income. At the turn of the century, less than 10 percent was employed in farming, which accounted for less than 7 percent of the income.

[47] Mingay, G.E. (1998*) Rural life in Victorian England.* Stroud, Sutton Publishing.

Marriage to Sarah Kipling

John was about 20 years old when the family moved from High Shipley to Harperley and it was there that he met Sarah Kipling, the daughter of Joseph Kipling, a farmer from Stackholme. Stackholme was a remote farm in Lunedale, about 25 miles from Harperley, so it seems likely that Sarah was employed at Harperley Farm, perhaps as a dairy maid judging by her later success at agricultural shows: for example, Sarah won first prize (15 shillings) for "Best Stand of Ornamental Butter" at Crook Agricultural Show in 1869.[48]

4-2 St Romald's, Romaldskirk, the Cathedral of the Dales, where John and Sarah were married in 1846

John and Sarah were married by licence[49] on 3rd October, 1846 at Romaldkirk Parish Church, the "Cathedral of the Dales", in Teesdale. In June that year, the Corn Laws were repealed and Prime Minister Robert Peel was forced to resign – those who were disappointed at the repeal of the Corn Laws took their revenge on Peel by blocking his Coercion Bill which would have given the Crown special powers to deal with the agrarian violence in Ireland. This violence was the product of destitution in Ireland and was greatly exacerbated in 1846 by the onset of the Great Hunger.

The Rev Richard Reade presided at the ceremony and the witnesses were John's brother Frank Sanderson of Low Harperley, and his sister Elizabeth. It was just over 4 years after this happy event that Elizabeth died at the age of 26 of 'water in the chest'(See p.72).

John and Sarah first lived at Stackholme with her parents, Joseph and Jane. The farm is situated just beyond what is now Selset Reservoir on a tributary of the River Lune, which itself feeds the River Tees. Just over 3 miles away across Hunderthwaite Moor is Baldersdale where Hannah Hauxwell's family lived for generations.

Sarah, five months pregnant at the time of the marriage[50], gave birth to a boy on February 20, 1847 at Stackholme. He was christened Joseph after Sarah's father. In 1848, the family moved to a farm at Marshall Green, Witton-le-Wear, about 2 miles from Hamsterley. It was shortly after they arrived here that their second child, Margaret, was born, followed in 1850 by another son, John.

---

[48] *Newcastle Courant*, September 10, 1869

[49] Marriage by licence removed the necessity for banns to be called: it avoided 3 weeks delay and retained more privacy for the family, understandable given that Sarah was already pregnant.

[50] For country people, pregnancy before marriage was not unusual and not a cause for shame if marriage ensued.

4-3 Sarah Sanderson, née Kipling in mourning dress, possibly1876.

John, Sarah and family stayed at Marshall Green for 5 years, moving two miles up the Wear to Black Hall Lodge near Harperley in May 1853 and farming there until 1858. By 1861 they had 10 children and had moved another two miles up the Wear to Bradley Hall, a 430-acre farm two miles downriver from Wolsingham.

That same year Prince Albert and Elizabeth Barrett Browning died, the debate took place at Oxford University on Darwin's theory of natural selection between Thomas Huxley and Bishop Wilberforce, and on September 26 the first British Open Golf Championship was held at Prestwick.

There was much happiness when their 11th child Caroline was born in 1863, but their "beloved daughter" died at the age of 9 months. By 1871, with the farm having grown to 670 acres, 9 of their children were present: Joseph, a shepherd, John, an agricultural labourer, Jane, Frank, Thomas, Sarah Ann, Elizabeth, Mary Isabella, and Ruth Kipling[51].

4-4 Bradley Hall where John Sanderson farmed, 1859-1879.

[51] "Ruth" was a Kipling family name.

Their eldest daughter Margaret was by this time a mother of two infants and married to John Nicholson of East Broomshiels Farm, Lanchester.

During 1871, the first Bank Holiday was introduced (on Whit Monday), trade unions were given legal recognition, the Royal Albert Hall was opened by Queen Victoria, Henry Morton Stanley met David Livingstone in Africa, and the Rugby Union was founded.

Bradley to Broomley

In 1879, John and Sarah Sanderson, together with son Thomas and daughters Elizabeth[52] and Ruth Kipling, moved fifteen miles north to Broomley, a 780-acre farm in Tynedale, Northumberland. The former tenant George Angus had died the previous year and his famous herd of shorthorns had been sold at auction.

As age took its toll, John increasingly handed over the management of the farm to his son Tom. In 1881, Tom drove 24 head of cattle 12 miles from his brother Joseph's farm at Lumley Ling to Broomley. Not long after he and his cattle had crossed into Northumberland at Allensford, Tom was stopped by PC Peter Spratt and charged with a breach of the cattle disease regulations, i.e., transporting livestock across the county boundary without authorisation. Tom Sanderson explained at Hexham Petty Sessions that his brother had applied to the Wolsingham magistrates for permission to move the cattle but they were unable to do anything. Given the circumstances, the Bench took a lenient view and fined him one shilling per head and costs.[53]

It was at Broomley Farm that John died aged 76 on Saturday, 16 July 1897, just under a month after Queen Victoria's Diamond Jubilee. He had been a successful farmer, prospering "where others would have faltered and failed", and enjoyed a comfortable lifestyle. David Eveleigh has noted that a holding of 500 acres was considered the threshold for membership of the middle-class and that many large farmers had lifestyles which were indistinguishable from that of the landed gentry[54].

The *Northern Echo* carried a glowing obituary:-

> We regret to record the death of Mr John Sanderson, formerly of Bradley Hall, Wolsingham, but latterly of Broomley, near Stocksfield-on-Tyne, which occurred on the 16th inst., after nine weeks severe illness, which proved fatal, notwithstanding the assiduous attention and skill of his medical advisers. Previously he was a strong, hale, and hearty man. He was 76 years of age. The interment took place at St Peter's Church, Bywell, on Monday. The funeral service was conducted by the Rev. C.P. Sherman, Hexham, assisted by the Rev Mr Stenhouse, Stocksfield. A large concourse of sorrowing relatives and friends followed his remains to the grave. He leaves a widow, four sons, and four daughters (all married), and several grandchildren to mourn his loss. Last year Mr and Mrs Sanderson celebrated their golden wedding. During the former part of his life, Mr Sanderson occupied the farms of Marshall Green, Black Hall, and Bradley Hall, near Wolsingham and Witton-le-Wear, but 18 years ago he removed to Broomley, where his demise took place. He was one of the most prominent and practical agriculturalists of his day. Energetic, shrewd, and far-seeing, his mind fostered no fads, but with a broad, clear and comprehensive grasp of agriculture in all its branches, combined with sound judgement, a quick perception,

[52] Elizabeth died at the age of 22 in 1880.

[53] *Newcastle Courant,* June 10, 1881

[54] Eveleigh, D.J. (1996) *The Victorian Farmer.* Princes Risborough, Bucks, Shire Publications.

and a keen insight into men and things, he determinedly persevered, and prospered where others would have faltered and failed, and few men have been rewarded with greater success in the farming industry. He was not an extreme politician, but always took an ardent and intelligent interest in municipal and parochial affairs, and was at various times during his life a member of the Board of Guardians, Highway Board, &c. He was possessed of a strong will and great force of character. He had a remarkable and striking personality, and his example and bearing were a great source of inspiration and courage to all who came in contact with him. Being of a genial disposition his advice was often solicited and freely given in cases of arbitration, &c., amongst his neighbours. He was honest and upright in all his dealings, gentle and unassuming, kind hearted and sympathetic, and it was his greatest pleasure to render help or do an act of kindness to those in need. The words which Robert Burns wrote in memory of his father may be appropriately applied here. He was a loving husband, a gentle father, and a generous friend.

> His was the heart that felt for human woe,
> And his the heart that feared no human pride.
> The friend of all, to vice alone a foe,
> And ev'n his failings leaned to Virtue's side."[55]

The trustees and executors of John's Will of £5,553 12/1d[56] were sons John and Thomas Sanderson. His wife Sarah was bequeathed:-

> ...all the household furniture plate linen china glass books pictures prints wines spirits provisions and other household effects belonging to me at the time of my death absolutely... and the trust monies....in the first place to pay my said wife an annuity of Sixty pounds during her life by equal half yearly payments the first of such payments to be made at the expiration of six calendar months from my decease. I direct that a proportionate part of the said annuity shall be paid down to the day of the death of the said annuitant.

The Will's reference to "…plate, linen, china, glass, books, pictures, prints, wines, spirits, provisions, and other household effects…" provides evidence that John Sanderson and his family were doing very well and enjoying the benefits of Victorian consumerism, despite the agricultural depression since 1875.

The residue of the trust monies was divided amongst his surviving children: John, Thomas, Francis, Margaret (Nicholson), Jane (Vickers), Sarah Ann (Baty), Ruth Kipling (Watson) and Joseph. John sought to ensure that there was proper provision for any offspring of his then childless daughters, Janey and Sarah Ann.

John's widow Sarah remained in Broomley village after John's death. At the 1901 Census, she was an 82 year-old 'Retired Farmer Living on Own Means', cared for by two of her grand-daughters: name-sake Sarah Sanderson and Margaret Jane Sanderson, the children of her eldest son, Joseph. Sarah Sanderson née Kipling died in 1905 at Broomley aged 86 years. Her Will was administered by her daughter Janey Vickers.

---

[55] *Northern Echo*, July 22, 1897

[56] The relative economic impact of £555,4 in today's terms is £3.3M (www.measuringworth.com)

A True Son of the Northern Dales

Born in High Shipley, close by the Wear
To a family of farmers who held him so dear
Maid Sarah Kipling one day heard his pleas
They married in Romaldkirk, close by the Tees
And after a lifetime exceedingly fine
John died at Broomley, close by the Tyne.

4-5 John Sanderson of Broomley (1821-1897)

5. THE FAMILY OF JOHN SANDERSON OF BROOMLEY

FJS had contact with and great admiration for a number of John Sanderson of Broomley's children and grandchildren. However, he did not know anything about his great uncle, the patriarch of the Tynedale Sandersons, who died seven years before he was born.

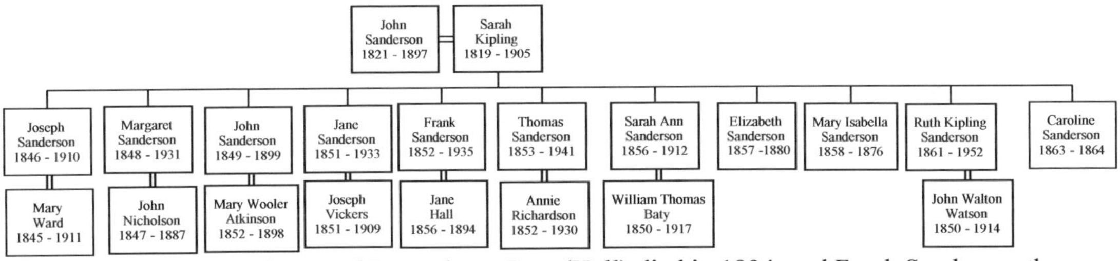

5-1 Family of John Sanderson of Broomley. Jane (Hall) died in 1894, and Frank Sanderson then married Florence Lumsdon in 1900, and after her death, married Maud Lumley in 1921.

John Sanderson of Broomley and Sarah (Kipling) had 11 children, and there are now thousands of descendants, many still involved in farming in the North-East of England and others who moved away, including many descendants in Saskatchewan, Canada. John and Sarah established a successful dynasty and on the testimony of FJS, the Hamsterley Sandersons had great admiration and respect for their Tynedale cousins. The focus here is on those members of John and Sarah's family who were known to FJS and who were mentioned in his reminiscences recorded in April 1980.

5-2 Frank, Ruth Kipling, Janey and Tom Sanderson in October, 1927.

The Trials of Janey

Jane Sanderson, the eldest daughter of John and Sarah, was born at Marshall Green, Witton-le-Wear in 1851, the year of the Great Exhibition in Hyde Park, and was given the name of her Aunt Jane Sanderson who was so tragically burnt to death at school when John was 13 years old in 1834 (See p.63).

5-3 Janey Vickers née Sanderson, circa 1901

5-4 Joseph Vickers of Tow Law

Through strong family connections Jane, known as Janey throughout her life, would have come into contact with her Vickers cousins on many occasions during her childhood. One contemporary was Joseph Vickers, her second cousin, whom she married in October 1875 at St Thomas's Church in Stanhope. The Best Man at the wedding was Joseph's younger brother, William Vickers of Pease Myers, and the other witness was her closest brother Frank Sanderson of Nafferton.

Joseph and Janey first farmed 600 acres at Tunstall House, Wolsingham, and in 1882 Joseph established Tow Law Auction Mart.[57] By the mid-1880s, when it would have become evident that they were unlikely to have children, they adopted Mary Annie Vickers, the daughter of Joseph's brother William whose wife Sarah (Petty) had recently died at the age of 36.

By the 1890s, Joseph, Janey and young Mary Annie had moved to Elm Park (also known as Helme Park), a palatial house near Tow Law. Joseph's prosperity was growing and Janey must have enjoyed much happiness raising her adopted niece, a happiness that was not to last. In March 1897, Mary Annie took ill and was admitted to Westholm nursing home in Bishop Auckland. The following month, Mary Annie died of pneumonia, aged 13 years, and was buried at Stanhope. Mary Annie must have been the pride and joy of Joseph and Janey, and one can only imagine the heartbreak that her death would have brought to the Vickers' family. And as if that were not enough to endure for one year, John Sanderson, Janey's father, died three months later at Broomley Farm.

Avoiding a Scandal

Sadly, unhappiness for Janey continued long after the deaths of Mary Annie and her father. Amongst the cards in my grandmother's postcard collection was one received at Pond House at Christmas, 1911. It was a postcard of a seated young girl with the message on the reverse, "With Best Wishes for Happy New Year, from All at Elm Park" (See p.47). FJS explained to me that the photograph was of Jennie Hamilton Vickers, and he recounted in whispered tones how she came to be the adopted daughter of Janey Vickers, a story later confirmed by Minnie Farrage, née Vickers, whose father Lawrie had featured in this family drama over one hundred years ago.

[57] For a detailed account of the life of Joseph Vickers, see my book, *Life and Times in Victorian Weardale: The Letters of Francis Vickers* (2012) – available from Amazon.

It is a story of infidelity and its remarkable consequences, of Joseph's affair with a maid and his desperate and ultimately successful efforts at damage limitation, of the rapid transformation of a young nephew from apprentice at Bainbridges to property-owning auctioneer and businessman, and of Janey's dignified forbearance and generosity of spirit in the face of what must have been an extremely stressful experience.

Joseph Vickers of Tow Law was a very powerful figure in County Durham by the time of his father Francis's death in 1903. Tow Law Auction Mart had become a great success, one of the most popular marts in the North, largely because of Joseph's reputation not only as an expert judge of stock but also as a "born talker", an expert auctioneer. With hundreds, sometimes thousands of stock sold at the weekly sales and special sales, and a commission of eight per cent on the selling price, Joseph had become a very wealthy man.

Not only was he wealthy, but also he was widely admired for his integrity and fair-dealing, necessary qualities for a successful auctioneer. And he was a high profile public figure, a Justice of the Peace, a prominent Freemason of the Tow Law and Crook Lodges, a County Councillor for Tow Law and Wolsingham, a member of the Weardale District Council, and a member of the Joint Hospital Committee for Infectious Diseases. He frequently chaired meetings and made speeches throughout Weardale. In short, he was a model Victorian farmer, businessman, and politician, proud of his success and widely admired for his outstanding achievements and his rectitude.

5-5 Elm Park, Tow Law, the home of Joseph Vickers and Janey (Sanderson)

His unblemished reputation in Weardale and beyond came under threat when, not long after his father's death, he embarked on an affair with a housemaid at Elm Park. The threat became serious when the housemaid, Mary Elizabeth Hamilton, informed him in the Spring of 1905 that she was pregnant with his child.

Mary Elizabeth came from a well-known Wolsingham family: her grandfather was a maltster and innkeeper at the *Bay Horse* in Upper Town and her father Joseph, a tailor. As a 19 year-old in 1901, she worked as a maid in York for William Thomas Baty, a locomotive foreman originally from Waskerley near Wolsingham, and his wife Sarah Ann née Sanderson, Janey Vickers' sister. Also present was the Baty's 18 year-old nephew Arthur Vickers, the son of William Vickers of Howl John and Margaret, the sister of William Thomas Baty

Mary Elizabeth gave up her service to the Batys in York, probably returning to Weardale to work for Joseph and Jane Vickers at Elm Park when her father became seriously ill in 1903. Joseph Hamilton died of pulmonary phthisis, now known as tuberculosis, in January 1904 at the age of 55. With Joseph likely to have been ill for several months before his death, Mary Elizabeth may have secured service at Elm Park so that she could be close to the family during a difficult time.

One scenario thereafter is that her employer Joseph Vickers, a man of similar age to her father, and a man of a "social, kindly disposition", may have provided a shoulder to cry on in her grief, and that the comfort he provided at a stressful time developed into a closer relationship.

Whatever the circumstances, as soon as Joseph learned of the pregnancy, he was naturally desperate to avoid a scandal in the family, preserve his reputation, and act as honourably as possible in the circumstances not only towards Mary Elizabeth Hamilton but also to his wife Janey. He had a lot to lose and needed to call on all his considerable political experience to manage this extremely delicate and problematic situation.

He quickly decided that the best solution was to keep the problem "in the family": he needed to find a way to incorporate Mary Elizabeth into the Vickers family, thereby protecting not only her reputation but also his own, and giving him the legitimate means of keeping in touch with, and perhaps supporting, the child.

To keep it in the family he sought to persuade one of his young nephews to marry Mary Elizabeth, offering Thornley Hall Farm, Tow Law, as an inducement. First he asked his nephew, Minnie Farrage's father, Lawrie Vickers if he would marry Mary Elizabeth, but Lawrie was already engaged to Annie Siddle[58] and declined the invitation. He then travelled to Newcastle to see Lawrence William's cousin Tom Vickers where he was working at Messrs Bainbridge Department Store - which incidentally had been founded by Eastgate-born Emerson Muschamp Bainbridge in 1838. It is not known how long Tom pondered the proposition, but the arrangement may well have been sealed not only with the promise of the farm but also with Joseph formally adopting his fatherless nephew and offering him an immediate partnership in Tow Law Auction Mart Company Ltd.[59]

Thomas Herbert Vickers, described as an Auctioneer on the marriage certificate, married Mary Elizabeth Hamilton, Domestic Servant, on September 19, 1905 at Thornley Parish Church. They were married by licence, thus avoiding the need for banns which would have caused delay and drawn unwanted attention to the wedding. It is noteworthy that the witnesses at the ceremony were Joseph Vickers himself and Frank Sanderson of Nafferton, the brother of Janey Vickers whose prime intent would have been to protect and support his favourite sister.

[58] Lawrence William Vickers married Annie Siddell (sic) in Houghton-le-Spring in 1906

[59] The Tow Law Auction Mart became a limited company on November 3, 1904.

5-6 Believed to be Mary Elizabeth Hamilton. Fashionable and attractive, perhaps Joseph Vickers had little difficulty in persuading his nephew to marry her.
(Courtesy of Francis Vickers White)

Joseph, a God-fearing man who for the most part had led an exemplary life, will have found the ceremony stressful. Any relief he felt when no just cause or impediment was declared will have been overtaken by an even greater feeling of relief once the minister pronounced that Thomas Herbert and Mary Elizabeth were Man and Wife.

Whatever Joseph felt on that day, to the outside world appearances and family honour were officially preserved, although there would have been the inevitable gossip in such a close-knit community where everyone tended to know everyone else's business. The *Auckland Chronicle* appeared to acknowledge this, reporting that the marriage had been "the subject of much interest,"[60] when the family would clearly have wished for a low-profile event.

Family members and close acquaintances will have certainly known the truth: Mary Elizabeth's puzzling pregnancy and the late and abrupt emergence of Newcastle-based Tom Vickers as the intended bridegroom would have raised questions and set tongues wagging. And no doubt to her great personal distress at the time, Janey will have known only too well of her husband's infidelity, particularly given that Mary Elizabeth was living at Elm Park before her marriage.

5-7 Thomas Herbert Vickers preserved family honour (courtesy of Francis Vickers White

And what of the feelings of Mary Elizabeth Hamilton when she found herself pregnant by Joseph? She will have known that such a

[60] *Auckland Chronicle*, September 21, 1905

prominent public figure who traded on his integrity and trustworthiness, would be desperate to avoid a scandal and that there would be no question of him giving up his marriage. Whatever she felt, she must have quickly agreed to Joseph's plan to find her a husband.

Less than four months after the wedding Mary Elizabeth gave birth to a girl, Jennie Hamilton Vickers, on January 13, 1906, at Elm Park.

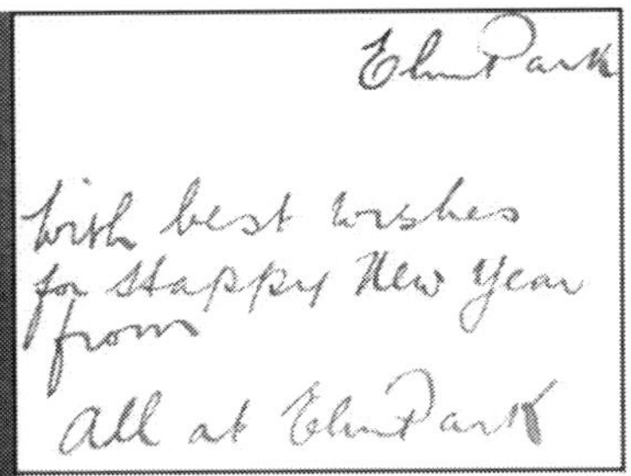

5-8 A postcard ofJennie Hamilton Vickers at Elm Park sent by Janey Vickers to Frank Sanderson at Pond House, Hamsterley, in 1911.

It is not known whether Thomas and Mary Elizabeth developed an affection for each other during their marriage, or whether it remained a strictly business arrangement. To the outside world, they will have presented themselves as man and wife, but in reality they may have been "keeping up appearances".

We will never know the full story, but we do know that Tom's life was transformed: the career at Bainbridges abandoned, he was now a young farmer, an auctioneer at Tow Law Mart, and living at Thornley Hall with a wife and child he had acquired through an arrangement with his uncle.

Francis Vickers of Belle Vue who died in 1903 was spared the discomfort that may have accompanied these events, but what of his wife Mary? The family may have considered it wise to keep Mary in the dark, given her age and sensibilities. If so, she will have delighted in the birth of Jennie Hamilton Vickers as a great granddaughter rather than the granddaughter she was.

Tom Vickers' life was further transformed less than three years after the marriage when Mary Elizabeth Vickers succumbed, like her father before her, to Pulmonary Tuberculosis on 27th October 1908 at Thornley Hall, the death being reported by her brother-in-law, Francis Edwin Vickers who had been present at the death. Her unacknowledged mother-in-law, Mary Vickers née Bowman of Belle Vue House, was spared some sadness: she died a few months before Mary Elizabeth and 18 months before the death of her eldest son.

Jennie Hamilton Vickers was adopted by Janey and Joseph at Elm Park, less than a mile from Thornley. To the world at large, Joseph and Janey had, admirably, adopted Jennie Hamilton Vickers following the tragic death of her mother. Janey may have felt at least some initial discomfort about this, but for Joseph, notwithstanding the sadness and regret he would have felt at the untimely death of Mary Elizabeth, it was a remarkably convenient outcome.

Given that there were no direct descendants to inherit his considerable wealth, is it possible that Joseph deliberately set out to produce a direct heir through his relationship with Mary Elizabeth? It is possible but unlikely, as the potential ruinous consequences would have been obvious to him, whereas the fortuitous solution he found could not have been foreseen. Nor could he have foreseen the tragedy of Mary Elizabeth's early death, which presented him with the opportunity to adopt Jennie Hamilton Vickers and make her a major beneficiary under his Will. There is some irony in the fact that Janey the surrogate mother was actually related by blood to Jennie because of the earlier connection between the Sanderson and Vickers families: they were second cousins, once removed. And Joseph's untimely death on Boxing Day, 1909 at the age of 58 meant that Janey assumed the sole responsibility for raising Jennie Hamilton Vickers.

In his Will, each of Joseph's nephews and nieces received cash and shares in the Tow Law Auction Mart Company Limited. In addition, Lawrence William Vickers of Belle Vue was given Joseph's house and land at Park House, Stanhope. And true to a promise he had made several years earlier, Joseph declared:-

> I give devise and bequeath unto my said nephew Thomas Herbert Vickers my farm known as Thornley Hall and Thornley Grange Tow Law aforesaid together with all the implements live and dead agricultural stock thereon and all the articles upon the said farm for his own use and benefit absolutely.

The only proviso was that his wife Janey should be allowed to live rent free at Thornley Hall if she wished. The greatest part of the detailed Will is devoted to ensuring that Janey had sufficient funds for "maintaining, educating and bringing up in a manner suitable to her station in life my adopted daughter Jennie Hamilton Vickers".

Tom Vickers was the natural successor to his uncle at Tow Law Auction Mart which remained in the Vickers family until it closed in September 2005. In 1911, Tom married policeman's daughter Florence May (Florrie) Snowdon at Stanhope St Thomas. Thereafter, he steadfastly maintained the public version of the events concerning his first marriage, that after his wife's death, he had given up his daughter to his uncle for adoption, and that Jennie Hamilton Vickers was a half-sister to the children of his second marriage. In legal terms and in the eyes of the Church, Tom's position was the correct one, but in reality, Jennie was his first cousin, and first cousin once removed to his children.

Janey Vickers was still at Elm Park in 1911, looking after 5 year-old "niece" Jennie Hamilton Vickers with the assistance of two servant girls. By the end of the First World War, she had moved with her adopted daughter to Hexham to be near to her brothers, Frank and Tom Sanderson. Frank's son John Thomas Sanderson and his daughter Jenny once went to stay with Janey Vickers at Broomley Villa, Hexham in 1920. Jenny was getting ready to go to a dance when her father said, "Your Auntie wants you." Jenny went to her great aunt's room and was stunned to receive a cheque for £100[61]. That was a lot of money in those days, but Joseph Vickers had left what was a considerable fortune of £22,000 to Janey.

5-9 Jenny Sanderson: £100 surprise from Aunt Janey

Janey died at Broomley Villa in August 1933, aged 82 years. In her Will, drawn up in 1926, her adopted daughter Jennie Hamilton Vickers was bequeathed her furniture and household effects, linen, jewellery and other personal effects, with the residue of the estate, after expenses, being divided equally between brothers Frank and Thomas Sanderson.

5-10 Janey Vickers née Sanderson at Elm Park in 1910

[61] £100 in 1920 would have the purchasing power of over £3,500 in 2013

Significantly, in a Codicil to the Will drawn up 4 months before her death, Janey bequeathed Broomley Villa "together with the land and buildings belonging thereto" to her beloved adopted daughter, Jennie Hamilton Vickers.

5-11 Ruth Kipling Watson née Sanderson (right) with eldest son John Sanderson Watson, and her sister Janey in 1890.

The Trials of Ruth

Ruth Kipling Sanderson was born in 1861 at Bradley Hall, Wolsingham and married Weardale farmer and auctioneer John Walton Watson at Hexham in 1886. Ruth would not have anticipated her husband's ability to attract notoriety throughout his life.

FJS recalled being puzzled that a prefect and the best boxer at Barnard Castle School, Anthony Watson[62] brought him a fruitcake to school one day. "What the bloody hell's he giving me the cake for?" he mused. He subsequently discovered that Anthony's mother Ruth was his father's cousin.

The fact that Anthony was the best boxer at school was perhaps not surprising, considering his father John Walton Watson was a combative giant of a man, 6'4" tall and 22 stones.

He was well known in the dale for his prodigious strength, and a man not to be trifled with. His grandson John Ross told of him regularly picking up and carrying two 16-stone bags of cement under his arms as if they were feather cushions at Wolsingham Railway Warehouse.

From the time of his marriage to Ruth Sanderson, there are newspaper accounts of his court appearances, mainly in connection with alleged threats and assaults against those who had crossed him or his friends.

On one occasion at Brough Hill Fair, John Snowdon, a farmer friend of John, had bought some cattle from two Irishmen. But after the deal was done, the Irishmen made the mistake

[62] Anthony's son Wilson Watson has a Barnard Castle School Cup won by his father in 1917 for Putting the Shot.

of demanding more money with threats. Mr Snowdon was not a big man and was greatly relieved when John Watson saw what was happening and promptly picked up each of them by the scruff of the neck, one in each hand, banged them together and dropped them in a heap on the ground.

On another occasion, he was fined for assault on a policeman. He had been denied a right of way for his sheep and was met at the gate by the policeman who prevented him from passing. Incensed by the perceived injustice, John Watson knocked down the policeman and put his foot on his neck.

A Fracas and a Horse-whipping in Weardale

5-12 "I learned him not to do so"
John Walton Watson

On Friday January 17th 1890 at Stanhope Town Hall, there was much excitement in court when Joseph Dawson, a carrier from Ireshopeburn, and John Walton Watson a farmer and cattle-dealer of Redgatehead, came before the Justices of the Peace, Mr Charles J Backhouse and Dr Charles Arnison. Dawson and Watson had accused each other of assault, and many spectators were present to witness the proceedings.

At the outset, John Walton Watson admitted assaulting and pulling Joseph Dawson out of his cart, but Mr Charles Dix for Dawson stated that it was not just ordinary assault as it had been preceded by Watson making a threat to one of Dawson's brothers that he would "let the blood out of Dawson before night", and then afterwards boasting about it.

It was also pointed out that Watson's counter-claim of assault had only emerged some days after Dawson's summons.

Dawson's evidence was that as he travelled down the dale in a heavy cart, Watson followed him in a spring trap. Near Westgate, Watson jumped out of the trap, took off his coat and challenged him to a fight. When Dawson refused, Watson pulled him out of the cart, struck him, knelt on his body and threatened to murder him on the spot. Dawson managed to get hold of a stone and said he would use it if Watson came near him again.

He claimed that he then drove off but that Watson came alongside him again and flogged him with a horsewhip for quarter of a mile before driving ahead. Under questioning by Mr

John Proud for Watson, Dawson denied agreeing to fight, denied using his horsewhip, and said that he had not spoken to Watson for four years and didn't know why the altercation started.

Several witnesses were called, one of whom was William Vickers of Pease Myers, the Stanhope Waywarden. It was obvious that William was a reluctant witness, perhaps not least because John Walton Watson's wife Ruth (Sanderson) and his brother Joseph's wife Janey were sisters. He said that on the day of the alleged assault, he and his brother Joseph, the owner of Tow Law Mart, had spoken with John Watson at the mart. Watson explained to them that a man had been "ill-using old Willy Bell", a 60 year-old pony breeder from Upper Weardale, and that he had "learned him not to do so". Watson had not mentioned a stone, but claimed that he had been 'brayed' with a whip by Dawson.

On oath, Watson said that when he asked Dawson about ill-using Old Willy Bell, Dawson asked what he had to do with it. Watson then left his trap at Dawson's invitation and was struck on the hand with the butt end of Dawson's whip. He claimed he took a stone from Dawson who then reached for a knife. Questioned by Mr Dix about the relative strength of himself and Dawson, Watson replied that he was prepared to lift weights against him. Mr Dix replied "London's the place for strong men!", and Mr Proud interjected, "My client could lick Sandow out and out if he had the chance!"

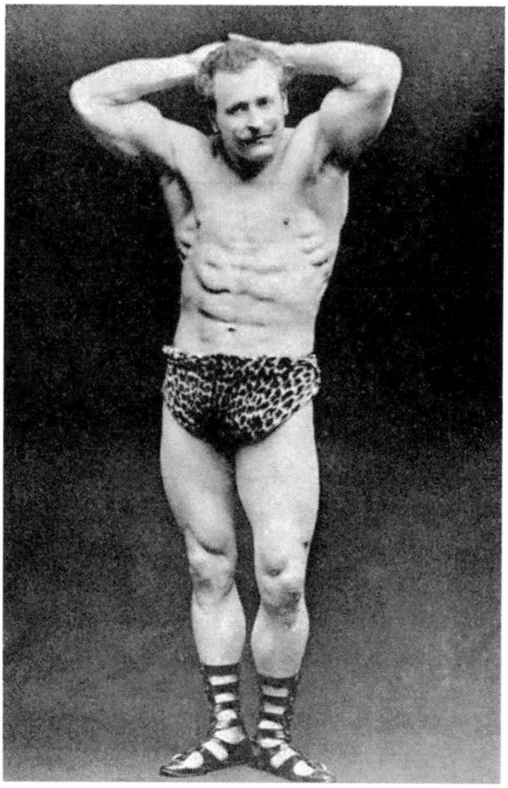

5-13 Eugene Sandow: "My client could lick Sandow…"

Sandow was a Prussian strongman who had caused a sensation two months earlier in London when he had beaten "Samson", celebrated as "the strongest man on earth". His extraordinary feats were reported in the local press and he actually performed at Bishop Auckland Town Hall in October 1892.

The Bench noted that Watson had admitted the assault and, concluding that it was not as bad as made out, they fined him 20 shillings with costs. The case brought against Dawson was dismissed.[63]

Seven and a half years later, Joseph Dawson was near Ireshopeburn in his cart when he was overtaken, knocked down and run over by a trap, and was struck in the back by the shaft of the trap, sustaining a compound fracture of the ribs.[64] There is no suggestion that John Walton Watson was driving the trap.

---

[63] *Northern Echo*, January 18, 1890

[64] *Northern Echo*, October 30, 1897

Some of his workmates did tempt fate - there was the time he was locked in a room, and when he tried to lift the latch by inserting his finger through the hole in the door, his workmates whacked his finger with a stick. What happened after he got out of the room is not recorded.

5-14 Sisters united in widowhood in 1920s: Janey Vickers and Ruth Kipling Watson

Compassion for those less fortunate was not one of his virtues. A family story is that once he returned home to find a tramp about to have a bowl of soup which had been prepared for him by Ruth. To John, the tramp was one of the "undeserving poor" who was a charge on rate-payers like himself, and so he promptly took the bowl and made the unfortunate tramp sit there and watch while he himself enjoyed the soup.

Ruth herself was a talented embroiderist, evidenced by a Quilt made for her wedding in Tow Law, Co Durham, c1886. It is now in the Textiles Collection at Bowes Museum, Barnard Castle.

Frank Sanderson of Nafferton

Much admired as a farmer by FJS, Frank (pictured overleaf) was born at Marshall Green, Witton-le-Wear, in 1852. Frank had all of his eight children by his first wife, Jane Hall, daughter of Thomas Hall, a farmer from Tow Law: Edith, George, William, Margaret Jane, Fred, Sally, Francis and John Thomas. He married Jane on February 21, 1874 at Satley

Parish Church with John Nicholson, his brother-in-law as Best Man and his sister Janey the Bridesmaid. At the time of his marriage, he was farming at Broomshiels, but by 1881, he had moved to Manor Farm near Lanchester and his sister Margaret and her husband John Nicholson had taken over the tenancy of Broomshiels.

Frank's wife Jane died in 1894 aged 39 years at Little White Farm near Brancepeth.[65] In 1900, Frank married Florence Lumsdon, and after her death, he married Maud Lumley in Sunderland in 1921.

Shortly after his father's death at Broomley in 1897, Frank moved from his native County Durham to Nafferton, according to FJS one of the finest farms in Northumberland. His brother Tom took the tenancy at Broomley, which was about 3 miles from Nafferton.

5-15 Frank Sanderson (1852-1935)

5-16 The 1908 photograph in question is of Eleanor Eliza Sanderson and her brother FJS, "a fine little chappie".

The Tynedale Sandersons kept in touch with their Weardale cousins. A postcard sent by Frank Sanderson of Nafferton to Frank Sanderson of Hamsterley in late December 1908, says:-

To wish you a Happy New Year. I think it is the photo of yr two children I have got. If it is, we think they are very good indeed.
The boy looks a fine little chappie.

Frank retired to live in Hexham where he suffered a coronary thrombosis and died in 1935, aged 82 years. After almost 40 years in Tynedale, his good standing in the South Northumberland farming community was evident from the obituary in the local newspaper:-

[65] In 1922, Frank Sanderson of Hamsterley's wife Edith died, also at the age of 39 (See p.145)

DEATH OF AN OCTOGENARIAN FARMER

One of the best known farmers in the district, Mr Francis Sanderson, died at his home, 6, St Cuthbert's Terrace, Hexham, on Monday.

Mr Sanderson, who was 82 years of age, was a member of one of the best known farming families in the North. He was born at Black Hall Lodge, near Witton-le-Wear where his father was then farming, and afterwards, removed to Bradley Hall, near Wolsingham, where Mr Sanderson commenced his active farming career. He afterwards took the farm of Manor House, near Lanchester, and also farmed Littlewhite, near Brancepeth. About 36 years ago (in 1898), he took over the tenancy of Nafferton, one of the best known of Lord Allendale's Tynedale holdings, and probably the largest farm in South Northumberland. He farmed here until his retirement a few years ago, when his son (Mr J.T. Sanderson) succeeded him.

Mr Sanderson took no part in public affairs, but was deeply interested in all matters connected with agriculture. He served for a long time on the committee of management of the Tyneside Agricultural Society, and was a steward. He was a well-known judge, and regularly judged the implements of the Tyneside Show at Hexham, and he was also a prominent judge at ploughing days in the county and Durham. One or two ploughing days under the auspices of the Tyneside Agricultural Society were held at Nafferton.

Mr Sanderson belonged to a long-lived family. Three brothers besides himself, farmed on Tyneside, viz., Mr Thos. Sanderson, who farmed Broomley, Stocksfield; the late Mr John Sanderson who was in the occupation of Anick Grange; and Mr Joseph Sanderson, of Watch Currick, and formerly of Ouston, Whitfield.

Mr Sanderson was married three times, and he is survived by his widow, and a family of three sons and three daughters.

5-16 Frank Sanderson with his children: from left:
George, Edith, John Thomas, Sally, Fred, Maggie, Willie, and Frank Jnr

A Keen Horseman

Frank Sanderson of Nafferton's son Frank Jnr was a keen horseman and won many cups at point-to-point on an outstanding horse called *Nafferton Lad*. For example, on April 13th 1905, Frank Sanderson Junior on *Nafferton Lad* won the *North Hexham and Braes of Derwent* Point-to-Point.

5

5-17 Frank Sanderson Jnr of Nafferton with *Nafferton Lad* and some of the Cups won at Point-to-Point. c. 1908

The horse was in its hey-day in the early years of the 20th century up to 1910, after which it was retired from racing to live out its days on the farm. When the First World War came, good horses were in demand for the forces, and *Nafferton Lad* faced the prospect of being drafted for the Western Front. The family couldn't bear the thought of this great horse going to war and were left with the sad decision to have him put down. As painful as this was, the family felt that there was no other alternative.

A Bit of a Swankpot

Another son, John Thomas Sanderson, born in 1874 at Bradley Hall, took over the tenancy at Tunstall House where his Uncle Joseph Vickers had farmed, and eventually farmed at Nafferton Farm after his father had retired to Hexham. He married Jane Story in 1898 and had two children: Jack who married Nancy Reed, and Jenny (Thompson).

5-18 John Thomas Sanderson (1874-1945)

FJS recalled that John Thomas was "a bit of a swankpot". Evidence from photographs showing John Thomas sporting an elegant waxed moustache (left) lends support to FJS's observation. However, he did not stand on his dignity too greatly, as Nancy Sanderson née Rogerson recalled John Thomas's blue budgerigar perching on his moustache, a novel and no doubt amusing party piece.

FJS remembered John Thomas coming to Hamsterley regularly, before, during and after the First World War. He would first visit his Aunt Janey (Vickers) at Elm Park and then continue on to Pond House, Hamsterley where he would visit his father's cousin and namesake Frank Sanderson. Meanwhile, his wife Jane would go to see her friend, Mary Ann Spence née Gipps in the village – Mary Ann was the daughter of Harry Gipps, a farmer and former landlord of the *Cross Keys*. FJS remembered John Thomas as having a good sense of humour and that he was a very kind man. He died in 1945 aged 71 years.

After Frank Sanderson of Nafferton's death in 1935, the links between the Tynedale and Weardale branches of the family, already weakened by the death of Edith Sanderson in 1922, were effectively severed for almost half a century: in 1980, first myself and then FJS and his second wife Joan, visited Jack Sanderson, the g. grandson of John of Broomley, at Stocksfield. Also present was Jack's sister Jenny (Thompson) who had received the surprise £100 gift from Aunt Janey in 1920.

5-19 William Sanderson with wife Jessie, Gordon and Lawrence

William Sanderson

Born in 1883 in Lanchester, William farmed at Nafferton. He married Jessie Dods in 1919 and had two sons, Gordon and Lawrence. Lawrence, the youngest son, pictured here sitting on his mother's knee, died tragically in an accident with a gun at Nafferton Farm just before Christmas in 1929. He was 5 years old. The next day, 23 December, Coroner Phillip W Dodds concluded that Lawrence had died of "Shock following gunshot wounds to the head accidentally received. Lived half an hour." Although it was clearly an accident, cousin Jack Sanderson, the owner of the gun, suffered a lifetime of regret as a consequence. The impact on the immediate and wider family of this terrible event can barely be imagined. His father William, a noted horseman and farmer, finished his working life driving a brewer's dray in Darlington.

Fred Whitfield, the grandson of Sarah Elizabeth Whitfield née Sanderson, and Lawrie's first cousin once removed, recalled:-

> The impact of this accident was handed down through the generations. When I was 11 or 12, I was given my first (and only) shotgun, a 410 gauge; the handing over was preceded by a lecture on safety and what had "befallen poor Lawrie" and the first few times that I went out I was told to "Remember Lawrie". When I went away to school, I never saw the gun again.

Farmers routinely hold shotguns for pest control and for shooting game, and there is inevitably the ever-present danger of accidents. Lawrence died in 1929 and ten years later, another tragic accident with a shotgun at Crook's Altar Farm, Eastgate, resulted in the death of two people (See p.109) And FJS remembered a sharp lesson he received about gun safety from Old Tom White at Harperley in 1920 (See p.60).

Thomas Sanderson of Broomley

John of Broomley's son Tom Sanderson, described by FJS as a great character, was born in 1853 at Black Hall Lodge. He was farming with his father at Broomley when he married Annie Richardson from High Fotherley in 1883. When his father died in 1897, Tom stayed at Broomley.

5-20 Tom Sanderson with Annie and their children Annie and Jack in 1890

Their granddaughter Kath Douglas née White, remembered them well.

Tom she described as *'canny'*, i.e. a nice person, whereas her grandmother was 'very severe', meaning that she was probably quite anxious by nature. Kath recalls that when her grandparents came to stay, Annie had a stool placed under the stairs where she could sit during thunderstorms, as well as a little stool for her grandson Harry so that he could keep her company.

She also recalls that her grandfather had a yearning to travel but was never able to do so because of Annie's reluctance.

5-21 Tom Sanderson at Broomley in 1905.

FJS particularly liked and admired Tom and his brother Frank. "They were 'go-ers', very good farmers", he said. Tom in particular was a strong character. In addition to Broomley, Tom also acquired three sheep farms, Ayhope Shield (See p.213), Honeybee, and Ruddy Carr which FJS visited several times. On one trip to Ruddy Carr, a farm 3 miles north-west of Hamsterley on the edge of Pikestone Fell, FJS recalled seeing 17 dead sheep laid at the back of a wall. He also stayed at Broomley Farm as a young boy, and the only thing he could remember was an enormous pig, bigger than he'd ever seen before or since.

Tom Sanderson had two sons and two daughters- William Anthony (Willie), Sarah Evelyn, John Thomas (Jack), and Hannah Richardson, but FJS only spoke of Willie, and Hannah who married Tom White.

Willie Sanderson was born at Broomley Farm in 1892. A bachelor, he was " great fun, a good singer", at his best in convivial company (See p.130). FJS recalled that Willie often stayed at Ruddy Carr, as did his father Tom, and John Story's wife cooked for them.

John Story, son of a shepherd from the Bewcastle Fells in Cumberland and a shepherd himself, moved to Wolsingham in 1878. First he worked for the Wooler family as a shepherd at Harthope Farm, Wolsingham, and 10 years later, moved to nearby Ruddy Carr which was tenanted by Tom Sanderson. The cook at Ruddy Carr, John Story's wife Mary (Cowan), was the daughter of another Bewcastle shepherd.

The death of Tom Sanderson at the age of 86 in 1941 took its toll on Willie, as FJS recalled:-

> When Tom died, the farm was finished. Willie was no good then. He moved to Scotland and went out on a bicycle one day, went to the river and was drowned. They found the bike...

Willie Sanderson of Crichton Royal, Dumfries was last seen alive on 16 July 1955. His body was found three days later in the River Nith at Dumfries. Administration of his Will was granted at Newcastle-upon-Tyne in 1956 to Hannah Richardson White, the widow of Tom White and Sarah Evelyn Pratt née Sanderson, wife of Fleetham Watson Pratt.

Hannah Richardson Sanderson and Tom White

FJS knew Tom White junior, the husband of his second cousin, quite well. He also recalled that Tom's brother Harry had been in the yeomanry before the First World War, and had a gun in the house. FJS once went to stay at Harperley where Harry and Tom's father Old Tom White was farming, and he recalls:

Harry gave me his gun. I went to the kitchen door and held the gun up and pointed it at Old Tom White. By God, you've never heard anyone shout so loud - he frightened me to death! It's a wonder I didn't pull the bloody trigger!!

It is easy to imagine the scene as the teenage FJS pointed the gun at genial Old Tom White who then subjected him to a sharp lesson about not pointing guns at anyone. Fatal accidents with guns, particularly within the farming community, were common, leading to great emphasis on safety. In 1914, a correspondent described "a man of a Roman Father type[66] who thrashed his son for even pointing a stick at him, and so nipped in the bud the habit of pointing things."[67]

5-22 Hannah Sanderson and Tom White junior on their Wedding Day in 1908.

Perhaps Frank Sanderson of Hamsterley had not conveyed the message to his son contained in Mark Beaufoy's poem, *A Father's Advice*, written in 1902:-

> If a sportsman true you'd be, listen carefully to me...
> Never, never let your gun pointed be at anyone.
> That it may unloaded be matters not the least to me.
> For all the pheasants ever bred will not repay one man dead.

[66] In Ancient Rome, the father's authority was absolute. The father could even go as far as whipping his children, selling them into slavery, or even killing them if they did not obey his wishes.
[67] *Essex Newsman*, May 30, 1914

Tom and Hannah White had six children: Thomas Arnold, John Sanderson, William Henry (Harry), Sarah Annie, Mary Kathleen (Kath), and Maurice Geoffrey (Geoff).

Kath recalled her father and mother:-

> My father was very strict – I suppose he had to be with three sons to keep in order. But he spoiled me. I remember sitting on his knee as a child, whereas my sister never did. He was also a very fair man – not so long ago, a man who used to work on the farm at Fotherley said to me, "he was the fairest boss I ever had."

Then the War came and he died in 1940 – the Germans started dropping bombs on Newcastle during his funeral. Life was difficult after that – I had to work on the farm and I hated it, it's not the same when it's not your farm.

> My mother was a good mother, although not the lovey-dovey type. She was very domesticated and taught us a lot when we were young. She was very loyal to the family - she never criticised anyone in the family to an outsider and never criticised one family member to another.[68]

5-23 Mr Tantobie Richards, the Egg-collector

Kath had happy memories of her time at Fotherley before her father died. One memory is of Mr Richards, the Egg Collector from Tantobie, a village 10 miles away on the outskirts of Stanley, Co Durham. Mr Richards visited Fotherley every week and was known to the family simply as 'Tantobie'.

[68] Francis Vickers White of Wolsingham recalls his Aunt Hannah as quite tall, slim, always smartly turned out and he was taken by the dangly earrings she always wore.

Tom White died in 1940 aged 61, and according to his obituary in the *Newcastle Journal*, he had been "one of the most industrious and successful agriculturists in the Tynedale district". The obituary continues:-

> A noted breeder of Border Leicester sheep, his stock was sought after by many flock owners for crossing purposes, and an expert judge, his wide knowledge of all farm stock was often requisitioned in the show ring.
>
> As an exhibitor, Mr White met with great success at local shows and famous representatives of the Fotherley flock won him many high honours in local show yards.....evidence of the high value of his stock was the fact that he won a silver challenge cup at Edmondbyers show outright, by virtue of three successive championships with Border Leicester ram lambs. Mr White was also the proud possessor of a silver cup which he had won outright at the North Tyne and Redesdale show at Bellingham.
>
> A genial and familiar figure at Hexham and other marts Mr White was ever ready to give sound advice on farming matters.
>
> ...Mr White leaves a widow, four sons and two daughters, two of his sons being engaged in farming.

Evidence of the respect in which he was held by members of the farming community was shown by the large gathering of mourners at the funeral at Healey on Tuesday afternoon. St John's church couldn't hold all the mourners – many stood outside the church "in reverent groups" while the service was proceeding.

Sheep shearing and marking at Hill Farm, Weardale, in 1888. ***Sent by Mr. White, Riding Mile on Tyne. Northumberland.***

5-24 The above photograph was taken at Ruddy Carr (not Hill Farm) 1888, and was sent to a newspaper by Tom White junior, son-in-law of tenant Tom Sanderson.

6. THE PLOUGHMEN

> The sounds of England, the tinkle of the hammer on the anvil in the country smithy, the corncrake on a dewy morning, the sound of the scythe against the whetstone, and the sight of the plough team coming over the brow of a hill, the sight that has been seen in England since England was a land...[69]

Such sounds and images would have very familiar to great grandfather Frank Sanderson who was born on 3rd July, 1828 at High Shipley, just north of Hamsterley, and baptised on Sunday, 16th November at St James Church in Hamsterley. That year the Duke of Wellington became Prime Minister, Daniel O'Connell was elected MP for County Clare, London University was founded, Thomas Arnold became Headmaster of Rugby School, and the Marble Arch was built.

Frank was the youngest of John and Margaret's seven children, and was born when his father was 46 and his mother 43 years old. His maternal grandfather was Francis Vickers (1749-1822) of Pease Myers and young Frank was named after him. It was thus through the Vickers' connection that "Francis" became a family name for the Sandersons in 1828. Incidentally, "Francis" remained a popular Vickers' family name – for example, as well as grandfather Frank Vickers, Frank of Low Harperley also had an Uncle Frank Vickers (1793-1877) and two cousins of that name[70]. Francis remains a Vickers and Sanderson family name to this day.

Accidentally burnt to death in school

FJS spoke movingly of a traumatic event from the 1830s.

In 1834, when his grandfather Frank Sanderson of Low Harperley was 6 years old, the family suffered a great tragedy that was to haunt him for the rest of his life.

Nationally, 1834 was notable for the introduction of the New Poor Law which required parishes or unions of parishes to house the poor in workhouses. In return for their food and clothing, inmates had to work each day, and children received some schooling. Many likened the new system to "Prisons for the Poor". It was also the year that the Tolpuddle Martyrs were victimised to discourage the British working-class movement, and when slavery was abolished in the British Empire. And 1834 was also the year in which there was a great fire in London and a small deadly fire in Hamsterley.

> In the early evening of 16 October 1834, to the horror of bystanders, a huge ball of fire exploded through the roof of the Houses of Parliament, creating a blaze so enormous that it could be seen by the King and Queen at Windsor, and from stagecoaches on top of the South Downs. In front of hundreds of thousands of witnesses the great conflagration destroyed Parliament's glorious old buildings and their contents. For those who watched the destruction through the night it was the most staggering occasion of their whole lives.[71]

---

[69] From *On England*, by Stanley Baldwin

[70] Frank Vickers (1809-1901) of Dean Head and Francis Vickers (1821-1903) of Belle Vue.

[71] Text from www.parliament.uk/worksofart

6-1 *The Palace of Westminster on Fire, 1834*

This great fire caused many serious injuries but remarkably, there was no loss of life. In December at Hamsterley School, a small fire took the life of a young girl, Jane Sanderson.

Jane was born in 1826 and was close to her brother Frank. They attended the village school in Hamsterley together – less than 2 miles from their home at High Shipley.

In rural communities children helped out on the land at busy times of year which meant that in the spring and summer months and in October during potato picking, attendance would be poor at the school, but at this slack time of year on the land, many of the village children would have been present.

On a cold Monday morning in December 1834, Jane was playing hide and seek with her classmates during a break from lessons. She was chasing the other children and they locked her in the classroom to prevent her catching them. Classrooms in those days had open fires without fireguards and Jane came too close to the fire. Her dress caught alight and she was quickly engulfed by the flames. Jane was trapped in the classroom, and the other children believed that she was play-acting when they heard her screams for help. She would have had extensive burns and must have experienced excruciating pain and suffered terribly.

A Village in Mourning

The Burial Register records that Jane "accidentally burnt to death in the school". She died on Monday, December 8, 1834, aged 8 years, and was buried in Hamsterley churchyard on 11th December. Given the circumstances surrounding Jane's death, and the fact that she was only a child, there would have been much shared grief in the village and an exceptional attendance at the funeral.

A verse from a poem written in 1835 aptly conveys the great sadness at the funeral of a child:-

Under the shroud of the sullen cloud, beneath the darkest sky,
The gathering breeze, through leafless trees, blows heavy in the wild;
The sound of measured steps is heard – the grave stands yawning by –
They go, in sad procession slow, to the funeral of a child.[72]

The family mourners would have included parents John and Margaret Sanderson, and numerous aunts, uncles, and cousins, mainly represented by the large Vickers family from Stanhope. The funeral would also have been attended by villagers, more distant relatives and friends of the family, as well as farm workers and other associates from the farming community.

The funeral procession would have been led by pall bearers, followed by the hearse containing the coffin pulled by black horses, and then followed by the mourners in carriages. The procession would have made its way at walking pace from the Sanderson farm at High Shipley on to the main road, and then at a brisker pace through Bedburn and up Bedburn Lane to Hamsterley. Then the cortege would have slowly made its way through the village past the *Cross Keys*,[73] and to St James' Church, half a mile beyond the village – a total distance of 2½ miles.

At the end of the funeral service, the ceremony concluded at the graveside in the churchyard with only the men remaining to witness the actual interment. Then, family and friends would have returned to High Shipley for a feast.

After the burial, the period of mourning varied depending on a person's relation to the deceased, so in the case of Jane's parents, the period would have been at least 9 months, whereas for her brothers and sisters, 6 months would have been sufficient.[74]

Poet and philosopher Samuel Taylor Coleridge, political economist TR Malthus, and essayist Charles Lamb also died in 1834 but, unlike Jane Sanderson, they each had had a long life in which to fulfil their promise.

A Common Victorian Tragedy

Pamela Horn[75], writing about schools in Victorian times, reports that:-

> …heating was normally provided by an open fire at one end of the room, but the warmth thrown out was often inadequate in the winter months, and the children were almost too cold to work. (p.57)

Perhaps it is significant that the tragic accident happened on a Monday during the winter when the teacher would have had the fire blazing in order to heat the building after a cold weekend[76]. And given that children at the time tended to be somewhat 'overdressed', it is easy to imagine how a child, seeking the warmth of the fire on a cold day, would have strayed too close to the flames without realising the danger.

---

[72] Adapted from A Child's Burial in Spring, *Belfast Newsletter,* May 5 1835

[73] "*Cross Keys*" refers to the Papal Arms - originally, this inn was under the patronage of the church, and would provide refreshment for those attending services and other functions

[74] Alirangues, Loretta M. *Funerary Practices in the Victorian Era* (morbidoutlook.com)

[75] Pamela Horn (1995) *Labouring Life in the Victorian Countryside*. Stroud, Sutton Publishing

[76] A Report from a school in Devon in 1894 reads, "The thermometer stands at 24½ deg.F, 10 o'clock, fires lighted 2½ hours". Quoted in P. Horn (1995) Labouring life in the Victorian countryside Abingdon, Fraser Stewart (p.57)

Where the teacher actually was when this terrible event was happening is not known, but there must have been questions asked, given that the tragedy occurred whilst the children were unsupervised. The first schoolmaster after the school opened in 1822 was the curate, the Reverend Thomas Gibson. His successor as curate was the Reverend James George Milner and it is possible that he was the teacher in charge of the children in 1834. If so, then he is likely to have sustained criticism for his failure of care, especially as he already enjoyed a less than cordial relationship with prominent members of the parish. Less than two months before the tragedy, he had been involved in bad-tempered exchanges with the Vestry Men, one of whom was John Sanderson, Jane's father. (See p.21)

Alexander Macaulay, MD, described circumstances in which people received burns:-

> The worst burns that occur arise from the burning of inflammable gases, from gunpowder, from the boiling over of hot fluids, as painters' oil, or fluids in laboratories; *from the dresses of females taking fire*...and such like accidents.[77]

There are many reports from the nineteenth century of young children being burnt to death, and 1834 provided some typical examples. In February, a Coroner's Inquest recorded a verdict of "Accidental Death" after 8 year-old Barbara Piper from Hexham was burnt to death.[78] In June, a five year old child "belonging to Mr Hope of Kay's Burn, near Witton Gilbert", was burned severely by a fire and died within a short time.[79] In November in Richmond, "a little boy of the name of Wells" was sitting near the fire, when by some means his clothes caught the flame, and he was so dreadfully burnt that he died the next day." His father had tried to put out the flames and ended up in hospital.[80] But parents were not always close at hand in such circumstances: A return from the City and Liberty of Westminster indicated that in 1834, no less than 100 children had died from burns, "chiefly owing to their parents leaving them alone in a room with a fire in it"[81]

Young children would often be left in the care of older brothers or sisters whilst the parents were either at work in the fields or else the father was out at work and the mother was on an errand. In March 1834, it was reported that:-

> ...a poor woman by the name of Fox, residing in Robinson's Lane, Sunderland, had occasion to leave her children in her house by themselves while she went to the market. During her absence, a fine little boy, about five years of age, set his clothes on fire, and was so dreadfully burnt that he died the next morning.[82]

Decades later, such tragedies were still common. A Warwick doctor reported that in the 1860s he had attended 8 cases where the clothes of a child had caught fire, with 4 cases proving fatal.[83] In 1874, the shocking death of Alice Mary Pettitt was reported:-

> The child, who is five and a half years of age, had been left in the house by herself at Wolsingham, and whilst breaking some coals behind the fire, her pinafore became

[77] Macaulay, Alexander (1831) *A Dictionary of Medicine: Designed for Popular Use*. Edinburgh, Adam Black

[78] *Newcastle Courant*, February 15, 1834

[79] *Newcastle Courant,* June 14, 1834

[80] *Newcastle Courant*, November 22, 1834

[81] *Newcastle Courant,* March 14, 1835

[82] *Newcastle Courant*, March 29, 1834

[83] Pamela Horn (1997) *The Victorian Country Child*. Stroud, Sutton Publishing (p.20)

> ignited, and as there was no assistance at hand, she was burned in such a serious manner about the lower part of her body that she only lingered seven hours, when death put an end to her sufferings.[84]

In 1875, a 5 year-old girl from Fletwell in Norfolk died "after severe suffering from being burnt". Her mother was working in the fields and the girl was being looked after by her 10 year-old brother. The boy had left the house briefly to get some fuel and the young girl had "by some means got her clothes on fire, and ran out of the house all in flames".[85]

In Jane's case, she was left alone, not by her parents, but by the teacher at the school. How tragically ironic that 8 year-old Jane, supposedly safe at school in the care of the *in loco parentis* schoolteacher, should suffer such a terrible fate.

The Enduring Impact on the Family

Christmas came exactly two weeks later but there would have been no sense of celebration in the Sanderson household. The death of Jane certainly left its mark on the family. FJS recalled that when he was a young boy at Hamsterley, his grandfather Frank, who was at school with Jane on the fateful day, wouldn't let anyone go near the fire:-

> My grandfather had a big armchair in the kitchen and no-one was allowed to be any nearer the fire than the armchair. If I got too near the fire, he would give us (sic) a stroke with his stick.

It is remarkable and telling that FJS knew all about the death of his great aunt, and was able to recount the sad event with great clarity and some emotion in 1980, almost a century and a half after it happened. He was very well aware of the impact it had made on his grandfather and his lifelong anxiety about open fires. He never got over it.

An insight into the likely trauma experienced by Jane's brothers and sisters, not least 8 year-old Elizabeth and 6 year-old Frank, at the horrifying death of their sister is provided by the recollections of nature writer William Hudson. When William was 6 years old, his dog died, and he recalled in later life how astonished he was "at the intensity of feeling" he experienced, "the terrible darkness it brought on so young a mind", and how the event awakened him "from that beautiful dream of perpetual joy". In other words, the death of his dog had confronted the previously carefree William with his own mortality.[86]

For Elizabeth and Frank, this confrontation with mortality must have been particularly traumatic in that the death of a sister, more so it would be imagined than the death of a favourite dog, will have given them a premature acquaintance with the notion of death being applicable to themselves.

As Wordsworth noted:-

> --- A simple child
> That lightly draws its breath
> And feels its life in every limb,
> What should it know of death?

---

[84] *Northern Echo*, April 11, 1874

[85] Pamela Horn (1994) *Op cit*

[86] Quoted in P. Dudgeon (Ed) 1992 *The Country Child* London, Headline Pub Co, p.50

These words from a poem *We are Seven* were written in 1798 when Wordsworth was 18 years of age. The poem records a conversation between a man and a young girl whose sister and brother had died. Another of the verses could so easily relate to the terrible suffering of Jane Sanderson:-

> The first that died was sister Jane;
> In bed she moaning lay,
> Till God released her of her pain;
> And then she went away.

6-2 William Wordsworth

A poem from the 1830s addressed to mourning children gives an insight into the way people at that time were offered Christian consolation when faced with the death of a child:-

> Weep not, young mourners – weep not tears of sorrow,
> "She was so good!" – If so, how fit to die!
> Remember, that for her there dawns no morrow,
> But one of endless happiness on high!
> Weep not for her; since pure and undefiled
> Her summons found her. Weep not; for the child
> ...
> The bell has ceased and dust to dust is given!
> Weep not for one who now may smile in Heaven![87]

Many parents would take comfort from such consolation but many others would have their faith severely challenged: how could it be part of God's Plan that an innocent child should be taken from them? The verse below from *A Child's Burial in Spring* expresses this emotion:-

> Then rose in my rebellious heart unhallowed thoughts and wild,
> Daring the inscrutable decrees of Providence to scan –
> How death should be allotted to a pure, a sinless child,
> And length of days the destiny of sinful man![88]

Frank Sanderson of Low Harperley's cousin, Francis Vickers of Belle Vue, lost three of his children in infancy, and in his search for comfort and meaning, converted to Primitive Methodism where reunion of family and friends in the afterlife was keenly anticipated.[89]

---

[87] From *The funeral of the charity child* by Harriet Maria Gordon Smythies, 1835
[88] A Child's Burial in Spring, *Belfast Newsletter,* May 5 1835
[89] For more detail, see my book *Life and Times in Victorian Weardale: The Letters of Francis Vickers*, published in 2012.

The Samplers

Elizabeth Sanderson was two years older than her sister Jane and in 1834, they would have been practicing their needlework by hand-stitching numbers, letters of the alphabet, and simple images onto a piece of cloth called a sampler. A sampler survives which mentions Jane Sanderson. It was either originally Jane's sampler and completed by one of her sisters, most probably Elizabeth. Or it was Elizabeth's tribute to her beloved sister, as it was often the case that a sampler would commemorate the death of a (young) member of the family.

Victorian Samplers

> *On the walls of cottages in out-of-the-way parts of the country, in wayside inns and old farmhouses, may frequently be found very lovely and elaborate specimens of the half-forgotten art. The owners, as a rule, have not the remotest idea that any value attaches to the faded piece of needlework, nor do they imagine that ladies would be eager to transfer them to their boudoirs and artists to their studios. The verses on the samplers are very interesting in most cases but nearly all have a melancholy tinge despite the fact that the majority are worked by tiny fingers.*[90]

6-3 Sampler in memory of Jane Sanderson (1826-1834) Courtesy of Jon Preston

The sampler contains the typical embroidered numbers and letters of the alphabet, together with a variety of simple images of ships and weeping willow trees. It also indicates where the family lived, SHIPLEY, and the year of Jane's death, 1834. Along the bottom of the sampler is recorded:

JANE SANDERSON.
AGED.8.DIED.DEC^{r}.10th

The Burial Register and the memorial stone in Hamsterley churchyard record the date of death as Dec 8th. The most likely explanation for the discrepancy is a faulty recollection of the date by the family when the sampler was being completed, perhaps 2 or more years after Jane's death. We do know that Jane suffered burns on Dec 8th, so if the date on the sampler is correct, it would mean that Jane suffered for two days with terrible burns.

---

[90] *Northern Echo*, November 13, 1899

There is also a sampler created by Jane's sister Mary who was born at Ravensford on July 17, 1815 (See p.24). Mary records that the sampler (See below) was "wrought by me" in 1827 when she was 12 years old. However, the third line appears to contain at least some of the initials of her brothers and sisters, with the last one being "FS". Her brother Frank Sanderson was born in July 1828 which suggests that Mary was working on the sampler until at least 1828.

6-4 The Sampler of Mary Sanderson (1815-1856). Courtesy of Jon Preston

Another example of a sampler being worked on by more than one daughter comes from the Kipling family of Stackholme in Lunedale (See p.35).

Mary Kipling's ◆ Sampler ◆ Aged 15 ◆ daughter ◆ of Joseph ◆ and ◆ Jane
Kipling ◆ July ◆ 20 ◆ Year ◆ of ◆ Our ◆ Lord ◆ 1821 ◆

Sarah Kipling Aged 14 ◆ 1833

Thou, who didst with love and blessing,
Gather Zion's babes to thee,
Still a Saviour's love expressing,
These, the babes of Zion, see.[91]

Mary Kipling, born on July 20th 1806, worked on the sampler when she was 15 years old in 1821, and it was completed by her sister Sarah (Sanderson) in 1833 when she was aged 14.

6-5 Mary and Sarah Kipling's Sampler, last worked on in 1833.

[91] *The Sunday School Teachers' Hymn-Book*, London, Sunday School Union, 1824

The Victorian Era

Three years after Jane Sanderson's death, and when Frank was nine years old, Queen Victoria came to the throne. Pamela Horn, in her book *Labouring life in the Victorian countryside*[92], comments;-

> When Queen Victoria came to the throne in 1837 the majority of her subjects were countrymen, dependent for their livelihood on agriculture and upon the vagaries of the seasons and of harvest yields. Despite the spreading influence of northern industrialism, rural life and the village community still dominated English society. The ploughman and his horses tilled the soil, the seeds were sown, and in due time the crops were gathered. Other members of the rural community, such as the country craftsmen - carpenters, wheelwrights, blacksmiths, millers and saddlers - served the needs of the farmers and were reliant upon agricultural prosperity for their own well-being. Together they formed a tightly knit group, integrated for the carrying out of a particular task - the cultivation of the soil and the raising of stock - and for them mutual dependence and co-operation were essential. Farming was still a labour-intensive industry and at harvest time the whole village would turn out to bring in the crops safely.

Frank Sanderson of Low Harperley's early experience of life in a small farming community would have been just as described by Pamela Horn - a closely-knit, not to say parochial community with a common dependence on agricultural prosperity. By the time Queen Victoria had been on the throne for 10 years, Frank moved with his parents (John and Margaret), brother John, and sister Elizabeth from High Shipley to Low Harperley, just over a mile north across the River Wear. Shortly afterwards, elder brother John married Sarah Kipling from Stackholme, Lunedale (See p.35) and moved out of the family home, leaving Frank to manage the farm alongside his elderly father.

Towards the end of October in 1850, Frank lost his second sister who would have provided him with so much companionship and guidance during his growth to adulthood. Elizabeth, who was unmarried, died at the age of 26 at Harperley, with her sister Mary Stephenson present at her death. Elizabeth died of "water in the chest", i.e., Hydrothorax. Also called dropsy of the chest, it is a collection of water in the chest, one or both lungs being affected at the same time:-

> When dropsy in the chest (occurs), the patient labours under a difficulty of breathing, especially when lying down; and the pulse is feeble, and commonly irregular ...This complaint commonly proves fatal, and probably there is no means of cure, except by evacuating the water, by an opening into the chest; an operation which is always precarious, and commonly more dangerous as the disease which it is intended to relieve.[93]

In 1851, Frank and his parents were farming 160 acres at Harperley. His sister Mary was also living at Harperley with her husband John Stephenson and their children. Frank's older brother John had moved from Stackholme, Lunedale to Marshall Green, Witton-le-Wear and was farming 180 acres with the help of 3 labourers. As mentioned earlier, Frank's

---

[92] Published by Fraser Stewart, Abingdon, 1995

[93] *Encyclopaedia Britannica,* 1823

eldest sister Margaret and her husband Joseph Hall were farming at Monkfield in South Bedburn, and at the time of the census, they had a visitor, Margaret's uncle, William Sanderson. William was born in Stanhope Parish in 1778, "the bastard son of John Sanderson", born a year before John married Hannah Grey in Hamsterley.

The Double Wedding in 1855

The Crimean War in which England and France allied with the Turks against Russia commenced in 1854 and ended in September 1855 with the fall of Sevastopol. Frank Sanderson of Low Harperley and Eleanor Alderson of High Shipley would probably not have paid much attention to this well-reported war, being quite pre-occupied as they were by the preparations for their marriage. Frank would have known Eleanor from at least the mid-1840s when the Alderson family took over the tenancy of High Shipley, and the Sandersons moved the short distance across the River Wear to Harperley.

Preparing for the marriage would have been a particularly welcome distraction for Eleanor who was coming to terms with her mother Eleanor's death at High Shipley in January 1854. On Saturday, February 17 1855, just over 3 months after the magnificent but tragic Charge of the Light Brigade at Balaklava, Frank and Eleanor were married at St James Church in Hamsterley in the presence of John Sanderson and John Kirton Nattress.[94] The Reverend W.K. Milner presided, having recently become caretaker curate for his father James George Milner, the Perpetual Curate of Hamsterley (See p.22). If Eleanor senior had been alive, she would have been doubly proud on that severe winter's day in 1855 because it was a double wedding: Eleanor's sister Ann married George Bell, a farmer's son from Lanchester. FJS recalled that George Bell's son John kept the *Commercial Hotel* at Bishop Auckland (replaced by the *Castle Hotel*).

A month after Frank and Eleanor were married, Charlotte Bronte died. And later the same year, David Livingstone discovered the Victoria Falls in Southern Africa.

Life on the Farm

In Christopher Wood's book about paintings of English country life[95], he observed:-

> The English countryside must have looked at its most beautiful in the mid-nineteenth century. It was the last golden age of English agriculture, the period when 'high farming' was at its peak, employing a work force of two million people. Before the agricultural depressions of the 1880s and 90s, which were to drive so many people away into the towns, it was a time of general prosperity. The land had never been so intensely cultivated, and never employed so many people. Very little machinery was used and chemicals were unknown. All farm work was done by men and horses, using methods that had hardly changed for centuries. The countryside must have looked greener, lusher and more idyllic than it is possible to imagine now. Roads were mostly small and unsurfaced, and the only traffic was horse-drawn. Villages

[94] FJS believed that the Nattresses were related to the Sandersons. In fact, they were related to the Aldersons, John Kirton Nattress being the husband of Jane Alderson, Eleanor's elder sister.

[95] Wood, Chrispoher (1988) *Paradise Lost: Paintings of English Country Life and Landscape 1850-1914*, London, Barrie & Jenkins.

> were bustling, industrious places, full both of farm workers and of local craftsmen, and with a strong local culture and dialect (p.19).

This golden age of general prosperity for two decades from the early 1850s was certainly enjoyed by Frank and his brother John. They were successful tenant farmers and, just as their father had done when he died in 1865, were able to pass on the fruits of their success to their children.

Souden gives the following insights into the kind of work Frank would have been doing on the farm:-

> Whereas the farm worker in the fields is a rare and solitary sight today, in the early Victorian countryside the fields might be busy with people all year round. Only late in the century, when livestock became more important in England's rural economy and machinery began to make its presence felt, did field work begin to play a less prominent part in the business of farming.[96]

Harvest Time

Harvesting was also a special time on the farm. As David Souden observes:-

> The harvest was an immense activity. The entire neighbourhood was involved, from farmers to itinerant workers, from fit men and their wives to their children and aged parents. The harvest in mid-Victorian England involved more workers than at any previous time.

6-6 This cartoon from *Punch* in 1879 depicts a mounted landlord talking to a tenant farmer. There was never a photograph of Frank Sanderson of Low Harperley, but this is how he might have looked - with gaiters, frock coat, white whiskers and pipe, and with no hint of deference to the landlord. He would have been about 50 years old and probably wearing spectacles by that time.

[96] Souden, David (1991) *The Victorian Village*. Collins & Brown, p.84.

6-7 Harvesting in Victorian times (from painting by HH Parker)

Flora Thompson, born in an Oxfordshire hamlet in 1876, recalls life on the farm in the 1880's, giving a description of harvesting which would have been very familiar to Frank Sanderson of Low Harperley and his family:-

> In the fields where the harvest had begun all was bustle and activity. The scythe still did most of the work and they did not dream it would ever be superseded.
>
> After the mowing and reaping and binding came the carrying, the busiest time of all. Every man and boy put his best foot forward then, for, when the corn was cut and dried it was imperative to get it stacked and thatched before the weather broke. All day and far into the twilight the yellow-and-blue painted farm wagons passed and repassed along the roads between the fields and the stack-yard. Big cart-horses returning with an empty wagon were made to gallop like two-year-olds. Straws hung on the roadside hedges and many a gate-post was knocked down through hasty driving. In the fields the men pitch-forked the sheaves to the one who was building the load on the wagon, and the air resounded with Hold tights, and Wert ups, and Who-o-as. The Hold tight! was an empty cry; sometimes, in the past, the man on top of the load had not held tight or not tight enough. There were tales of fathers and grandfathers whose necks or backs had been broken by a fall from a load, and of other fatal accidents afield, bad cuts from scythes, pitch-forks passing through feet, to be followed by lockjaw, and of sunstroke; but, happily, nothing of this kind happened on that particular farm in the 'eighties. At last, in the cool dusk of an August evening, the last load was brought in, with a nest of merry boys' faces among the sheaves on the top, and the men walking alongside with pitch-forks on shoulders.[97]

[97] Flora Thompson quoted in *The Country Child*, p18. P Dudgeon (Ed)

Speed the Plough

As is the case today, one of the most important aspects of field work in Victorian times was ploughing, and the Victorians recognised the importance of ploughing matches, not just as recreation for the ploughmen and amusement for the spectators, but for encouraging excellence in an activity vital to the national interest:-

> It is generally held that good ploughing is essential to good farming, good farming is essential to good crops, and good crops are essential to national prosperity. Therefore, in encouraging ploughing matches, we shall be doing the nation at large a real and lasting benefit. A good ploughman may be made better by friendly competition with his fellow ploughmen, and a better man may become the best, because these competitive trials are healthy stimulants and assist in developing the talents of the competitor.[98]

The ploughman would take great pride in his work:-

> Ploughmen could be discovered strolling out on a Sunday to cast a critical eye over the fields of neighbouring farms, and they would take part in ploughing matches at country fairs and shows. A good furrow had to be as straight as a die, and the overall effect as tidy as might be.[99]

Just over a year after Frank was married, one Wednesday afternoon in February in his 28th year, he won a Silver Cup at the Harperley and Helme Park Fair for his prowess in ploughing.

[98] *Chelmsford Chronicle*, April 21 1871

[99] Souden, David (1991) *The Victorian Village*. Collins & Brown (p.84)

6-8 The silver cup won in 1856 by Frank Sanderson of Low Harperley

The cup is inscribed with the message:-

"SPEED THE PLOUGH"

PRESENTED
TO
Francis Sanderson
THE BEST
PLOUGHMAN
at the
Harperley and Helme Park
PLOUGHING MATCH
27th Feb^{y}, 1856[100]

Staffordshire pottery mugs often carried a traditional verse in the early Victorian period, including the reference to "God speed the plough":-

God Speed the Plough

O happy is the farmer and free from all care
Who rises every morning to breathe fresh air
And hears the birds singing from every green bough.
No life like the farmer's who follows the plough.
Success e'er attend him and plenty and peace
May the seeds that he sows with blessings increase
May health still around him its comforts bestow
Long life to the farmer and God speed the plough.

Frank Sanderson was an excellent ploughman and an excellent farmer, as evidenced by a report of an exceptional crop of oats in August, 1871:-

> The crops in Weardale are everywhere looking well. The hay harvest is nearly reaped, and is most abundant, and with the exception of that first cut getting a shower or two, has been well won, and will vie both in quantity and quality with the best seasons on record. From Witton-le-Wear to Stanhope the corn fields present one of the most pleasing sights seen for some years and should the fine sunny weather of the

[100] FJS hosted a dinner party at *The Royal Hotel*, Clacton, Essex, on 27th February 1956 on the 100th anniversary of the ploughing contest. In 1978, he deposited £100 in a Building Society, to be drawn in 2056 to celebrate the bicentennial of the contest.

> last few days continue, harvest operations will partially commence on the course of a week, as we saw a field of barley on the Bradley Farm almost ready for the sickle. Harvest will not, however, become general for three weeks. All descriptions of grain crops are good in this district and the straw of same unusually luxuriant. On a farm at Harperley, under the management of Mr Frank Sanderson, in a field near the lodge, a head of oats was plucked which measured 6 feet eight inches, and was one inch in circumference round the stem, and contained 190 corns. This monster stalk was in a 12 acre field, and the average length of the straw could not be less than 4 feet 6 inches or upwards. On this farm, there is another field of eight acres, next the railway station, equally luxurious.[101]

It was not only the harvest plans that were disrupted a few days later when, on Friday, 18th August, the Wear Valley experienced a violent thunder storm. The storm was at its height when, at 4 o'clock in the afternoon at Knavesmire, a remote farm just south of Hamsterley, 30 year-old Matthew Wilkinson and his wife (and first cousin) Margaret, together with their infant son Joseph, were in the kitchen having tea. Suddenly, there was a blinding flash of lightning immediately followed by "a fearful crash of thunder". Alarmed, Matthew, and Margaret carrying the child, ran out of the house to check the stock in the nearby farm building. Returning to the house, they had almost reached the doorway when they were hit by another terrible flash of lightning. Neighbours who saw the house in flames quickly responded:-

> On arriving there the house was completely enveloped in flames. Mrs. Wilkinson lay outside the door on the ground, insensible, her husband, with his head resting upon her knee, quite dead, and a child by his side struck blind with lightning....Mr. Wilkinson was killed instantaneously, while his wife and child were blinded and rendered insensible.... Measures were adopted to save some of the furniture, but being an old building with a thatch about a yard in thickness, the cottage burnt very rapidly, and little property was rescued. The farm buildings and the stock were saved, and the fire prevented from spreading beyond the house, only three gable walls of which remained.[102]

It was reported that "on Saturday the poor woman died on that day from the effects of her injuries, and little hopes are entertained of the child's recovery". However, Margaret and Joseph survived: ten years later, Margaret was living at Wether Hill Windmill with her widowed mother, her son Joseph, and another son, eight-year-old Matthew, his age suggesting that Margaret was in the early stages of pregnancy when her husband died. Margaret died at Wether Hill in 1892 and is buried at Hamsterley.

Ransomes' Ploughs

Ransomes of Ipswich was foremost during the Victorian period in producing prize-winning ploughs. They designed new ploughs for the plough-trials at the Royal Agricultural Show at Newcastle in 1864 but they realised that the ploughman and the horses are as important as the plough itself, so they sought a skilled ploughman to join up with their team of Suffolk horses. In 1863, they hired James Barker, a 36 year-old Essex man

---

[101] *Newcastle Courant*, August 18, 1871
[102] *Teesdale Mercury,* August 30, 1871

who had a great local reputation as a ploughman. Barker competed for them not only in the Newcastle trials but afterwards in plough trials wherever they were held up and down the country. Ransomes won five prizes at the Newcastle Show, and during the same year, fifteen out of twenty All-England prizes, all with the newly designed ploughs and the new ploughman. At the Tynemouth Manor and District Ploughing Match in 1865, it was reported that:-

> Messrs Ransomes of Ipswich…carried off first honours, competing with one of the ploughs of this celebrated firm. Their ploughs, there being three on the ground, were greatly admired and the success of their representative, James Barker, was hailed with much satisfaction.
>
> Before the match, James Adams, the agent for Ransomes, indicated that if Barker won, he would not be accepting the prize money, as Ransomes did not wish to compete for prizes at local ploughing matches. The prize would therefore be given to the second ploughman.[103]

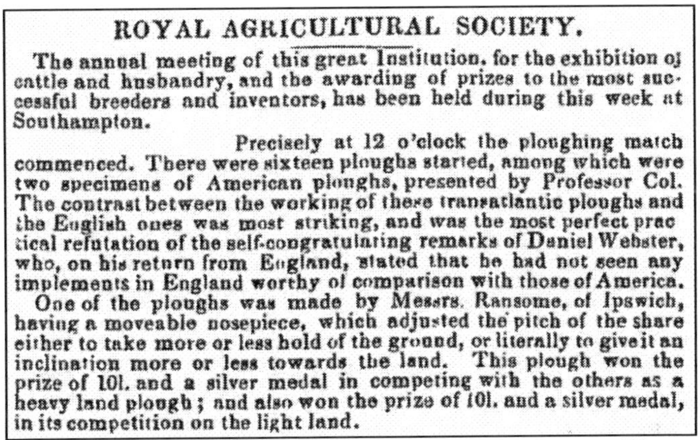

ROYAL AGRICULTURAL SOCIETY.

The annual meeting of this great Institution, for the exhibition of cattle and husbandry, and the awarding of prizes to the most successful breeders and inventors, has been held during this week at Southampton.

Precisely at 12 o'clock the ploughing match commenced. There were sixteen ploughs started, among which were two specimens of American ploughs, presented by Professor Col. The contrast between the working of these transatlantic ploughs and the English ones was most striking, and was the most perfect practical refutation of the self-congratulating remarks of Daniel Webster, who, on his return from England, stated that he had not seen any implements in England worthy of comparison with those of America.

One of the ploughs was made by Messrs. Ransome, of Ipswich, having a moveable nosepiece, which adjusted the pitch of the share either to take more or less hold of the ground, or literally to give it an inclination more or less towards the land. This plough won the prize of 10l. and a silver medal in competing with the others as a heavy land plough; and also won the prize of 10l. and a silver medal, in its competition on the light land.

6-9 Ransomes winning ploughing prizes in the 1840's[104]

Two years later at the same event, Barker won again, and again the cash was "generously returned" for the man who came second.[105] Ransomes was obviously aware of the fact that their man Barker, a full-time professional ploughman, was for the most part competing against lowly farm labourers not used to competing in ploughing matches. By winning and voluntarily forfeiting the prizes in the local ploughing matches, James Barker generated much goodwill for the company, with himself and his plough standing "very high in the opinion of the public."

Ransomes and Barker kept winning ploughing matches in all parts of the country, generating much positive publicity in the press:-

> (The number of prizes won) certainly speaks well for their ploughs and their adaptability to all soils in every state of the weather.[106]

---

[103] *Newcastle Courant*, February 10, 1865

[104] *John Bull*, 29 July 1844

[105] *Newcastle Courant*, February 8, 1867

[106] *Newcastle Courant,* November 2, 1866

> At the conclusion of the Autumn Ploughing Match Season, at Goxhill, Lincolnshire, a spirited contest took place, the palm being carried off by James Barker, Messrs Ransomes' well-known ploughman; thus increasing the celebrity of that firm by winning their thirty-third prize this season.[107]

> Nothing could excel the skilful work of Messrs Ransomes' man with his wheel plough; it was generally admired, and it was not surprising to learn that he carried off the leading honours of the day.[108]

Plough Wars

By 1868, many ploughing societies, rather than being grateful recipients of the generosity of Ransomes, had changed their rules. Thus at the Fifth Annual Ploughing Match of the Bywell Ploughing Society at Nafferton Farm, it was announced:-

> Should the Servant of a Plough Manufacturer be the Winner of any Prize, he will be duly acknowledged as such, but the Money or Watch will be given to the next Successful Competitor.[109]

Despite the relentless public relations campaign carried out by James Adams and the champion ploughman James Barker, the first signs of discontent with Ransomes were evident in 1867 at the Bywell Ploughing Match. At the dinner after James Barker had inevitably won the Class 1 first prize, Mr Thomas Trotter, in proposing a toast to the successful competitors, stated that Ransomes should not have sent a man "whose great practice rendered it rather unfair for others to contend with him." He understood that they wished to promote their plough but pointed out that they could do so by "exhibitions for that purpose and competitions fitted for them." However, he acknowledged that James Barker could teach their ploughmen some lessons, as his work was "the admiration and wonder of all who saw him."[110]

Thomas Trotter's observations show the mixed opinions at that time in ploughing societies about the success of Ransomes. On the one hand, there was a feeling that Barker's well-practiced expertise in matches gave him a great and unfair advantage over his local competitors. On the other hand, he was recognised as an excellent role model, someone who could inspire the local ploughmen to be the best they could be. His inspirational qualities were enhanced by his personality, as highlighted in a newspaper tribute:-

> At the shows and matches no one who has met Barker can forget his broad and kindly smile, or the favourite sentimental songs with which he has enlivened many a company at a ploughing-match dinner after the labours of the day were over. A great feature of Barker's life has been that he has always conducted himself in such a way that, while being a favourite among his fellow ploughmen, he has, by his civility and good conduct, earned the respect of the farmers and others with whom he has come into contact.[111]

---

[107] *Newcastle Courant*, December 7, 1866
[108] *Newcastle Courant,* January 31, 1868
[109] *Newcastle Courant,* January 24, 1868
[110] *Newcastle Courant*, February 1, 1867
[111] A Champion Ploughman. *The Border Watch (South Australia)* July 14, 1886

THE PLOUGHING MATCH.

6-10 The Ploughing Match: *Illustrated London News,* July 16, 1842

There was a demonstration of Barker's ability to win hearts and minds at the Northumberland Agricultural Society Annual Ploughing Match in 1868 where he again won the main prize. Mr Jacob Wilson, in proposing "the successful competitors", observed that he believed that the farmers did not grudge "one single shilling either Mr Adams (Ransomes' Agent) or his man Barker took out of the county (Applause)."

Mr Adams, ever-mindful of a marketing opportunity, responded by stating that Ransomes "thought more of public opinion than gain, as instanced in the liberal way in which they have presented a plough (as a prize) for competition." This, he said, showed their good intentions, and that they did not seek advantage to themselves at the society's expense. He then received applause when he observed that every farmer "could not but acknowledge the superiority of finish and style" evident in Barker's ploughing. He concluded with a provocative promotion of Ransomes' ploughs:-

> I do not want to push trade but I believe that the ploughs I have seen this day were without exception the roughest lot I've ever seen (Laughter). I do hope that you will introduce a better plough – which would be to your credit and advantage.[112]

Of course, by "a better plough", he meant a Ransomes' plough.

[112] *Newcastle Courant*, February 14, 1868

Ralph Stothard in the Spotlight

Months later, the mutterings about James Barker's unfair advantage over local ploughmen had extended into a more generalised complaint about the business practices of Messrs Ransomes. At the Bywell Annual Ploughing Match in December 1868 at Hindley Hall, Ransomes' ploughs won all three prizes in Class 1 for "ploughs of any description", but the winning ploughman was not James Barker but 21 year-old farmer's son, Ralph Stothard[113] of Low Carr House, Durham.[114] Great Uncle Ralph's win prompted a flurry of correspondence in the *Newcastle Courant* about the "dishonourable" practices of Ransomes

William Smith, a 22 year-old farmer's son from Low Fotherley, wrote to the *Courant* to point out that three out of five ploughs made by local blacksmith William Arkley of Broomley won prizes, "an honour which even Ransomes could not boast of on that occasion." Defending local ploughmen and plough-makers, he continued:-

> I believe it is also the imperative duty of someone to expose the corrupt practices carried on at local ploughing matches. It is becoming customary amongst large implement manufacturers to give ploughs as prizes at such competitions, thereby putting into the hands of the best qualified workmen ploughs of their own make as an incentive to use them at future competitions; and also inducing well-known prize takers to lay their old ploughs aside, and use theirs, by paying all their expenses when attending such contests. Such an acknowledgement was made by two competitors at the above-named society's match at Hindley last week, one of whom ploughed with the celebrated James Barker's own plough, and had his instructions throughout the day, to assist him in satisfactorily performing his work. This was directly breaking one of the society's rules: that "no one assist, direct, or otherwise interfere with any competitor whilst performing his work.

He concluded that the object of the local ploughing matches should be to improve the skills of local ploughmen and encourage local plough-makers to produce better implements so that the farmer can go to the nearest village and "obtain an instrument worthy of his use."[115]

Having been accused of receiving expenses from Ransomes and instructions from James Barker during the match, Ralph Stothard wrote to the *Courant* refuting the allegations:-

> I have read with some surprise the letter of your correspondent Mr Smith, and, as I suppose his remarks about Messrs Ransomes would be referred particularly to me as the winner of the Champion All-England Prize, I beg most emphatically to deny the truth of any of them.
>
> In the first place, I was not engaged by them to plough, neither did they pay my expenses. Secondly, I did not use Barker's own plough, but one that I have bought of them and believe to be quite as good as the one he uses.
>
> And thirdly it seems strange that anyone should wish to deprive Barker of the same liberty of speech that all others enjoy at ploughing matches; although, as a practical

[113] FJS's uncle.

[114] *Newcastle Courant*, January 1, 1869

[115] *Newcastle Courant,* January 15, 1869

> ploughman, I do not believe advice from lookers-on does any good, and I don't remember altering my plough during the match in question by the advice of Barker.[116]

Publicity-minded Ransomes also felt compelled to respond:-

> The ploughs which we have occasionally given as prizes at ploughing matches have been gratefully received by the different societies to whom we have given them, and whatever subsequent gain to ourselves as an introduction of our ploughs, it is clearly so much out of our pocket at the time, and will, we feel sure, not be denounced as a "corrupt practice" by the majority of your readers.
> We do not think that any business man would blame us for trying to introduce our ploughs in a legitimate way, and we consider it is only true business policy to get them into the hands of good ploughmen, even when it involves them laying aside their old ones.
> If a man will oblige us by so doing, we see nothing 'corrupt' in making him a substantial acknowledgement, though we must deny having paid the expenses of any man at the Bywell match as stated by Mr William Smith.
> All we ask is a fair field, and no favour, and we consider it a greater honour to carry off prizes in the hands of local men with our ploughs, as at the Bywell match, than to win them with our own man Barker. We would just add that though our ploughs are well adapted for taking prizes at matches, the same plough, by a simple change of breast, being suited to both classes of work.[117]

In another letter published the same day, John Gregory, an agricultural implement maker from South Shields, aired his grievances against Ransomes. He referred to the Hindley Hall Ploughing Match when Ransomes, despite having persuaded the best local ploughmen to use their ploughs, had only a third place in the swing class. He pointed out that Ralph Stothard, who won with a Ransome plough in the Champion Class, had previously won prizes with a Howard's plough. And at Fulwell, his own ploughs had outperformed those of Ransomes. He concluded:-

> I hope at the Northumberland ploughing match next week that men will not be bought over in the way I refer to, but take ploughs they have won prizes with and let all makers stand on their own merits. I would be one of the last to allude to the above, only in duty to see Hornsby, Howard, and all local makers get every Englishman's right, that is "fair play."[118]

The following week, William Smith returned to the fray in an attempt to justify his allegations against Ralph Stothard. He claimed that Mr Stothard had told a "respectable gentleman" that he preferred his Howard plough but had used the Ransomes' plough because he had had his expenses paid. With regard to Ralph's subsequent denial that he had received expenses, and Ransomes' admission that they see nothing corrupt in offering a "substantial acknowledgement" to ploughmen who adopt their ploughs, he declared that he was "quite at a loss to know the difference, as they seem to be equivalent terms, nothing less

[116] *Newcastle Courant*, January 22, 1869
[117] *Newcastle Courant*, January 22, 1869
[118] *Newcastle Courant*, January 22, 1869

or more than six in the one and half-a-dozen in the other." Mr Smith appears to have a point.

And as to Mr Stothard's denial of having followed Barker's directions, Mr Smith resorted to sarcasm:-

> He denies having followed Barker's directions. Be this as it may, it is well known by the spectators present on that occasion, that such directions were given, regardless of the rules of the society; but, possibly, as he styles himself the champion at that match, he may have attained that degree of perfection which requires neither the assistance of Barker nor any other professional man.[119]

In his letter to the *Courant*, Ralph Stothard's defence was that although he did not deny that Barker was offering advice, he maintained that freedom of speech allowed him to do so, and that in any case he had taken no notice of any advice given.

Mr Smith concluded that if Ransomes was not corrupt, it was far from honourable in the way they induced good ploughmen to lay aside ploughs which were well adapted for ordinary farm use and which had brought then success in ploughing matches:-

> They ask for "a fair field and no favour" – Now, it can be no fair field when the best local men are bought up by their agents, whilst the village smith, who may produce an even more excellent implement, has not such resources to introduce his ploughs in this way. No one would blame them for introducing their ploughs by ordinary and honourable measures, letting their ploughs, with others, stand on their own merits; but the course they are adopting must of necessity bring down upon them the censure of every unprejudiced mind.[120]

The person responsible for "inducing" good ploughmen to adopt the Ransomes' plough, their agent James Adams, responded to the various allegations by continuing to cultivate the local ploughmen and the farmers:-

> I have attended these matches for several years for Messrs Ransomes, and know all the best ploughmen; besides this, I am happy to say I possess the friendship of many of the farmers, and it is them I have chiefly to thank for seeing our ploughs more freely used this year, coupled with the fact that the men know they are a very superior implement.
>
> Your readers will all admit that this a perfectly "fair play", and Mr Gregory is quite at liberty, if he thinks proper, to call on men using our ploughs and induce them to use his own instead, although I believe he would find it a difficult undertaking.[121]

In an Editorial, the *Newcastle Courant* offered its opinion:-

> What a battle about ploughs is going on among the farmers and agricultural implement makers! …Mr William Smith … alleged that the champion ploughman at Bywell (Ralph Stothard junior, Carr House) was "coached" by Ransomes' "own man Barker." These statements have been corroborated by some and denied by others; so that it is difficult to arrive at the truth of the matter. One can plainly perceive,

[119] *Newcastle Courant*, January 29, 1869
[120] *Newcastle Courant*, January 27, 1869
[121] *Newcastle Courant*, January 29, 1869

> however, that the conduct of every person at these competitions is not altogether so honourable as could be wished.[122]

Undaunted by the attacks on his integrity by John Gregory and William Smith, Ralph Stothard won first prize in the open competition, open to ploughs of any description at the inaugural meeting of the Washington and District Ploughing Society in 1869. At the Dinner, in the presence of inter alia, James Adams from Ransomes, and the disgruntled John Gregory, Ralph made a speech in which he firmly endorsed Ransomes' ploughs:-

> I have ploughed at a great many matches and have used a large number of different ploughs, but I must say that the one that I ploughed with today, and which was from the manufactory of Messrs Ransomes was the best and easiest that I have ever ploughed with in my life![123]

John Gregory continued to air his objections to Ransomes' business practices in the *Courant*, becoming ever-more personal in his attacks on James Barker. The *Courant* took the view that Barker had the positive effect of 'stimulating' local ploughmen by his presence at matches, and that they hoped to see them beating the great champion "upon his merits".[124] Mr Gregory however, reacting to James Barker being sent to teach farmers how to plough, observed:-

> His creeping pace is enough to petrify a lively body....Barker may make a piece of work to please the eye, but the most intelligent farmers say this class of work is not the best for a crop.[125]

Gregory also expressed his distaste for the way Ransomes cultivated people in pursuit of their business interests:-

> You will soon see who are wanting to be the leading characters, who they are who are running after the officials, trying to get into their good graces, writing good reports, standing chairmen at dinners, making long speeches about this wonderful firm, singing comic songs, and dancing – particularly if successful. Is there nothing rotten about all this? I leave myself in the hands of a discerning public, whether I am right or wrong.[126]

History proved John Gregory to be wrong. He, along with William Smith and others were swimming against the tide in their staunch defence of localism, the idea that local farming practice could be sustained by local blacksmiths and small local manufacturers in the face of the might of large-scale manufacturers. Ransomes not only had excellent products but also had the financial muscle to market these products aggressively and effectively.

[122] *Newcastle Courant*, January 29, 1869
[123] *Newcastle Courant*, February 2, 1869
[124] *Newcastle Courant*, January 14, 1870
[125] *Newcastle Courant*, January 28, 1870
[126] *Newcastle Courant*, February 18, 1870

6-11 Advertising Sign for Ploughs

Inevitably, small local plough makers gradually disappeared, whilst Ransomes prospered: by 1877, James Adams was able to state that Ransomes' ploughs were the standard implement of the County of Durham, with the majority of prizes at ploughing matches being won by local men using their ploughs.[127] It was another seventy years before Ransomes finally ceased manufacturing horse ploughs (1948).[128]

James Barker remained peerless as the champion ploughman of England until he retired from competition in 1879, having won £2,000 in prizes during his career.

Champion Ploughman marries Lizzie Sanderson

Ralph Stothard continued competing in and winning ploughing matches in County Durham before retiring from competition in the mid-1880s. Thereafter he maintained an active interest in ploughing matches, becoming a well-respected judge and a sponsor of competitions.

In June, 1887, there was a magnificent Jubilee Thanksgiving Service in Westminster Abbey to celebrate 50 years of rule by Queen Victoria. After weeks of celebrations, Victoria wrote in her diary, "Never, never, can I forget this brilliant year, so full of marvellous kindness, loyalty and devotion of so many millions." She had seen her country build the greatest empire the world had ever seen and she had given her name to an age when Britain was the dominant force in the world. Elsewhere, American scientists had succeeded in measuring the speed of light. In South Africa, Cecil Rhodes gained control of the world's diamond market with the intention of using the profits to build a white man's homeland in southern Africa. Nearer to home, Verdi completed his opera, *Otello*, and Tchaikovsky composed the ballet, *Swan Lake*.

---

[127] *Newcastle Courant*, January 26, 1877

[128] Evans, George Ewart (1960) *The Horse in the Furrow*, Faber & Faber

It was in this year that 38-year-old Ralph Stothard married 30-year-old Lizzie Sanderson (pictured below) at Brancepeth Parish Church. Lizzie's 18 year-old brother Frank Sanderson of Hamsterley was a page-boy, and her brother John of Burnigill was the Best Man.[129]

FJS heard from his father about a frightening incident at the wedding. Lizzie and Ralph were in the wedding carriage when the horses bolted. Immediately seeing the danger, Lizzie's father Frank jumped off the top of the carriage and averted a possible tragedy by grabbing the horses and calming them, an astonishing reaction from a man in his sixtieth year. It was fortunate that he was on the carriage because the carriage driver was in no position to do anything but hold the reins. FJS's father told him that the bride and groom were lucky they weren't killed.

Ralph and Lizzie had three sons: Francis Sanderson Stothard, Farmer and Butcher, William Henry Stothard, a Colliery Manager by the age of 20, and Ralph Edward Stothard, a Coal Merchant. William Henry was named after Lizzie's brother who had died so tragically in her arms when she was 18 and he was 4 years old. (See p.113)

6-12 Ralph Stothard and Elizabeth Eleanor Sanderson were married in 1887.

The Stothard and Sanderson families remained close. A postcard from August 1910 is evocative of those carefree days prior to the First World War. Posted from the Isle of Man, it was sent by William Henry Stothard to his Uncle Frank Sanderson of Hamsterley, who had just returned from a holiday in Whitby:-

> I have just arrived safe. Plenty of girls. Hope you all feel well after Whitby. Kind regards. WH Stothard.

[129] Prior to the wedding, Lizzie had been a housekeeper for her brother John at Burnigill Farm near Brancepeth.

6-13 “HS” refers to William Henry Stothard, but who are “WB” and “SG”?

Francis Sanderson Stothard’s son John had memories of his grandparents from the 1930s at Neville’s Cross. Lizzie was very thrifty: everything was under lock and key, even the sweets she occasionally gave to her grandchildren. He remembers her retrieving a key from under her petticoat to open the drawer where the sweets were kept. He also remembers her making rice puddings with egg and gathering all the chicken bones to make soup. His grandfather Ralph he remembers as hard of hearing, and keeping himself active by digging seven spits a day in the back garden, always leaving himself “a bit to do”. There were also a few hens in the garden and they often used to wander into the kitchen.

Ralph Stothard died in 1934 at Baliol House, Neville’s Cross and just under two years later, on Friday 14th February1936, Lizzie died at the age of 80 and was buried in St Cuthbert’s Churchyard, Durham.

Infant Mortality

In 1861, the year that Abraham Lincoln assumed the presidency of the United States and the American Civil War began following the breakaway of 11 states to form the Southern Confederacy, Frank Sanderson was a tenant farmer at Low Harperley, near Fir Tree, farming 350 acres, employing 2 labourers and 3 servants. He was with his wife Eleanor, 28, and two young daughters, Elizabeth Eleanor, aged 4 and born in Witton-le-Wear (Marshall Green), and Mary Ann, aged 4 months. Sadly, Mary Ann was dead within three years.

Also present were main servants Christopher Laverick, 17, and Dowson Snowdon, 16, House Servants Mary Nattrass, 19[130], Sarah Roose, 17, niece Jane Alderson, 12 (her brother Henry’s daughter) and parents John and Margaret Sanderson, 78 and 75 respectively. The Housemaid was Margaret Stephenson, aged 16, the daughter of Frank’s sister Mary who had died 5 years previously.

[130] It is possible that Mary was the sister of John Kirton Nattress, Best Man at the double wedding.

(Elizabeth) Eleanor Sanderson, Frank and Eleanor's first child, was born on March 16, 1857 at Harperley. This was the year of the Indian Mutiny, the year in which Prince Albert was created Prince Consort, and the year in which the Halle Orchestra was established in Manchester.

Frank and Eleanor's second child, Elizabeth Sanderson, was born in January, 1858. The choice of the name 'Elizabeth' for their second child is likely to have been a tribute to Frank's beloved sister Elizabeth, who had died in 1850 at the age of 26. When little Elizabeth herself died aged 3 months on April 10, 1858, the name was transferred to her 2 year old sister, Eleanor, who became Elizabeth Eleanor Sanderson.

Their third daughter, Mary Ann Sanderson was born in 1860 and died on December 20, 1863, aged 3 years, of diphtheria. Poor Mary Ann was the victim of "a virulent zymotic disease, caused by a micro-organism, in which the mucous membrane, especially of the throat and air passages, becomes coated with an exudation which forms a thick leather-like membrane". Her father Frank was present when she died, and reported the death. Mary Ann's death was followed in early Spring 1864 by the death of her cousin Caroline Sanderson at Bradley Hall, aged 9 months.

By the time of the 1871 Census, there were three sons (John, Frank and William Henry) and one daughter (Elizabeth Eleanor) at home with Frank and Eleanor.

John Sanderson was born at 12.30pm on 8th October, 1862. This year saw Bismarck become the leading minister in Prussia, Garibaldi attempting to seize Rome and a major cotton famine in Lancashire. Thomas Sanderson, their second son was born in December, 1864 and died on New Year's Day, 1865, of inflammation of the chest. He was 4 weeks old. Just over 4 months later, Thomas's paternal grandfather, John Sanderson, died at the age of 82.

Three months after the death from drowning of his maternal grandfather, William Alderson, Francis Sanderson was born in early May, 1866 and died on May 28, aged 3 weeks, of uncertified "convulsions". The second Frank, FJS's father Frank Sanderson was born on October 8, 1868 at Low Harperley. Sadly, although not unusual for the time, only one of his grandparents, his paternal grandmother Margaret Sanderson, was alive to celebrate the birth. By this time however, Margaret was 82 years old and ailing. She died 5 months later of bronchitis.

The other son present in 1871 was 4-months old William Henry (See p.113).

At the time of the 1881 Census, Frank senior was still at Low Harperley, aged 52, farming 366 acres. Also present were his daughter, Elizabeth Eleanor (Lizzie), aged 24, and Frank junior, aged 12, a scholar. His wife Eleanor was at their other tenancy, Hill House Farm, Brandon, with her son John, aged 18. It appears that Frank took over the tenancy of Hill House Farm in the late 1870s after the tenant Hugh Kirton, a well-known cattle-dealer, died from a short illness. The transfer of the tenancy was likely to have been facilitated by family connections: Eleanor's sister Jane was married to John Kirton Nattress and they had a son, Hugh Kirton Nattress, indicating close kinship between the Kirton and Nattress families.

A School Board for Wolsingham

Frank Sanderson of Low Harperley was a vociferous opponent of plans to introduce a School Board to Wolsingham in 1873-4. The 1870 Education Act, which made elementary education available to all children between the ages of five and thirteen, signalled the recognition that it was the duty of the Government to see that education was provided for all children. However, how education was delivered was still at the discretion of parishes, which could either fully adopt the Act or continue to deliver public elementary education by the voluntary religious societies: the British and Foreign Schools Society (Nonconformist) and the National Society (Church of England). By 1870, they provided education for about 1.7 million of the 2.5 million children of school age, and the Education Act was intended to fill the gaps.[131]

Frank Sanderson, farming at Low Harperley at the time, and other ratepayers in Wolsingham Parish will have been aware of the fierce arguments about the establishment of a School Board in Stanhope where a mass meeting of ratepayers had been held in December 1873. On one side was the 'undenominational' party, led by the Reverend Hugh Gilmore, a Primitive Methodist Minister strongly in favour of a School Board on the basis that schools were so badly managed that "more of the kind would be an evil rather than a good."[132] Those against a School Board argued that £2,000 raised by voluntary effort would be sufficient to put the district into "school efficiency", and that the parish would be burdened not only with the yearly expenses of a School Board, but also the costs of building schools, say £6,000-7,000, if a School Board was introduced. Despite the concerns of a noisy minority of ratepayers, the meeting voted overwhelmingly in favour of establishing a School Board, which was granted in early 1874 for Stanhope Parish.

Just before Christmas 1873, down the dale in Wolsingham, a public meeting of anxious ratepayers overwhelmingly rejected taking measures to remedy the shortfall in school accommodation in Wolsingham and Tow Law. A follow-up meeting on this issue was held in the Town Hall, Wolsingham on Friday, January 9th, 1874 with Mr Ralph Crossling presiding. As at the previous meeting, there was a large attendance of ratepayers, including Frank Sanderson from Low Harperley Farm.

Mr John Noble Lacey, a tailor from Wolsingham, was first called upon to address the meeting. He spoke passionately in favour of a School Board:-

> I hold it to be the duty of the State to see that every child is educated, so that the child might have a fair start in life, and put on an equality with those whose parents have the means of giving them a proper schooling. (Applause) I believe that a great amount of crime and a great amount of pauperism arises from the want of education, and the ratepayers, in considering the utility of School Boards, should not forget this – that in punishing crime and maintaining paupers they have to contribute to a very large extent. I believe that two thirds of the rates have to go to punish criminals and keep paupers. A report written by the Rev WH Holland demonstrates the high levels of illiteracy amongst prisoners, and the Registrar General's report records that in 1867 there were 179,154 marriages, and 37,879 of the men and 51,606 of the women signed the marriage register with marks. Think of that and the condition of a family brought up under the guidance of those persons.[133]

Seeking to allay concerns about the high costs to ratepayers of maintaining a School Board, Mr Lacey quoted costs in other districts in the North of England. At this point, Frank Sanderson, "amidst a good deal of hissing and applause", rose to make an objection.

---

[131] Harrison, JFC, (1990) *Late Victorian Britain 1875-1901*. London, Fontana, p.200.
[132] *Northern Echo*, December 19, 1873
[133] *Northern Echo*, January 12, 1874

Chairman: "We must have order, sir."

Frank Sanderson: "If you stick to the truth you will get order, but I… (renewed interruption)

Chairman, "We demand order"

Frank Sanderson: "You have called a ratepayers' meeting, but I think you want the biggest ratepayers to go away."

From the audience, "Hear, hear!", and "That's it!" mingled with loud hissing and shouts of "GO!"

Frank Sanderson: "We can all go, so Good Night!"

Frank duly left the room, followed by several friends, but it was not long before they returned. Brandishing a bill which announced the meeting, Mr Sanderson said the bill clearly stated that it was a public meeting whereas the chairman had told him and his friends that it was a private meeting – the implication being that, as opponents of the proposed School Board, their presence at the meeting was not desired.

On resuming his speech, Mr Lacey stated that in no instance did the rates reach 3d in the pound in other districts, nor would it in theirs. With this reassurance and with the support of Mr John Emmerson of Tow Law, the meeting passed a resolution pledging itself to do all in its power to obtain a School Board for the parish.[134]

In an editorial, the *Northern Echo* supported the case for a School Board:-

> In Tow Law and in Wolsingham there are 1477 children of school age. According to the Government returns, there is only accommodation for 1277. There is therefore an actual excess of 200 children more than can be educated if every existing school were filled to the door.(but it is also a fact that the existing schools will hold 300 more children than are in the habit of attending them) By the law of the land, they are bound to supply this deficiency…or else the Education Department will decide the question for the parishes by ordering the election of a School Board.[135]

It was recognised that it was not just simply a matter of increasing school accommodation, but that there was also a need to ensure that the children actually attended school. The *Northern Echo,* displaying scant respect for the town of Tow Law, ventured that:-

> We are unwilling to believe that even in Tow Law there can be found a man so base and so cruel as deliberately to desire that even a single child should be doomed to hopeless ignorance, let alone five hundred.

As well as farmers like Frank Sanderson, there were other prominent opponents of a School Board, including Wolsingham solicitor Mr John Dolphin, a conservative who was quoted as saying at the public meeting that the School Board would close existing (private) schools, thereby requiring new schools to be built at the expense of the ratepayers. The *Northern Echo* ridiculed Mr Dolphin's reported statement:-

---

[134] *Ibid.*

[135] *Ibid.*

> We hope Mr Dolphin is merely illiterate, and that it is only through his inability to read that he made this statement, for if he could spell his way through the Education Act, he has been guilty of misrepresentation so gross that it almost deserves another name

The newspaper pointed out to the denominational opponents of Board Schools that the Education Act "is based upon the principle of supplementing, not of destroying the denominational system of education".[136]

In a letter to the *Northern Echo,* Mr Dolphin claimed he had been misquoted. He had not said that the School Board would close the existing schools, but that existing schools would not necessarily be under the control of the School Board and, being private property, might be closed at any time, leaving the School Board to build new schools.[137]

John Lacey was quick to respond to Mr Dolphin's protestations:-

> Sir, I am glad to find that our townsman Mr Dolphin has made an attempt to extricate himself from the ludicrous position in which he placed himself by expressions made use of in his memorable Town Hall speech on the 24th of December. Whatever your contemporary may have reported, the gentleman's utterance on that occasion is sufficiently well remembered by the good people present on that evening, who, through being blinded by prejudice, or heated by party passion, laid themselves open to the shafts of ridicule, and some of their ignominious defeats will long be remembered with amusement in our midst. Would you allow me, Mr Editor, to examine the following wonderful statement Mr Dolphin owns to have made:- "That it did not follow that all the existing schools should be handed over to the School Board; and as most of them were private property, they might at any time be shut up, and then the School Board would have to erect new schools." I think the gentleman's new version verifies the old saying, "Out of the frying pan into the fire." I should like to lay before your readers how many private schools we have in Wolsingham. I have again looked over the list, and find only two which are presided over in a very efficient manner by two ladies. I find that our Wesleyan school receives Government grants, likewise our National school, therefore I hold that these schools are public, and not private schools. The only other school in our town is the Grammar School, endowed from time to time by bequests from the benevolent for the free education of the sons of poor people. Surely Mr Dolphin will hardly call this a private school. But allowing so absurd a statement to pass, and allowing that these are private property, does the gentleman not see that, under his own supposition, we had better be prepared, by the adoption of the Education Act, for so possible an occurrence as that of these private schools being suddenly shut up? In fact, with the honourable exception of the two ladies' schools and the Wesleyan School, the two other schools, for any real benefit arising from them, are as good as shut up already. To give your readers some idea of how much these two schools have contributed to the teaching of our children, I may mention that for a period extending over three years, the National upper or boys' school cannot boast an average attendance of twenty scholars, and for eight months of that time it was without a master, and for other five months of the time it was presided over by a person for whose competency for the task the less said

[136] *Northern Echo*, January 12, 1874

[137] *Northern Echo*, January 13, 1874

> the better. Our Grammar School, that formerly used to be crowded, and afforded free education for 24 scholars, has not had, for at least ten years, an average attendance of more than five. Therefore, I submit that to all intents and purposes those two schools are shut up already, a fact which proves to any unbiased mind the extreme necessity of at once forming a School Board.
> John N Lacey[138]
> Wolsingham, Jan 14, 1874[139]

Despite the objections of Frank Sanderson and his ilk, Wolsingham and Tow Law fulfilled the requirements of the Education Act of 1870 by providing education for all children in the district. And the problem of absenteeism was addressed with the passage of the Education Acts of 1876 and 1880, making it compulsory for all children to attend school to the age of 10, and then 14, unless they could obtain special exemption.[140]

Frank Sanderson's dissatisfaction stemmed from the notion that a School Board would impose a heavy burden on ratepayers, and particularly those like himself who paid the highest rates. Attitudes began to change after 1870, but many remained ambivalent about universal elementary education. Working class families needed children's wages to supplement meagre family incomes, farmers valued the cheap labour provided by children, and many establishment figures, clinging on to "Old Opinions", worried about the educated labourer becoming dissatisfied with his lot.

Old Opinions

Once we thought that Education
Was a luxury for the few;
That to give it to the many
Was to give it scope undue;
Thought it foolish to imagine
It could be as free as air.
Common as the glorious sunshine
To the child of want and care;
That the poor man educated
Quarrelled with his toil! Anon,
Old opinions, rags and tatters,
Get you gone! Get you gone![141]

Frank Sanderson of Low Harperley's irascible nature was displayed at the time of his opposition to the School Board proposals for Wolsingham. FJS described him as a very proud man who was liable to take umbrage if he felt slighted in any way:-

> Grandfather was a little bit sharp. He would never say sorry. He left Hill House Farm near Brandon to come to Hamsterley earlier than he had planned because he'd fallen out with "Old (Tom) Sedgewick." Mind you, that wasn't a surprise to me

[138] John Noble Lacey died in 1881 aged 54 years.
[139] *Northern Echo*, January 15, 1874.
[140] Pamela Horn (1976) *Labouring Life in the Victorian Countryside*. Macmillan, page 39.
[141] "*Old Opinions*, by Scottish poet Charles Mackay (1814-89)

> because I knew Old Sedgewick and he was a bully, a difficult man to deal with. His sons worked on the farm and they had a very hard time with him.

Old Tom Sedgewick was born in 1852 at Marshall Green and was still there in 1871, working as a blacksmith, alongside John Stephenson of Brancepeth who was farming 165 acres. Tom would have been well known to the Sanderson family: it is likely that Tom's father, also Tom, worked as an agricultural labourer for John Sanderson of Broomley before John and family moved from Marshall Green to Black Hall Lodge in 1853.

Frank Sanderson of Harperley's response to problems with Old Sedgewick was, "That's it! I'm not putting up with this any longer. I'm leaving!" This is reminiscent of FJS's reaction to the Scots, "I'd say, 'There's your Home Rule. Get it! Get on with it! Bugger the lot of you!'" In fact, by the 1890s when the great depression in agriculture was well established, it was not unusual for major disagreements to arise between tenants and between tenants and landlords. As Mingay (1990) notes:-

> With the depression came a breakdown in the old relationship between landlord and tenant. The landlord saw old tenants…throw up leases and depart. (p.65)

Old Tom Sedgewick remained at Brandon and died there in 1940.

Back to Hamsterley

Frank Sanderson of Low Harperley bought Pond House in Hamsterley for his retirement, at the same time buying several adjacent properties. The farm was auctioned at the *Cross Keys Inn* on April 17, 1895. After bidding peaked at £1030, the property was withdrawn from sale but Frank Sanderson, the highest bidder, soon afterwards secured the property.[142]

After Frank Sanderson left, his son Frank Sanderson of Hamsterley stayed on at Brandon for several more years until the turn of the century.

BY MR BAINBRIDGE

Farm at Hamsterley For Sale.

TO BE SOLD BY PUBLIC AUCTION, at the Cross Keys Inn, Hamsterley, on Wednesday, April 17th, 1895, at 5 o'clock p.m. prompt - Mr T. G. BAINBRIDGE Auctioneer -

All that Valuable FREEHOLD GRASS FARM, known as Pond House Farm, situate at Hamsterley, in the Count of Durham.

The Farm consists of seven Meadow and Pasture Fields, containing in the whole 34 acres or thereabouts, and lies to the south and is adjacent to the village of Hamsterley. There is a large House and good Out-buildings on the farm.

A portion of the purchase money can remain on mortgage of the property if desired.

The tenant will show the property, and further particulars may be obtained of the AUCTIONEER, New Shildon; or of

STILLMAN & BOOTH,
Solicitors, Bishop Auckland

6-14 Auction of Pond House, Hamsterley in 1895

[142] *Northern Echo,* April 19, 1895

FJS had positive memories of his grandfather. He recalled being given sixpence for sleeping in the same bedroom in a little bed and checking if he was okay in his old age. He remembered that he had white whiskers and only washed his face once a week on a Sunday in a bowl of water placed on the table. He also recalled that he always had a pipe in his mouth and yet never smoked more than an ounce of 'baccy' a week. An ounce cost 8d at the time (about 3p, and equivalent of about £3 in 2013).

Grandfather Frank used to play in the garden with FJS and Ella:-

> We used to play him up. There was this puppy and we'd go in the hayshed and roll in the hay, and this pup would tear our clothes, and grandfather would lock us in. And there was a beautiful walled garden at the back of Pond House, a wall 12 feet high with lots of trees trained up the walls. There were apple trees, and plums, and a gooseberry bush. We used to hide behind the bush and he would look for us. He knew where we were but he wouldn't let on. He would let us think he hadn't seen us.[143]

6-15 Pond House in 1914. Edith (holding dog), FJS, Frank, Ella, and a maid, most probably Olive Coatsworth. Olive, daughter of George and niece of Jos Coatsworth, the Hamsterley Poet, married William Weir in 1913.

The Five Franks

FJS remembered his grandfather's last days:-

> He took a stroke and lived a few days. I was going to school at Wolsingham at the time, riding a horse from Hamsterley to Wolsingham every day. We used to get up at six o'clock and have breakfast at half past six. We were having breakfast and we

[143] It was typical for adults to join in children's games such as blind man's buff and hide-and-seek

> heard him fall. He had got up, got dressed and was putting his tie on – his arm was raised and he fell down. I remember him being in bed and I went and gave him a kiss, and he laughed like hell at me giving him a kiss. He thought it was funny me giving him a kiss! Oh, I thought a lot about him. He was always good to me. He was a grand old man and I loved him.

When Frank died at Hamsterley House on Sunday, 21 November, 1915, of a cerebral haemorrhage, FJS recalled that there were 4 other Franks by his bedside:-

> There was Frank Stothard (grandson), my father Frank (son), Frank Sanderson who was Essie Wearmouth's husband (grandson), and myself (grandson).[144]

Other family members likely to have been present are his daughter Lizzie and his other son, John, together with Edie Sanderson, Ralph Stothard and Mary Eleanor (Enna) Sanderson. The next day's death notice in *The North Star* implored, "Friends please accept this intimation. His end was peace."

Frank had written his will in 1911, signing it with his mark. Perhaps he had never had cause to write anything since his schooldays and had forgotten how to sign his name. Or was it his eyesight? According to FJS, he was "stone blind" with cataracts after the turn of the century and this would have made it impossible for him to write effectively. Not long before he died, he had an operation to remove a cataract from one eye and he was able to see again. FJS remembers that he always wore glasses. He also had a frozen shoulder which meant that he could not lift his arm above his shoulder.

Beyond this sad occasion, great and tragic events were unfolding: 1915 saw the first landing of British, Australian and New Zealand troops on Gallipoli Peninsula, the second Battle of Ypres, the first use of gas by the Germans and the sinking of the British passenger liner, the *S.S. Lusitania*, by a German U-boat, with the loss of 1,195 lives.

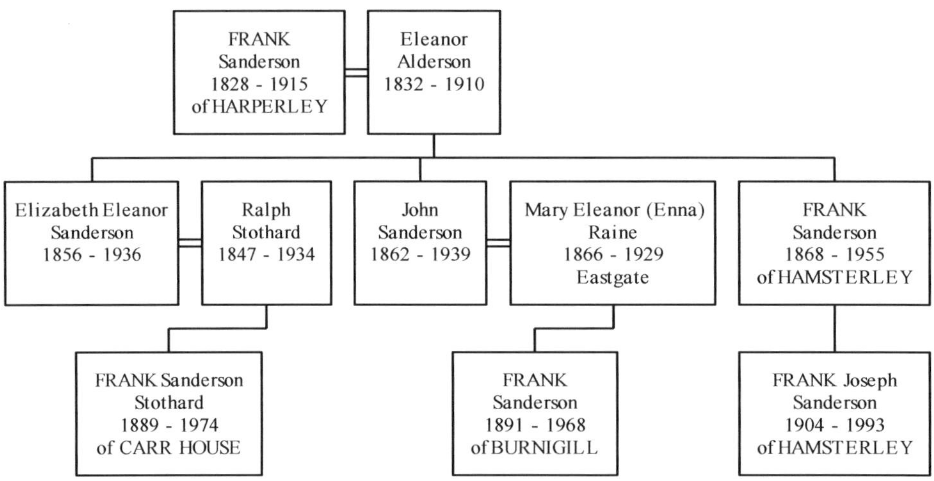

6-16 THE FIVE FRANKS: On 21st November 1915, members of the Sanderson family gathered at Hamsterley House. By the bedside when Frank died were four other "Franks".

[144] FJS's other grandfather Joseph Stephenson had died 6 months earlier (See p.160)

7. THE PRODIGAL SON

John Sanderson of Burnigill

John Sanderson, FJS's uncle, was born at 12.30 pm on Wednesday, October 8, 1862 at Low Harperley, about 2½ miles north of Hamsterley and about the same distance south of Tow Law. John was 6 years older to the day than his brother Frank, my grandfather. He was close to his elder sister, Elizabeth Eleanor and had a particularly close bond with his mother Eleanor.

7-1 John Sanderson of Burnigill, c. 1870

His early life was punctuated by family tragedies. Although the death of his sister Mary Ann when he was 13 months old would have made little direct impression on him, the same cannot safely be said about the deaths of brother Thomas when he was 2½ years old, brother Francis when he was nearly 4 and brother William Henry when he was 12 years old. He actually had the responsibility of reporting the death of William Henry to the Registry Office (See p.113).

By the 1870s, the family had two farms. On the day of the 1881 Census, Frank Jnr was with his father at Low Harperley, whereas 18 year old John was at Hill House Farm, Brandon with his mother. It was and remains quite common for parents to have favourites amongst their children, and it does appear that Eleanor favoured her first-born son and Frank favoured his youngest surviving son and namesake, the baby of the family.

Marriage to Mary Eleanor Raine

John went to school first at Thornley, a small village just over a mile from Low Harperley, and at Wolsingham Grammar School, and then qualified as a Vet before returning to run the second family farm at Hill House, Brandon. In the mid-1880s, his father Frank set him up at nearby Burnigill Farm, Croxdale after the long- standing tenant, Robert Cummings Coulson, had retired.

At Witton-le-Wear on Tuesday, 29th November, 1887, in the year of Queen Victoria's Jubilee celebration, John married Mary Eleanor (Enna) Raine.

Mary Eleanor was the eldest daughter of Hall Raine, a farmer from Crook's Altar Farm, Westgate.[145] The marriage itself caused friction in the family, perhaps because Mary

[145] Crook's Altar Farm was just over a mile north of Westgate and lies 1500 ft above sea level.

Eleanor and John were closely related – her mother Ann Stephenson and John Sanderson were first cousins. The witnesses were Ralph Stothard, the champion ploughman from Carr House, Durham who had married John's sister Lizzie seven months earlier, and Richard Pattison (husband of John's cousin Mary Stephenson, and Mary Eleanor's uncle), with the Rev Hodgson presiding.

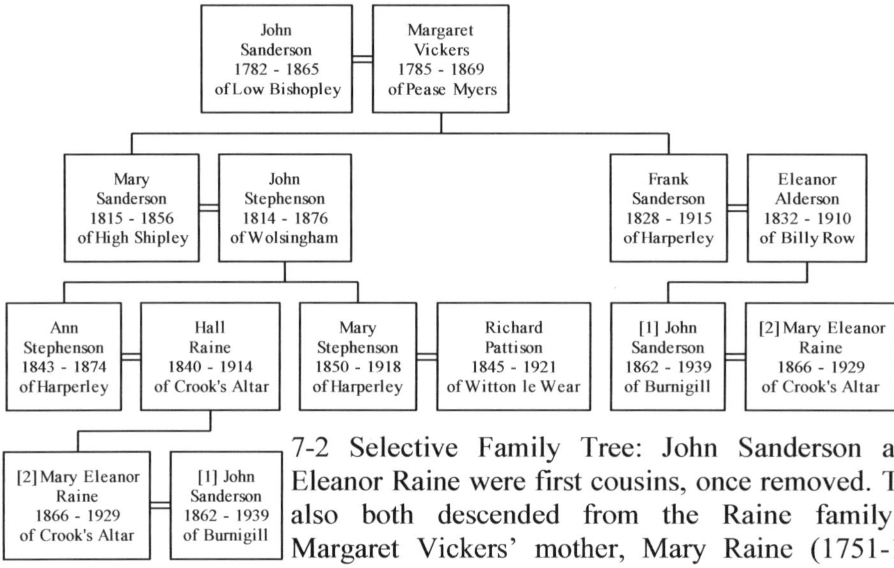

7-2 Selective Family Tree: John Sanderson and Mary Eleanor Raine were first cousins, once removed. They were also both descended from the Raine family through Margaret Vickers' mother, Mary Raine (1751-1833). In 1873, Richard Pattison, a witness at John and Mary Eleanor's wedding, had married Mary Eleanor's Aunt Mary Stephenson.[146]

Crook's Altar Farm

Mary Eleanor Raine was born at Crook's Altar Farm on 8 October 1866, making her exactly 4 years younger than John Sanderson and exactly 2 years older than brother-in-law Frank. She was in fact the eldest surviving child. Two of her sisters, both named Mary, had died at the farm in 1858 and 1860 respectively, both aged 1, and in February 1865, 1 year-old John Joseph Raine died. And on January 29 1866, 1 year-old sister Hannah died. This series of infant deaths is reminiscent of the tragedies experienced by Frank and Eleanor Sanderson in the same decade (See p.88).

7-3 Mary Eleanor Raine

[146] Thanks to Jon Preston for information about descendents of Mary Stephenson, née Sanderson

Crooks Altar, Weardale, County Durham

7-4 Crook's Altar Farm

Crook's Altar farm was built in 1811 in the manner of a 16th Century defensive bastle house: Frank Atkinson comments:-

Crook's Altar was built into a hillside with accommodation for cattle below and for the family above. One may assume that this was built along the old style, not as a response to the need for protection, but simply because it was the old way. Moreover, the warmth from the cattle below was doubtless communicated to the human beings above and this could well have helped to perpetuate the practice of living above the byre. Such buildings are traditional in the fullest sense of the word.[147]

Mavis McLean née Sanderson, the granddaughter of John and Enna Sanderson, related a tragic story about events at Crook's Altar in 1939 and her father's role in offering support to a distraught family (See p.109).

Highs and Lows

As mentioned above, John Sanderson began his married life at Burnigill Farm,[148] near Croxdale, and farmed 500 acres there until the late 1890s. His services as a Vet were widely sought throughout Durham, Cumberland and Northumberland. He also chartered ships to import cattle from Ireland, which he then sold at cattle markets in the north of England and Scotland. At this time, John was a successful

147 Atkinson, Frank (2001) *Life and tradition in Northumberland and Durham.* Otley, Smith Settle

148 Mavis MacLean commented in 2003: "In the 1920s a portion of Burnigill Farm was sold and the Bridge Inn was built. A few years ago the inn was flooded quite badly and subsequently lay derelict. Squatters moved in and things went from bad to worse. However, my brother (John Taylor Sanderson) – who loves a challenge – decided to buy the inn a few months ago..... John renamed the inn *The Honest Lawyer* – because he's never met one!

farmer. However, with his growing fondness of gambling and drinking, it is no great surprise that he was declared bankrupt by the turn of the century. After this setback, John was again set up by his father at Butsfield Burn Farm near Satley. About three miles north of Tow Law, Butsfield Burn Farm was within easy reach of the mart in Tow Law which John's cousin Joseph Vickers had established in 1882. But soon afterwards, his son William Henry died of croup in 1902 at the age of 5, a blow which might well have been the final straw for John, re-igniting his self-destructive tendencies. After the Butsfield Burn venture failed, he then worked erecting pylons all over the North of England for an electricity company. During these years, he also worked small farms in the Darlington and Gainford area, and at one time had a butchering business at Harrogate Hill, Darlington. In 1911, John moved to Letch House, a small farm at Morley, and 10 years later, he began farming at Eastbourne Farm, Woodland. It was there that Enna died in July, 1929, having suffered from cancer for about 8 years. She is buried in Woodland Cemetery.

FJS recalled how at hay time in 1928, Uncle John came to Pond House in Hamsterley and after helping with the haymaking, stayed overnight. The next morning he was restless, a little agitated and apparently reluctant to return home. Eventually FJS said to him, "What's the matter, Uncle?" John replied that he wanted to borrow £5 from his brother Frank because "our Mary's ganna get married".[149] Frank loaned him the money on the solemn promise that he would be repaid. FJS then took him home in the trap to Woodland. On the way, they stopped at *The Edge*, a pub on the outskirts of Woodland. Uncle John invited FJS to join him in the pub but he wouldn't go in as he was frightened that the pony might run away. His uncle brought out a pint for him and insisted that transport was no longer necessary as he intended to walk the rest of the way home. After he'd finished his pint, FJS duly returned to Hamsterley.

A year later, FJS and his father were passing John's house and called in for a cup of tea and to collect the £5.[150] John wasn't at home, but his wife Enna recalled that he'd come home somewhat the worse for drink, and had given her ten bob, claiming he'd backed a winner!

John's Annuity

As the first-born son, it would have been customary for John Sanderson to have been close to his father and to have figured prominently in his will. But in Frank of Low Harperley's will, drawn up on June 10, 1911, John was to receive the comparatively modest amount of 10/- per week (£26 annually), commencing at his father's death. John's brother Frank, the trustee, was to be responsible for the payments. Daughter Lizzie, on the other hand, was to receive a one-off legacy of £400[151] on her father's death, together with "all the household furniture and effects in my dining room and the bedroom above the same". Could it be that a 'drip-feed' annuity rather than a one-off legacy was to be paid to John because his father knew that his son would quickly squander the latter? Or was it because John had already had substantial money from his father to set him up as a farmer? It is of course difficult from this distance to establish whether the terms of the Will were wise and just, or whether they were manifestations of favouritism which worked to the disadvantage of John.

---

[149] In 1928, Elsie Mary Sanderson married George Gill, a farmer from Woodland.

[150] Borrowing £5 in 1928 would be like borrowing £255 in 2013.

[151] £400 in 1915 would be equivalent, in terms of purchasing power, to £28,000 in 2013.

Under the terms of the Will, Frank was to receive all his father's "stock and crops and implements of husbandry...absolutely" and all the residue of his personal estate and all his real estate on condition that he discharges his duties as Trustee, i.e., pays funeral and testamentary expenses, and pays the legacy to sister Elizabeth Ellen and the annuity to brother John.

John had been given financial support from his father to allow him to begin farming at Burnigill, described by FJS as "the best farm on Lord Boyne's Estate". But John's prodigal lifestyle was an obstacle to him making a success of the farming opportunities provided to him. In the words of his grandson, John Taylor Sanderson, 'he blew it', and in the process, testing the patience of his father and losing the sympathy of his brother Frank.

It must be remembered however that the golden age of farming ended in 1875 when prices fell and depression set in. Many farmers had become accustomed to relative prosperity in the preceding two decades and found difficulty in adjusting their lifestyles. Bankruptcies were common which means that John's financial difficulties in the latter part of the century were unremarkable. It can be reasonably argued that if John had farmed during the golden age like his Uncle John of Broomley, he would have stood a much greater chance of being successful, despite his errant ways.

His brother Frank, always careful with his money, appears to have taken a dim view of John's excesses. After his father's death in 1915, Frank began the payments to John of 10/- per week under the terms of the Will, but may have felt that it was a weekly waste of good money. John Taylor Sanderson remembers his father Alfred saying that the weekly payments only lasted for a short while:-

> John was returning from one of his binges - he would disappear for months on end - when he met his brother Frank in Bishop Auckland, and asked if he could borrow some money. Frank said that the only way he would give him cash was if he sold him his future right to 10/- a week under the Will. Apparently they went to a solicitor and John signed away his entitlement to £26 per annum for life. The sum paid was £80.

Eighty Pounds[152] in exchange for £26 per annum for life was a bad deal for John, and on a moment's reflection, Frank would have known that his brother was unlikely to hold on to this money for very long, given his lifestyle. John had agreed to sacrifice the steady if unspectacular income for a one-off payment of 3 year's-worth of the legacy. At least the 10/- per week had meant that the family had a regular income, whereas, in the event, it appears that the family were "left in poverty" as a result, and bad feeling remained for years afterwards. A view from John's side of the family was that it was "totally wrong and completely illegal" for Frank to have done this. Indeed, Alfred urged his father to take legal action against Frank, but he would never do it, saying only that "I could never do that to my brother."

From Frank's point of view, John was a ne'er do well who'd been given opportunities and had repeatedly failed. He was frequently asking to borrow money and didn't deserve sympathy. Whether Frank appreciated that the £80 would be squandered quickly and that in consequence the family would be left more vulnerable in the longer term is not known. It was all too easy for Frank to imagine that the payments were from his own pocket, rather

[152] £80 in 1925 is equivalent to over £4,000 today.

than reminding himself of how favoured he was under the terms of the Will. As it was, Frank, in his exasperation with his brother, overturned his father's wise and careful provision of an annuity for John.

The positive postscript to this sad story is that John did give up his destructive habits in later life, becoming a reformed character. However, he did not regain the prosperity of his young adulthood - there was no Will, suggesting that there was little in the way of inheritance for his children.

7.5 Ravensford Farm

Back to Ravensford

John moved to Ravensford Farm in 1936, 124 years after his grandfather John Sanderson had moved there with his bride Margaret Vickers. Twelve days after Britain declared war on Germany, he died at the farm on Friday, 15th September 1939, in his 77th year, of Cardiac Failure and Myocardial Degeneration. His son John, who was living in Evenwood at the time, was present at the death and informed the GRO. The following day, German troops surrounded Warsaw and Soviet troops invaded Poland.

The Funeral Service was held at St Mary's Church, Woodland on 18th September, followed by the burial at Woodland Cemetery. Thereafter, John's son Frank and daughter Lizzie farmed at Ravensford until Frank married Essie Jewitt née Wearmouth in 1945.

John Sanderson (1862-1936) did not pass through this world unnoticed. He took many wrong directions but no doubt had some fun along the way.

The Surviving Twin and the Maiden Aunt

One who never turned his back, but marched breast forward,
Never doubted clouds would break,
Never dreamed, though right were worsted, wrong would triumph,
Held we fall to rise, are baffled to fight better,
Sleep to wake.[153]

FJS made frequent reference to the family of his Uncle John. Most of the information I have about the family was provided in 1980 by Essie Sanderson from Toft Hill (Uncle

[153] Verse from *The Browning Birthday Book.*

John's daughter-in-law), and in 1996, by his grandchildren Henry Hewitson of Walworth and John Taylor Sanderson of Benton who wrote to me with recollections in 1996:-

> My father's family, whilst being relatively poor, were full of character and I was fortunate in being close to many of them in my youth. In the 1950s, most of my holidays were spent with my Aunt Lizzie and her brother Uncle Edgar; they lived in a small rented semi-detached stone cottage next to the Methodist Chapel just off the village green in Hamsterley. I believe the house was owned originally by Frank Sanderson (of Low Harperley) and then by my Great Uncle Frank Sanderson of Hamsterley. Incidentally, it was one of the last houses in County Durham to be connected to an electricity supply. I even remember the village public water pump on the green and the installation of a cold water supply in the house. I spent many a happy hour contemplating my future on the earth netty at the end of the garden.
>
> I can still feel the frost on the end of my nose whilst waking up in the cold bedroom on a winter morning, then the period spent motivating myself to get out of a warm high feather bed at 5 am each morning to begin my part-time milk job on Mr Collingwood's farm on the top of the bank leading towards Hamsterley village. Aunt Lizzie had spent most of her youth bringing up the family, as her mother died young, and then acted as an anchor for the many problems which occurred in her immediate families' lives. Sadly, this life of self-sacrifice left Aunt Lizzie feeling under-appreciated and regretful. Whilst she was a puritanical maiden aunt, she was a great cook. I can still smell the fresh bread and the warmth of the open range in the living room. Bought cakes were sinful, Aunt Lizzie called them 'kett'.[154] The other downstairs room, "the best room", was always very cold, always immaculate, but never used. We had to pass through this fridge each night to access the staircase which led to the bedrooms.
>
> Aunt Lizzie would occasionally take me to the cinema in Bishop Auckland and if it was an exciting part of the film and I was on edge, she would always say in a loud voice, "not to worry, they are only play acting". It used to be better than comedy playhouse!

7-6 Aunt Lizzie thought that bought cakes were "sinful".

Elizabeth Jane (Aunt Lizzie) Sanderson was born at Burnigill in 1890. She was housekeeper to Lord Barnard for 20 years before having to leave to look after her mother at Eastbourne Farm, Woodland when Enna became ill with cancer in 1926. In 1938, she moved to Ravensford Farm with brother Frank and then retired to the cottage in Hamsterley where John Taylor Sanderson enjoyed carefree holidays.

Lizzie died in Hamsterley in 1971, having never married.

[154] 'Kett' or 'ket' is a dialect word meaning 'rubbish', and comes from the Old Norse word, 'kjot'.

Edgar Sanderson was born on October 3rd, 1896 at East Butsfield Farm. His twin brother William Henry died at the age of five of croup, the same illness that took the life of his Uncle William Henry in 1875 at the age of 4½ years. (See p.113).

Edgar left school at 14 and worked on various farms until he was 17. In 1914, he lied about his age and joined the Durham Light Infantry. He served in France and Germany for 4 years and was seriously wounded a week before peace was declared. He had wounds to his face and shrapnel through both feet. As Edgar (pictured left in 1915) was being stretchered from the battle field with his arms hanging over the sides of the stretcher, a German sniper shot him through both wrists. Critically ill, he was transferred to a hospital in Cardiff and was not expected to survive.

He did survive and was discharged from the army after serving throughout the War for 1/- per day, with no pension.[155] He then worked on farms in the Ripon area but had to be re-admitted to military hospital on a number of occasions because of the shrapnel still lodged in his wounds.

7-7 Edgar Sanderson in 1915

After his wife Hilda (Waite) died in 1935, Edgar lived with his daughter Elsie and sister Lizzie, first at Ravensford Farm and then at the cottage in Hamsterley until his death in 1964.

John Taylor Sanderson recalls that his Uncle Edgar was always full of fun and quite the opposite of "prim and proper" Aunt Lizzie:-

He had sustained horrific injuries during the First World War. But he always had a "glint" in his eye and would sit making rude remarks under his breath about Aunt Lizzie's friends. For example, when Mrs Main, a rather large nurse who lived over the green, was coming over to see Aunt Lizzie, Edgar would say, "Here comes the old fat arse again". Aunt Lizzie would have been mortified if only she had known.

Nellie and the Browning Birthday Book

John Sanderson's eldest daughter, Ellen Ann (Nellie) Sanderson (pictured overleaf in 1910) was described by her cousin FJS as "a nice woman, but she got a bad knee, housemaid's knee, and she died very young".

Nellie was born at Burnigill Farm in 1888. Unmarried, she lived with her grandparents at Home Farm, Harperley and then at Pond House, Hamsterley, working as their housekeeper. In her grandfather's will (1911), in what seems like an attempt to ensure that he is cared for

[155] Eventually, after a doctor took up his case, Edgar received a pension of 4s.6d per week

until the last, she was to receive all the furniture and effects in her bedroom "if she be living with me at the time of my death". However, in a 1914 codicil to the Will, Frank Sanderson of Low Harperley notes that:-

> Whereas since the date of my said Will I have given certain household furniture and effects to my said granddaughter Ellen Ann Sanderson and my daughter Elizabeth Ellen, now therefore I give and bequeath all my household furniture and effects to my son Frank absolutely.

7-8 Ellen Ann Sanderson (1888-1917)

John Taylor Sanderson has a wonderful book, *The Browning Birthday Book*, which originally belonged to his Aunt Nellie. It is a book for recording birthdays and each day is accompanied by a quotation from the works of Robert Browning. On the first page is recorded the signature of *'Miss N Sanderson'* and a message from John's father, Alf, "This Book belonged my Dear Sister Nellie, Born 1888, Died 1917".

The Browning quotation for Nellie's birthday is from *The Lost Mistress*:

> I will but say what mere friends say,
> Or only a thought stronger;
> I will hold your hand but as long as all may,
> Or so very little longer.

The Browning Birthday Book held more significance for Nellie than at first appreciated in that she shared an anniversary with Robert Browning. Nellie was born on 12 December, 1888, one year to the day before the celebrated poet died. The family would have been aware of the coincidence of dates from Nellie's first birthday and the book would have been seen as an ideal birthday present for Nellie when she was old enough to read and write. She died on April 26, 1917 aged 28, two years after her grandfather Sanderson died, and is buried in Hamsterley churchyard. Her death was caused not by housemaid's knee as FJS implied, but by peritonitis, brought on by a perforating stomach ulcer.

Another Frank

Frank Sanderson (pictured below with his wife Essie) was born in 1891 at Burnigill. He left school at 14 and worked for various farmers until he joined the army at the outbreak of the First World War. After serving in France throughout the War, he worked at various pits for several years and also looked after a small farm at Woodland. By the time of his marriage at the age of 54, he was farming at Glenholme Farm, Hamsterley. FJS recalled that his father thought a lot about his nephew.

He married Florence Esther (Essie) Jewitt née Wearmouth in 1945 (See p.143) and bought Hazledean Farm at Morley[156] before eventually retiring to Toft Hill because of ill-health. He died in 1968 aged 77 and is buried at Etherley Cemetery. I visited Essie in 1980 at Toft Hill, when she gave me some family photographs. Looked after in old age by her son William (Billy) Jewitt in Hamsterley, she died on January 5th 1999, aged 97.

7-9 Frank Sanderson and Essie née Wearmouth

[156] Hazledean was farmed for many years by the Lowson family.

John Sanderson

John Sanderson (1893-1985) was born at Burnigill Farm. He left school at 14, worked on farms until he joined the 6th Batt DLI (Reg No 3342) in 1915 and served throughout the Great War in France. After discharge, he worked down the pit, married Nora Mason in 1920 and had five children.

The Second World War took its toll on his family.

His son Norman served in India and North Africa and was captured in 1942 when Tobruk fell. He suffered shrapnel wounds and lost the use of his right arm, and was repatriated in 1943.

7-10 Cpl John Sanderson and Sgt Willie Nattress in 1915

John (Jackie) joined the Royal Air Force Volunteer reserve as a navigator and gunner and served in the Middle East until the invasion of Italy. In November 1942, his plane was shot down by "friendly fire" whilst it was trying to land at Malta - the plane's signal lights were damaged, so the plane could not identify itself. His name is engraved on the Malta Memorial on the island.

Jean, whose mother had died when she was 9 years of age, left school at 14 to look after her family. During the blackout on Christmas Day 1941, she was walking on a footpath between Evenwood and Cockfield at 9pm. An army lorry mounted the footpath, injuring her so seriously that she died that night. She was 17 years old. The Inquest conducted by John Brown Humes concluded that Jean died of:-

> Compression of the brain following Cerebral Haemorrhage accidentally sustained upon 25 December 1941 whilst walking on the road and being struck by an Army Motor Truck.

At this time, it was not possible to sue the Crown and John received no compensation for her untimely death. However, John's brother Alf pursued the case and managed to get him £150 compassionate grant from the Crown Office.

A Good Sort

Alice Sanderson, who was born in 1895 at Burnigill Farm, was described by her cousin FJS as "a good sort". On leaving school, Alice worked for several wealthy families in the Darlington area. FJS remembered that she was housekeeper at Westside for hay and straw dealer Ned Walker, and that Willie Nattress (See Fig 7-9) used to cut hay for him.

Alice married Harry Hewitson of Heighington in 1921, and they subsequently rented a farm at Burn House, Middridge, owned by Sir Anthony Eden. The land was eventually taken over to allow the building of Newton Aycliffe, and Henry, Alice and their two children, William and Henry, moved to Walworth.

7-11 Harry and Alice Hewitson

Alice was very well liked by her cousins. My father Henry, Auntie Ella and FJS were in close contact with the Hewitsons, and Ella's son Terry Atkinson remembers meeting "Auntie" Alice (his first cousin, once removed) frequently at the Monday Market Day at Darlington.

Alice died aged 78 and Harry Hewitson was 91 when he died.

My father Henry Sanderson would often visit the Hewitsons at Walworth, where he was remembered by Alice's son, also Henry, for trying repeatedly to ride a pony at the farm only to be outwitted by the pony's tactic of lying down every time he tried to mount.

When he was a butcher at Jackson's in Darlington in the mid 1940's, he used to deliver sausages to the Hewitsons by leaning out of the moving village bus and lobbing the sausages over the top of the bus onto their front garden. In case they hadn't witnessed the delivery, he would phone them later to check.

The Decorated Policeman

Alfred Stephenson Sanderson was born in 1901 at Butsfield Burn, 8 months after the death of Queen Victoria. He was named after his second cousin Alfred Stephenson Pattison, the son of Richard Pattison and Mary Stephenson (See Fig 7-2), who had died from fever a year earlier in the Boer War.

7-12 Alf with May (Taylor) and baby Mavis

FJS knew his cousin Alfie well when he was young but lost contact in 1925:-

> The last time I saw Alfie was in 1925 when (William) Henry Stothard (another cousin) and me had been to Newcastle Races. We met him when we were leaving the race-course.

Alf married May Taylor in 1929 and they had two daughters and a son: Patricia, Mavis, and John Taylor. John Taylor Sanderson had the following recollections of his father and mother:-

> My father Alf was an incredible man and was in the police force for most of his working life. We moved homes many times, a bit like nomads, moving all over County Durham which did not help my education. Whilst only reaching the rank of Detective Sergeant in the CID, he was a very good policeman and had the distinction of receiving more commendations than any other policeman in the Durham County Constabulary, a record I believe still stands today. Unfortunately, his work necessitated long hours and we saw little of him as we grew up. He was a drinker and a gambler but he totally reformed when he left the police force. He was very kind-hearted and kept in touch with all the family. My mother was a "saint" and showed us all much love and understanding. She was totally opposite to dad in that she did not drink or smoke. She established a natural affinity with everyone she met; I well remember being on bus journeys where total strangers would tell my mother their life stories. She came from a wonderful large working class family from Newcastle called Taylor."

Mavis MacLean, the South-African based daughter of Alfred Sanderson and grand-daughter of Enna and John, visited her brother John and her cousins Elsie Tipler and Henry Hewitson in the summer of 2003. Mavis recalled the time her cousins and their spouses Tommy Tipler and Connie Hewitson took her to see Crook's Altar in Upper Weardale:-

> It was beautiful day but even on such a day we were aware of its remoteness and the bleak fells – and the wind blew and blew. Crook's Altar is now just a heap of stones – no semblance of a building. I said to Elsie that it was incredible that somehow or other, Annie Raine (Enna's half-sister) had got herself from there to America in about 1900. Elsie looked around her and said quite seriously that if she had lived there, she would also have got herself to America, even if she'd had to swim there. It was very bleak[157].

A Very Sad Accident

Crook's Altar had a more recent and tragic connection with the family, as Mavis explained:-

> My father Alfred Sanderson was a policeman stationed at Eastgate at the beginning of the Second World War, and it was at this time that he paid his first visit to Crook's Altar. He was very friendly with a family of farmers called Dalton who farmed Snowhope Close and another farm at Eastgate. Johnny Dalton, the eldest of 6 brothers and sisters, helped run the farms in Eastgate and his wife helped her mother

[157] It was 'bleak' in the summer of 2003, but generally it was much more bleak in a 19th Century Weardale winter when Enna was growing up.

Mary Elizabeth Elliot run the Elliot farm at Crook's Altar. Johnny's eldest son had recently had his 18th birthday and his parents had given him a gun as a present. Shortly afterwards, the boy was staying with his mother and grandmother at Crook's Altar and had been out shooting. It had been raining and his mother told him to clean the gun when he came into the kitchen, and this he did. However, he didn't realise that there was a cartridge left in the gun – the gun went off and shot his mother in the leg. He thought he had killed her and went outside and blew his brains out. His mother died on the way to hospital. Not surprisingly, Johnny Dalton was utterly distraught and suicidal, and my father really helped him at this time. Perhaps because of the tragedy, no one ever wanted to stay there afterwards, hence the present day heap of stones.

7-13 Alf Sanderson was stationed at Eastgate in 1939. The pose with cigarette in hand was not unusual for the time.

This heart-rending story related by Alf Sanderson to his children not many years after the event has been recalled remarkably accurately by Mavis. The Daltons farmed at Snowhope Close and had been there for many years – they were present there at the time of the 1911 Census: farmer William Dalton, aged 56 and originally from Cumberland was with his 40 year-old wife, Ann (Emerson) whom he had married in 1891. Also present were Elizabeth Atkinson, William's widowed sister, and 5 children, the eldest being 19 year-old John William (Johnny) Dalton.

Johnny Dalton, a farmer who became a prize-winning dales pony breeder, married schoolteacher Mary Annie Elliott from Stanhope in the summer of 1919, and in early 1921, their son, also John William (Willie), was born. Willie became one of Weardale's best known young farmers. In 1936, he won a Shield for coming first in the Durham County Speaking Competitions at Darlington and took part in several County speaking demonstrations. His youthful achievements will have made his parents very proud, and his prodigious talent promised a fulfilling future.

In early 1939, Willie celebrated his 18th birthday, and the events described by Mavis occurred two months later at the 143-acre Crooks Altar Farm (owned by the Elliot family), with both young Willie and his mother Mary Annie dying of gunshot wounds on Monday, October 9 1939, shortly after the outbreak of the Second World War.

The tragic events were reported in *The Northern Echo* the following day under the headline "SHOOTING TRAGEDY ON LONELY FARM: Weardale Mother and Son

Killed".[158] After the shootings farm servant Norman Parker ran to Westgate village 1¼ miles away but was overtaken by quarry workers on bicycles who were able to phone for medical help and the police.

Dr John O'Hara travelled the six miles from Stanhope and arranged for 45 year-old Mrs Dalton to be taken by ambulance to Newcastle Infirmary. Sergeant Dawes from St John's Chapel and Chief Inspector Thomas Fowler from Stanhope also attended the scene.

The Inquest

At the inquest in Westgate on 11th October, the farm-hand Norman Parker recalled that Willie had left him in the byre while he went off to shoot moles and plovers, and he was still in the byre when he heard gunshots from the direction of the house. He went to the house and saw Mary Annie lying wounded and then found Willie lying dead in the paddock with terrible head injuries.

Maurice Robinson, a quarryman from Westgate, gave first-aid to Mary Annie who exclaimed:-

> This is a sad accident Maurice. It wasn't me to blame. I could not help it. Willie was just rubbing the gun and it went off.

It is noteworthy that in her state of shock, Mary Annie imagined that people might think that the accident was somehow her fault.

The principal witness, described not surprisingly in the circumstances as "a pathetic figure", was Mrs Mary Elizabeth Elliot, the 69 years old mother of Mary Annie. She recalled that when Willie returned to the house, the gun was wet and his mother asked him to clean it. Willie started to clean the gun with a rag, and as Mrs Elliot turned her back, she heard a gunshot, followed by her daughter crying out "Oh Willie!" before collapsing on the floor. Willie immediately ran out of the house, with his grandmother shouting after him, "You have not hurt your mother. Come back." After another gunshot, Mrs Elliot went outside and found Willie lying dead in the paddock. Her view was that Willie was unfamiliar with the gun and had become frightened after shooting his mother. It is easy to imagine how utterly distraught Willie would have been about what he had inadvertently done.

Willie's Death Certificate, received from John Edward Brown Humes (Coroner for Darlington Ward), records that he died in the Paddock at Crook's Altar, Westgate-in-Weardale, Stanhope, aged 18 years, of "gunshot wounds of the brain, self-inflicted whilst the balance of his mind was disturbed". Mary Annie was pronounced dead later the same day at Royal Victoria Hospital in Newcastle, her life having ebbed away on the ambulance journey from Weardale. Mr Brown Humes declared that Mary Annie died of "shock and haemorrhage following a gun-shot wound in the left leg caused by the accidental discharge of a shot-gun by the son of the deceased". In a closing statement, he expressed his great sympathy for Johnny Dalton:-

> In these days, when we have so much tragedy all around us, we may be pardoned for thinking that a man so little deserving of it should be doubly bereaved in this dreadful manner. He has lost a devoted wife and a brilliant son.

[158] *Northern Echo*, 10 October, 1939

Great Shock for Walter Dalton

The *Northern Echo* reported that "there is a younger brother, who returned home from school only a short time after the tragedy." Walter Dalton, who was twelve at the time and showing the same academic promise as his older brother, vividly recalled the tragic events of over 70 years ago. He was a pupil at Wolsingham Grammar School and despite having had scarlet fever the previous summer, was "top lad" in his class, for which achievement his father bought him a new bicycle. On October 9th 1939, he took the train from Wolsingham to Stanhope where he collected the bike and then cycled to Crook's Altar Farm. On the way, he encountered the distressed farm servant, Norman Parker, who was running down to Westgate to summon help. Walter recalls:-

> It was terrible for the family. All Willie ever wanted to do was to be a farmer. On that day, he saw that a mole was making a mess of a field, so he grabbed father's gun[159] and went out and shot it. When he got back to the house, the gun was wet from the rain and he was cleaning it with a rag when it went off. The family left Crook's Altar Farm that night and never went back.[160]

Walter recalled that PC Alf Sanderson, stationed at Eastgate, was very friendly with his father. This meant that although, given the terrible events, he will have had a formal role as an investigating officer, he would also have provided much-needed sympathy and support for the Dalton family at this time. Walter also incidentally remembered that Alf was a very good snooker player.

Three quarters-of-a-century earlier, Mary Eleanor Raine spent her infancy at Crook's Altar but had moved to Witton-le-Wear by the late 1860s. By the time of the 1881 Census she was 14 years old and living in Whitworth, near Spennymoor with her 41 year-old father, a Butcher, and two brothers and a sister, Annie. At the time of Mary Eleanor's marriage to John Sanderson in 1887, John Hall Raine was described as a labourer, suggesting perhaps that his butchering business had foundered. By the 1891 Census, he was a Farm Servant in Merrington Village, and Annie was a domestic servant at Hill House Farm, Brandon, working for her uncle, Frank Sanderson of Low Harperley. Annie subsequently worked as a servant for George Manners of Westerton before migrating to America. According to family accounts, she had an eventful life, becoming a dresser to Hollywood stars and marrying, and eventually divorcing, a German inventor of hydraulic jacks. After a brief visit home in the late 1930s, Annie returned to America and was never heard of again.

FJS briefly mentioned two other children of John and Enna: Battling Bertha (1905-1985) who married Norman Hall, a farmer from Woodland in 1925, and Eleanor Margaret (Dollie) Sanderson (1897-1974) who married farmer and colliery owner Harry Coates in 1923 at Cockfield.

---

[159] Walter recalled that it was "a good gun", made by FJ Smythe, Gunsmiths of Darlington. He also stated that it was his father's gun, and not a birthday present for Willie.
[160] Walter Dalton spoke to me about the tragic events of 1939 in 2013.

8. A CANNY OLD FELLA

In 1868, Disraeli became Prime Minister on Lord Derby's retirement but was replaced by Gladstone following the Liberal triumph in the December General Election. The first Trades Union Congress was held in June, the Metropolitan District Railway was opened in London and the last public execution was held in London in May.

On 8 October, 1868, Frank Sanderson was born at Harperley. He was the seventh child of Frank Sanderson of Low Harperley, also a seventh child, and Eleanor née Alderson. His namesake had died in infancy in May 1866.

Frank was 10 years younger than his sister Lizzie and 6 years younger to the day than his brother John, which meant that as the baby of the family, he would have received plenty of attention and affection from his parents, at least until William Henry Sanderson was born in 1871.

The Life and Death of William Henry

Frank's early life was spent at the Home Farm, Harperley where he would witness the painful illness and tragic death of his little brother William Henry in the summer of 1875 – reminiscent of the experience of his father, also a 6 year-old at the time, witnessing the death from burns of his 8 year-old sister Jane in 1834 (See p.63).

As 1870 drew to a close, Eleanor Sanderson was imminently expecting her eighth child. The feelings in the household at Harperley will have been of anticipation and excitement at the prospect of a new addition to the family mixed with a deeply felt apprehension based on tragic family experience. Of Frank and Eleanor's seven children, four, including their first child, had died in infancy or early childhood and two of the surviving children, Lizzie and Frank, suffered from chronic chest complaints.

Just after the turn of the year, William Henry Sanderson was born at Harperley Farm. His Christian names were Alderson family names. As the months passed, everything seemed to be going well for William Henry, and Frank and Eleanor will have gradually replaced the unremitting apprehension during the child's infancy with feelings of optimism as they celebrated his third and then his fourth birthday. The bond between the child and his family would have been increasingly strong. Lizzie and John were by now in their teens, and, although William Henry and his brother Frank, just over 2 years older than him, were not exceptionally robust children, they were holding their own.

Or so Frank and Eleanor thought. Just at the time when William Henry would be developing fast and displaying the energy and curiosity of the typical 4 year-old, he developed croup. Also known as diphtheria, croup is a throat condition, occurring usually in children, and most commonly in boys. Macaulay (1831) provided a vivid 19th century description of a deadly disease:-

> The symptoms of croup are the following: After exposure to cold and wet, the patient is seized with shivering, restlessness, and a difficulty of breathing, which goes on increasing, and is accompanied with cough, of a peculiar barking hollow sound, ...febrile symptoms of great severity appear; the face is flushed, the pulse is strong, the thirst urgent, the anxiety is great, and there is a throwing back of the head to

> escape suffocation and to favour respiration; which, besides being much interrupted by the painful fits of coughing, is performed with a hissing sound, as if some soft substance were in part obstructing the windpipe. There is present also a degree of swelling and sore throat, and the pain of this in swallowing adds to the sufferings of the patient. As the disease advances, the face becomes livid and swelled; the respiration becomes more shrill, and is performed with greater difficulty and at longer intervals, till it at last ceases altogether…sometimes thick purulent-looking matter is spit up, or pieces of a substance resembling a membrane. Croup consists in the inflammation of the mucous membrane of the trachea, by which there is a secretion of a very tenacious matter, and this occasions a contraction of the passage for the air. A degree of spasm also not infrequently attends.

In the pre-Victorian period, if an emetic didn't work, the remedies were:-

> …to put the child in a warm bath, to apply a number of leeches around the upper part of the windpipe, to give purgative medicines, and, if the child be full and strong, it may be proper to take a quantity of blood from the arm." Macaulay added that "we trust to emetics, bleeding, blistering and complete evacuation of the bowels.[161]

Not surprisingly the mortality rate was high, and treatment remained rudimentary until as late as the 1920s when an effective vaccine was developed. Such was the helplessness of families faced with this affliction that people sought a cure through superstitious practices. For example, it was said that some old women of Staithes in Yorkshire believed that three drops of a black cat's blood was "a sovereign cure for croup".[162] In Maine, New England, there was a belief that a nutmeg pierced and hung on a string round the neck prevented boils, neuralgia, and croup.[163]

William Henry's condition worsened despite the best efforts of the family to nurse him back to health.

Although the event happened almost 30 years before he was born, FJS recounted the heart-rending story with great emotion, his eyes becoming misty and his voice a whisper and wistful with the telling:-

> William Henry was about four, he was younger than my father. He died on Aunt Lizzie's knee saying all the while, "Rock me harder, rock me harder" as she cradled him in me grandmother's rocking chair.

The image of this poor little boy, my Great Uncle William Henry, in his sister's arms, with hoarse cough and laboured breathing, exhorting her with his faltering voice, "Rock me harder", is precious but almost too much to bear.

The Death Certificate indicates that he died of croup on June 22, 1875. His 12 year-old brother John was present at the death and was also the informant of the death, a big responsibility for one so young.

---

[161] Macaulay, Alexander (1831) *A Dictionary of Medicine: Designed for Popular Use*. Edinburgh, Adam Black

[162] *Newcastle Courant*, May 28, 1898

[163] *Newcastle Courant*, June 25, 1892

The Death of William Henry[164]

Oh William Henry, come to Lizzie
Let me hold you close and warm
I will soothe you, I will rock you
So to keep you safe from harm

Can the circle be unbroken,
bye and bye Lord, bye and bye?
There's a better home awaiting,
in the sky, Lord, in the sky

Rock me harder, dearest Lizzie
Oh rock me harder just once more
For I am tired, and oh so weary
And my throat is oh so sore

Can the circle be unbroken,
bye and bye Lord, bye and bye?
There's a better home awaiting,
in the sky, Lord, in the sky

William Henry, he is gone now,
Lord you never heard my prayer
as I rocked him like a baby,
in my mother's rocking chair

Can the circle be unbroken,
bye and bye Lord, bye and bye?
There's a better home awaiting,
in the sky, Lord, in the sky.

Unfortunately, such vivid re-telling of family events which occurred long ago is unusual these days: not only are families more dispersed, with younger members having less contact with their older relatives, but also there are so many alternative leisure pursuits: the cosy family evenings by the fireside when parents and grandparents would entertain each other and the children with songs and stories of the old days are a thing of the past.

The fact that FJS knew the story so well gives an indication of the impact of the death of William Henry on the family. His death, along with those of his two brothers and two sisters, would have presented the ultimate test of the Christian faith of Frank and Eleanor. Child deaths were a quarter of all deaths and the Churches responded by producing 'consolation literature' (See also page 68) to explain the deaths from a Christian viewpoint, and encouraging the bereaved to seek consolation through their faith. Mourners were urged to see the child's death as:-

> …a trial intended as a spiritual challenge which could purify the parents' souls. Grieving parents were informed that this trial would teach them the lesson of submission to God's will, but were informed that this would not be easy. Some of them…might even harbour rebellious thoughts against God in their grief. Authors of consolation literature refrained from addressing the problem that such a terrible trial

[164] After a 1930's American folk-song popularised by the Carter family.

could be interpreted as God's punishment, though that was how many sorrowing parents perceived it.[165]

Parents were also encouraged to believe that blessedly, God, in an act of mercy, had taken the innocent child away to glorious heaven from a world of sin, temptation, pain and sorrow. Whether Eleanor in particular found real consolation from her faith is uncertain, but one imagines it will have become increasingly difficult for her to accept that God might require yet another death, the death of a precious four-year old child. When she was 21 years old, her mother died, and thereafter the repeated devastating loss of her children may well have caused her in some ways to withdraw from the world. Certainly, family accounts suggest a lady who was somewhat remote and unworldly in her later years at least.

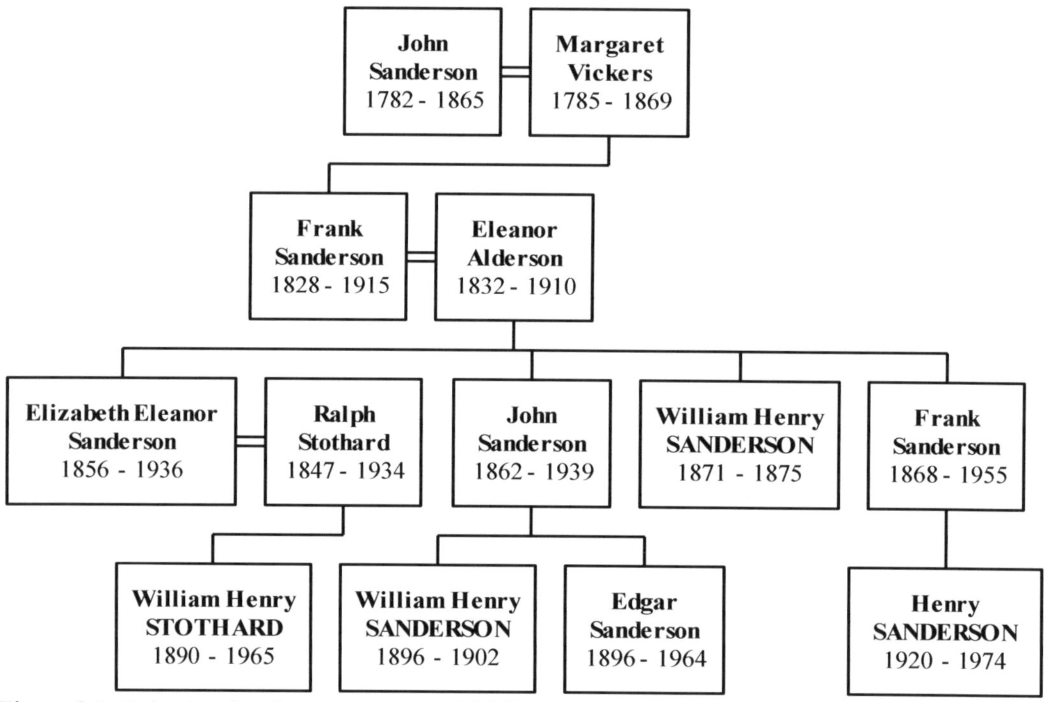

Figure 8-1: Selective family tree, showing "William Henry" family members.

The profound effect of William Henry's death is evidenced by the perpetuation of his Christian names in the family. His sister Lizzie who had nursed him in the rocking chair married farmer Ralph Stothard, and their son, William Henry Stothard, was born in 1890.

After gaining a Colliery Managers Certificate in 1914, he worked for the Consett Iron Company, becoming manager at Chopwell Colliery (1918), Plenmeller Colliery, Haltwhistle (1927), and Newbiggen Colliery, Northumberland (1930). After the creation of the National Coal Board in 1947, he continued managing at Newbiggin until 1950, at which time he became a mining agent for the Northern Division of the NCB until his retirement in 1956.[166]

165 Jalland, Pat (1996) *Death in the Victorian Family*. Oxford, OUP.

166 Details from the Durham Mining Museum website.

William Henry Stothard was visiting his cousin Ella Atkinson née Sanderson at Acrum House Colchester when he died in 1965.

8-2 William Henry Stothard (1890-1965)

William Henry Sanderson's sister-in-law Mary Eleanor Sanderson née Raine gave birth in 1896 to twin brothers Edgar and William Henry, the latter dying at five years of age in 1902 at Butsfield Burn. His Death Certificate reveals the cause of death, by a fateful coincidence, "Membranous Croup". How distraught must the family have felt to have named a child in memory of his departed cousin, only to have him also struck down by the same affliction at the same age?

Frank Sanderson of Hamsterley's youngest son (my father) was christened "Henry" – perhaps the family felt it would be tempting fate to name another child "William Henry" after the untimely deaths in 1875 and 1902.

Frank's early ill-health

Several other children in the family suffered from chest complaints, and given the infant mortality in the family, and the cruel death of William Henry, it is understandable that the family went to great lengths to ensure that their remaining children survived. Lizzie's asthma was manageable, but there was such concern about the chronic respiratory problems experienced by Frank that his father sent his youngest and favourite son to Bournemouth for treatment in 1889. FJS recounted the story:-

> My father was bad (ill), you know, when he was 21 and they thought he was going to die. His lungs weren't working properly and they thought he had consumption. He went to Bournemouth - that was the place to go. He was 9 months at Bournemouth, in lodgings and having treatment from a doctor every day.

Bournemouth: the healthiest resort in all the land

Bournemouth was undoubtedly the place to go. It had progressed from a quiet undeveloped early-Victorian backwater to a popular up-market resort by the 1870s. It became particularly known as a resort for invalids with chest disease, people going there "for health, not gaiety." One of the largest sanatoria in Europe was established right next door to the *Mont Dore Hotel* which had its own supply of seawater to enable various kinds of bathing for its guests. Press reports helped Bournemouth raise its profile in the North-East:-

> The climate of the north-east coast has long been noted for the prevalence of the piercing north-east winds which are so trying to invalids with chest disease, or who are threatened with consumption. Even during the present month of May …the

weather we are experiencing is not to be compared to that which prevailed at Bournemouth in the month of February. It is somewhat to be regretted that such a little gem of a town, which is admired by all who visit it, should be quite unknown and nearly unheard of in the Northern Counties. As the question "Where is Bournemouth?" is so often asked, I may begin by saying that it is situate on the coast of Hampshire, and within a very short distance of the boundary of Dorset, having the ancient town of Christchurch on the east and the little fishing port of Poole on the west. Between these two towns the English Channel forms a bay, and thus the town of Bournemouth is sheltered from storms …while it possesses a beautiful sea view. It is only thirty years since Bournemouth began to have a local habitation or name. It was in the year 1854 that it was discovered that the climate was the finest and mildest in England.

8-3 Illustration of Old Bournemouth, 1856. From Watson-Smith, S. (1934) *The Book of Bournemouth*. Pardy & Son.

In addition to its mildness, its atmosphere has another advantage of equally great importance to invalids, and that is the exceeding dryness. The soil is sandy, and after a shower there is no mud, and visitors can take a walk without the least inconvenience.

Such is the mildness of the Bournemouth climate that in February the seats on the cliffs were frequently occupied by convalescent ladies reading in the open air, and enjoying the sea breeze and a warmer sun than has been experienced in the north in the present year….One of the great advantages enjoyed by invalids is the shelter provided by the innumerable pine trees for which the district is noted and the aroma from which is regarded as most beneficial to sufferers from diseases of the lungs.

The Bourne Valley has been transformed into beautiful pleasure grounds which are open to the public, and are the favourite haunt, like those at Saltburn, of the more

delicate class of visitors – the stronger class preferring to ramble along the high cliffs and enjoy the ever-changing scenery.
The town is almost entirely composed of spacious villas of almost every description of architecture. Ample accommodation is provided at the various hotels and boarding houses for the visitors.
Bournemouth is most noted as a winter residence, but even in the summer months visitors can find shelter from the sun, and a gentle refreshing breeze is ever blowing from the English Channel.
Bournemouth – the healthiest health resort in all the land.[167]

One famous resident of Bournemouth in 1884-87 was novelist Robert Louis Stevenson who, somewhat strangely by today's fashions, actually moved there from the South of France for health reasons. He bought a house which he named Skerryvore,[168] and lived there for three years, during which time he wrote *The Strange Case of Dr Jekyll and Mr Hyde*.

8-4 Robert Louis Stevenson (1850-94)

8-5 Pen and ink drawing of Invalids' Walk in Bournemouth Gardens (1890) by Harry Furniss.

[167] *Northern Echo*, May 15, 1880
[168] Skerryvore was named after a Scottish lighthouse built by RLS's grandfather

Bishop Lightfoot's Example

In 1888-89, Bournemouth was much in the news in Bishop Auckland and district. The widely-respected Bishop of Durham, suffering from a lung infection, travelled to Bournemouth in November 1888 and convalesced there for several months:-

> Bishop Lightfoot's invalid quarters at Bournemouth consist of a private villa residence, situate among pine trees, on the East Cliff. The house is opposite the residence occupied for some months last winter by the Queen of Sweden. His Lordship takes an airing on the cliff almost daily in a bath chair.[169]

By early spring, the positive reports of an improvement in his health would not have gone unnoticed by the Sanderson family:-

> The improvement in the Bishop's health has continued in a most satisfactory manner. He is now able to get out of his bath chair without undue fatigue, and the symptoms which at one time caused the gravest anxiety have disappeared.[170]

By May 1889, the Lord Bishop was sufficiently recovered to be able to return to Bishop Auckland:-

> Nothing in the nature of a public reception is contemplated to signalise the arrival of Bishop Lightfoot at his Episcopal seat at Auckland Castle… He will leave Bournemouth tomorrow for London, remain in the metropolis all night, and travel by saloon direct to Bishop Auckland on Friday.[171]

It is quite possible that this good news about the bishop encouraged Frank Sanderson of Low Harperley to send his son to Bournemouth in the autumn of 1889. The 350-mile journey from Weardale to Bournemouth would have been demanding at the time, taking most of the day to complete. He would have taken food with him and also had the benefit of toilets which had been introduced to trains in 1881. It must have been quite an adventure for a country boy to travel so far by train, with Robert Louis Stevenson's words describing it well:-

From a Railway Carriage

Faster than fairies, faster than witches,
Bridges and houses, hedges and ditches;
And charging along like troops in a battle
All through the meadows the horses and cattle:
All of the sights of the hill and the plain
Fly as thick as driving rain
And ever again, in the wink of an eye
Painted stations whistle by.

---

[169] *Northern Echo*, November 30, 1888
[170] *Northern Echo*, March 2, 1889
[171] *Northern Echo*, May 22, 1889

It would have been a far more formidable journey to contemplate sixty years earlier in the pre-railway days and would have taken the best part of a week to complete. It would have been even more difficult in the early part of the 18th Century when roads were generally appalling – smothered in dust in summer and deeply rutted and muddy in winter. The journey from York to London along the Great North Road could take as long as 8 days, which means that a journey from Weardale to Bournemouth could easily have taken two weeks. Not that such a journey at that time would have been contemplated by a farmer's son from Weardale: horizons were limited, rarely extending beyond the parish boundaries for many people. Frank Sanderson of Hamsterley's grandfather, John Sanderson of Bishopley (1782-1865) would have been one of the more widely travelled locals, but in the 1820s, is likely to have experienced only infrequent visits to Newcastle, and more regular visits to the markets in Darlington and Bishop Auckland.

8-6 Bishop JB Lightfoot (1828-1889)

Soon after Frank arrived in Bournemouth, Bishop Lightfoot's health deteriorated again and he returned to the south coast in early November. Less than two months later at the *Imperial Hotel*, a short distance from Frank's lodgings, the Lord Bishop passed peacefully away:-

> Dr Lightfoot died at a quarter to four this afternoon …Up to Tuesday evening he seemed to be progressing favourably, but a change for the worse then ensued, and his recovery soon began to feel almost hopeless… He (died) without having regained consciousness…the immediate cause (of death) being acute congestion of the lungs.[172]

[172] *Northern Echo*, December 23, 1889

His body was returned from Bournemouth to Durham for the funeral on December 27th. The first part of the funeral service took place at Durham Cathedral, and then the hearse and a score of mourning coaches set off to Auckland Chapel for the concluding rites:-

> It is seen that the whole route, along the Bailey, across picturesque Prebend's Bridge, and well out of the city, is lined with people, who reverentially uncover as the body is slowly drawn away….Every house on the road has its blinds drawn, every shop its shutters up, and the people assemble in scores on the roadside. At Spennymoor the inhabitants turned out in their hundreds, and in every way that was possible to them manifested their sorrow at the loss of the distinguished prelate who, during the course of his episcopacy, had done so much for the practical religion in his diocese both by high Christian example and noble deed.[173]

The news of the Lord Bishop's original positive experience of Bournemouth may well have been an inspiration to Frank and his family, and so his death may have been equally dispiriting. Nevertheless, Frank over-wintered in Bournemouth, but eventually became disillusioned with his treatment and increasingly bored and homesick. He had had an opportunity to relieve the boredom when he received a message from his 27 year-old brother John who wanted him to come to London to have a night on the town. But Frank declined, probably because he felt that "a night on the town" with John would prove too costly – even in his early twenties, Frank seems to have formed a view of his older brother as prodigal in his ways.

In desperation at the lack of improvement in his health, he went to consult another doctor in the late Spring of 1890. FJS explained:-

> My father said to the doctor, "Now look, I want you to examine me and if I'm going to die, I want you to tell me I'm going to die, but I don't want to die in Bournemouth, I'm sick and tired of Bournemouth. I want to go home."

The doctor asked him what he did for a living – "A farmer! Well, <u>that</u> couldn't be better - get a dog and take it out, shout at your dog and get your lungs working - and use plenty of pepper on your food."[174]

Presumably the logic was that pepper would make him sneeze, thereby exercising his lungs. Pepper aside, I do recall that he had a great liking for salt, a habit that would be discouraged today on health grounds.

According to FJS, his father quickly got over his respiratory problems and, apart from a broken collar-bone and a brief bout of chilblains, he never had a day's illness for the rest of his life.

FJS spoke of his Uncle John "drinking like a fish", but his father also liked a drink:-

> He had too much whiskey one night at the *Cross Keys* and came in and fell over the bloody stable lamp in the scullery. But he was never bad, never had a cold, and was never croaky like me.

Paraffin lamps had been introduced in the 1860s and provided the only means of lighting in Hamsterley at the time.

---

[173] *Northern Echo,* December 28, 1889

[174] FJS's account, April 1980

After another evening of over-indulgence at the *Cross Keys*, FJS recalled:-

> He came home and sat down to have supper and I said, "Where's your teeth?" My father, who hadn't noticed they were missing, said, "I know where I've left them! They're in the toilet at the Cross Keys. Go and get them for me!"

Frank once offered some practical health advice to Jackie Cousins, who worked for Dick and Ella Atkinson at Low Staindrop Field House and Acrumbouts of ill Farm, West Auckland. Jackie remembered having chilblains one winter in the 1940s and, on the advice of my grandfather, ran 150 yards down a snow-covered track in his bare feet. His chilblains quickly disappeared, never to be seen again. This 'hair of the dog' advice probably stemmed from practical experience within the family of attempting to cure chilblains in this fashion, which conjures the amusing image of my grandfather, and perhaps his father before him, running around Hamsterley in the snow, barefoot. In fact, given the significant number of family members over the generations who have died of ailments such as bronchitis, diphtheria and pneumonia, is it not possible that some of them succumbed after desperately attempting to cure chilblains?

Courtship and Marriage

When his father bought Pond House in Hamsterley for his retirement in 1895, Frank Sanderson of Hamsterley stayed on at Brandon for several years. He was there in 1898 when he made a Servant's Agreement with Rachel Jones of Hunwick Lane Ends. Rachel was 14½ years old and was to be employed from 24th November for a period of six months, for which she would receive the sum of £3 - 10/-, plus board and lodging.

In 1911, Rachel was housekeeper for George Southern Smailes, a schoolmaster at Rowlands Gill.

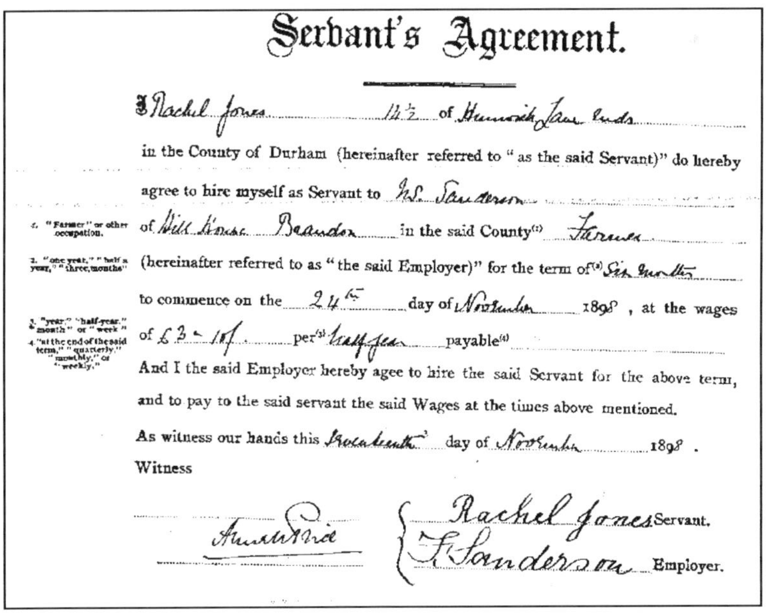

Servant's Agreement.

I Rachel Jones 14½ of Hunwick Lane Ends in the County of Durham (hereinafter referred to "as the said Servant)" do hereby agree to hire myself as Servant to W. Sanderson of Hill House Brandon in the said County(1) Farmer (hereinafter referred to as "the said Employer)" for the term of(2) Six months to commence on the 24th day of November 1898, at the wages of £3 - 10/- per(3) half year payable(4)

And I the said Employer hereby agree to hire the said Servant for the above term, and to pay to the said servant the said Wages at the times above mentioned.

As witness our hands this Seventeenth day of November 1898.

Witness

[illegible]

Rachel Jones Servant.

F. Sanderson Employer.

1. "Farmer" or other occupation.
2. "one year," "half a year," "three months"
3. "year," "half-year," "month" or "week"
4. "at the end of the said term," "quarterly," "monthly," or "weekly."

8-7 Servant's Agreement from 1898 between Frank Sanderson and Rachel Jones, aged 14 ½ years.

The first time Frank met Edith Stephenson of Bedburn was when she was riding in a trap with her father and he was riding on horseback to Hamsterley from Brandon to see his father. Joseph Stephenson asked him, "Who might you be?" Frank replied that he was going to visit his father at Pond House. "Oh, you're his son, are you", said Joseph. Joseph, and no doubt the precocious Edith, were interested in this eligible bachelor, but it was a while before Frank saw either of them again.

By 1903, Frank Sanderson was living next door to his father in Hamsterley and engaged to Edith. Family postcards reveal that some of Edith's female friends viewed her impending marriage with mixed emotions – not only would there be feelings of excitement about Edith being married but there would also be envy amongst still unbetrothed girlfriends, and concern about the effect the marriage might have on the friendships.

8-8 Elizabeth Lowson's postcard to Edith, her "true friend".

The Lowson sisters[175] appeared anxious about their friendship with Edith: after they had received a letter from Edith in early February, 1904, their relief is palpable. Elizabeth Jane Lowson wrote on February 5, thanking her for the "long expected letter" and she endorses the picture of the Deer House, Auckland Park with the words:-

> "However rare true love is, true friendship is rarer."

This message can be taken as a not-too-subtle reminder to Edith not to forget her friend when she marries.

Evelyn Lowson wrote a day later with the message:-

[175] The sisters were Elizabeth J. (b. 1880 at Evenwood) and Evelyn (b. 1881 at Morley). Their father John was a colliery owner. One of the Lowson sisters was godmother to my father, Henry Sanderson (1921-1974).

I thought you had forgotten this part of the world all together, but am glad to hear that you are still alive.....From your Still Existing Friend.

8-9 Edith Stephenson in bowler hat with the Lowson sisters from Morley at Bedburn Hall Farm in c. 1900.

This message from Edith's "still existing friend" has a mildly pointed tone, with Edith being gently admonished for not being in touch.

At this time, Edith was only 20 years old and about to get married – her Lowson girlfriends were 2 or 3 years older and they might have felt slightly discomforted by their younger friend entering into wedlock ahead of them. In 1909, Evelyn Lowson married policeman Albert Ernest Brown, and Elizabeth Jane Lowson remained unmarried – in 1923, she was a 43 year-old Company Director and Secretary to Henry Lowson Ltd, a mining company based at Tower Lodge, Morley.

The excitement about the marriage is evident in a postcard to Edith from cousin Mary Jane (Jennie) Swinbank on 10 December, 1903. Postmarked Winston, and depicting St Hilda's Church, South Shields, the message reads, "Nice spot to be married at".

8-10 Nice spot to be married at...

On November 3, 1903, Edith received a German-made romantic card from Frank Sanderson of Hamsterley with the message:-

> "Come and let me kiss you in the dark. How would this suit(e)"

8-11 Come let me kiss you in the dark

In August 1904, the month that the *Entente Cordiale* was signed between Britain and France, settling outstanding territorial disputes, Frank married Edith Stephenson at Hamsterley St James in the presence of Edith's brother George Stephenson and close friend Rose Ellen Douglas, a schoolteacher and the daughter of schoolteachers from Woodland. The Vicar was H.T. Lovejoy, he having succeeded his uncle, the Rev J G Milner, in 1885. He remained at St James Church until 1905.

Honeymoon at Whitley Bay

Frank and Edith enjoyed a late honeymoon at Whitley Bay during the summer Bank Holiday in 1905. For anyone looking for lively entertainment in a fashionable seaside location, Whitley Bay was an obvious choice for people from the North East and Southern Scotland. In 1861, Whitley Bay, situated about 8 miles north of Newcastle-upon-Tyne, was an unremarkable coastal village with a population of about 300. But access was transformed when the railway station arrived the following year, and its population expanded rapidly. It became a popular Victorian seaside resort, attracting holiday makers from all parts of the North East and Scotland – and there were cheap rail excursions from many parts of the country.

8-12 Frank and Edith at the time of their wedding in 1904

A typical seaside holiday involved "…walks along the shore, donkey rides, bathing, band concerts, and Punch and Judy shows. For those women wishing to bathe in the sea, there were bathing machines which could be hired. These consisted of a wooden shelter on wheels which was dragged into the sea by a horse or a donkey. Within the enclosure, one could undress and change into one's bathing costume with absolute decorum and, for those not brave enough to actually swim, they offered a secure site from which to splash in the water."[176]

[176] Extract from Charles Keene (1823-91) *Mr Punch at the Seaside.*

8-13 Whitley Bay where Frank and Edith honeymooned in 1905

The postcard sent by Frank from Whitley Bay to his mother Eleanor in Hamsterley provides an indication of how popular visits to the seaside were:-

> Arrived safe, but lodgings hard to get. We can only stay here until Monday, so will have to seek some place by then. The place is full of visitors.
> Your sincere son, F Sanderson.

FJS and Ella

Their son Francis Joseph Sanderson (FJS), was born at Bedburn Hall Farm, the home of Edith's family, on August 16, 1904 (See p 219 ff for more detail on the life of FJS).

In 1907, the Second Peace Conference at The Hague failed to stop the arms race but did agree conventions on the rules of war and neutrality. It was also a momentous year for New Zealand: in September, the country became a dominion of the British Empire, and in December, fire destroyed the parliament buildings in Wellington. Other significant events included the founding of the Boy Scout movement by Lord Baden-Powell, the first showing of a cubist painting by Pablo Picasso, the court appearance of 57 suffragettes following violent clashes with the police, and the record five-day crossing of the Atlantic by the British Ocean liner *SS Lusitania.*

It was also the year in which FJS's sister Ella was born at Pond House, Hamsterley. Eleanor Eliza Sanderson, named after her Sanderson and Stephenson grandmothers respectively, was doted on by her parents. On 4 October, 1909, Edith and 2 year-old Ella had gone to stay with the Stothards at Carr House, Durham. Husband Frank, who'd stayed at home to look after the farm, wrote a rather touching postcard to his baby daughter:-

> Frankie thinks you are having a long holiday as he has nobody to play with at nights. Tell mother we are all going on alright.

Ella attended Hamsterley School until the age of 11, and transferred to Wolsingham Grammar School at the end of the First World War.

8-14 Ella with her mother in 1913

Having some fine times of it: holidays and leisure time

During the late Victorian and Edwardian eras, the family took advantage of the wider horizons made available with the advent of the railways. There are many instances of extended trips to the sea-side in the summer months and trips to spa towns, as well as frequent visits to relatives at, for example, Nafferton, Winston and Framwellgate Moor.

After their trip to Whitley Bay, Frank and Edith travelled to Harrogate and Knaresborough in late September. From there, Edith wrote to her cousin Jennie Swinbank who was staying at Bedburn Hall Farm and looking after FJS – who was about 13 months old at the time. The postcard depicts the House Boat Cafe, Knaresborough and contains the message:-

> How are you enjoying yourself. We are having some fine times of it. Give our love to all.

8-15 Having some fine times of it at Harrogate and Knaresborough

There

was the occasion (possibly May, 1913) that Frank, his sister Lizzie, and her husband Ralph Stothard were staying in Harrogate. FJS remembered that "Madame Pankhurst" the suffragette was in town at the time, actually staying in the same street, and his father was frightened at the prospect of bombs going off. This was understandable in that the suffragettes bombed the Chancellor Lloyd George's house on February 19, 1913, and Harrogate was one of the major towns in the suffragette campaign. It had long attracted middle-class women to take the waters and meet their friends, and thus a likely place for the suffragettes to carry out a summer campaign.[177] The fear made Frank return home sooner than he had planned, but he returned to Harrogate in the following August when the Great War began.

Particularly before the age of mechanisation, farming was extremely hard work and as recalled by Flora Thompson, sometimes very dangerous. Nevertheless, the tenant farmer and the farm workers would find time for amusement, particularly in the long winter evenings when there was less to do in the fields.

The village inn has for many generations played a large part in local life. Hibbert tells of the astonishing amount of alcohol consumed in these places during the 19th Century – in 1875, "the most bibulous year on record", 1.3 gallons of spirits and 34.4 gallons of beer was consumed per head of the population.[178] It is safe to assume that the 19th century Sandersons drank their fair share of this prodigious national consumption, and the tradition was enthusiastically continued into the last century. Frank Sanderson of Hamsterley for example was a regular at the *Cross Keys* in Hamsterley, on one occasion leaving his false teeth there and only realising their absence when he sat down for supper.

The pub was almost exclusively a male preserve until well into the 20th century, leaving the more liberated of women to find alternative amusement. Frank's gregarious wife Edith was a frequent visitor to the homes of friends and family, and also enjoyed attending and participating in concerts at the Mission Room in Hamsterley.

In a postcard message to her friend Lizzie Gray née Walton who lived at nearby Diddridge Farm, Edith asks:

> Are you coming up to the concert in the Mission Room on Sat night – if so, come and have tea with us."

Hibbert describes some of the ways in which families amused themselves during the 19th Century:-

> There were jigsaws and all kinds of games to play, card games and board games, paper and pencil games, whist and loo, piquet and Pope Joan, halma, solitaire and corinthian. Above all, there was patience, and there was music.[179]

Playing cards was a favourite past-time of Frank Sanderson of Hamsterley, an activity he was still enjoying in his 70s when he visited my maternal grandparents at St Helens Auckland in the 1940s. He also liked a game of dominoes; when he was living with daughter Ella at Low Staindrop Field House before World War II, he would often go to High Staindrop Field House for a game of dominoes with Charlie Hankey.

---

[177] Crawford, Elizabeth (2013) *The Women's Suffrage Movement in Britain and Ireland: A Regional Survey*, Routledge.
[178] Hibbert, C. (1987) *The English: A Social History*: 1066-1845. London, HarperCollins. p.622
[179] Ibid p 625

8-16 Frank Sanderson Jnr of Nafferton, with violin

Several members of his cousin Frank Sanderson of Nafferton's family were capable musicians – Frank's sons John Thomas and Frank Jnr played the violin and the latter also played the organ. FJS's grandfather Joseph Stephenson played the violin.

FJS revealed that his father was a good pianist:-

He learnt to play himself without any lessons at all. We had many very pleasant evenings when friends came in and my father would sing all these old songs. I remember many of them.

Willie, the son of Thomas Sanderson of Broomley, was a great singer according to FJS. One of his favourite songs, which was obviously great fun to sing in convivial company with a pint of beer in hand, was *"Good Old Doctor Shelly"*[180]

The song is about a roguish doctor, perhaps best described as a quack. The first verse ran:-

Oh I'm a doctor you can see, and one of great renown
I only charge a tanner cash instead of half-a-crown
I cure mumps, the whooping cough, the measles and the flu
you can pay me by instalments if you give an IOU."

This was followed by the chorus which everyone would join in singing:

I'm Shelly, Good Old Doctor Shelly
No matter what complaint you've got
I can cure you on the spot
If you've got a pain, in your dermi-kelly
Just trot old Tommy round to me
I'm Good Old Doctor Shelly.

The skills gained in farming were sometimes put to use in leisure time. Thus at agricultural fairs, my g. grandfather Frank of Low Harperley and his son-in-law, Ralph Stothard of Carr House were very successful in ploughing contests. Ralph competed at

[180] Recorded at Vesey Farm in April, 1980. Uncle Frank sang the song with some relish, recalling that cousin Willie Sanderson used to sing it about 60 years previously. The genre, if not the song itself, survives today in rugby clubs throughout the world.

national standard and Frank won a ploughing cup at the Harperley and Helme Park Fair in 1856 (See p.76 ff). The former was also an accomplished billiards player.

Until well into the 20th century, the Hamsterley Hoppings[181] took place every year and was the most noted fair of its kind in County Durham. It was originally called the "Feast of the Dedication", taking place on the feast day of St James, the Saint to which the parish of Hamsterley is dedicated. It took place over 2 days and included events such as cricket, wrestling, dog trials, quoits, foot races, and ass races, all for prize money. Many villagers as well as visiting competitors and spectators would participate in the festivities.

During the 20th Century, first the radio, then cinema, followed by television, dominated the lives of many people, arguably to the detriment of family life. So, despite the relentless hard work, the frequent ill-health and the lack of modern comforts, our forebears did have enviable social lives – hours by the fireside talking or making music, village concerts where everyone would play a part, and wide and frequent mutually supportive contact with relatives and friends.

An Encounter with a Murderer

FJS recalled, "I remember the time my father took two hosses to Newcastle Fair."

In October, 1909, Frank Sanderson of Hamsterley took two horses to Newcastle Autumn Horse Fair to sell, riding one and leading the other for the twenty-mile journey. He sold them to someone he knew and took a cheque for them. At the Fair he met cousin Frank Sanderson of Nafferton in Tynedale who persuaded him to accompany him to the Town Moor where he wanted to buy some Irish heifers. When they returned to the horse fair, a man who my grandfather had assumed to be a friend of his cousin asked him if he would buy a colt for him. "It's round here, behind the tents, you buy it and I'll pay you", the man said. Frank quickly replied, "No, I'll buy it for you but you pay for it!" as he followed the man behind the tents.

At this point, a second man who was holding two horses grabbed him and shook him. Frank immediately knew what was happening: they were after his money and the man had shaken him to see if he had any gold coins, to hear the rattle. He wrestled free and ran underneath the tent ropes, grabbed his saddle, bridle and tackle, ran for a cab and travelled to Central Station. He was still frightened when he got home.

A few months later, on Friday, March 18, 1910, there was a murder on a train between Newcastle and Morpeth[182]. A porter at Alnmouth station was checking the carriages of the 10.27 am train from Newcastle and found the blood-stained body of 44 year old John Nisbet under a seat in the first compartment. He had five bullet wounds in his head. Beside the body was a return ticket from Newcastle to Widdrington.

Nisbet was a colliery book-keeper who delivered the pay to the men at Stobswood Colliery near Widdrington every fortnight. It was clear that Nisbet had been robbed, and it was later established that he had been carrying 231 sovereigns, 206 half sovereigns, £35 9s 0d in silver and £1 0s 6d in copper, all in a locked leather bag. The bag was later found, slit open with a sharp knife, at the bottom of a pit shaft at Hepscott Colliery.

---

181 'Hoppings' came from 'hopping and dancing'.

182 Details of The Newcastle Train Murder are contained in: Eddleston, J.J., (1997) *Murderous Tyneside – the executed of the 20th Century*, 81-99.

By March 21, the police had arrested John Alexander Dickman, a clerk turned professional gambler whom a witness had seen in the presence of Nisbet on the morning of the murder. It was established that he knew Nisbet and had travelled on the same train, although he had not come forward to say so. After it was discovered that Dickman was carrying £17 in gold, he was formally charged with the murder.

Dickman was tried at the Moot Hall, Newcastle, on July 4, 1910. After a trial lasting 3 days, the jury returned a guilty verdict, at which Dickman declared:-

> I can only repeat that I am entirely innocent of this cruel deed. I have no complicity in this crime. I have spoken the truth in my evidence and in everything I have said.

THE NORTHERN ECHO, THURSDAY, 7 JULY, 1910

DRAMATIC SCENES

Close of the Train Murder Trial; the Prisoner Protests his Innocence

DICKMAN CONDEMNED.

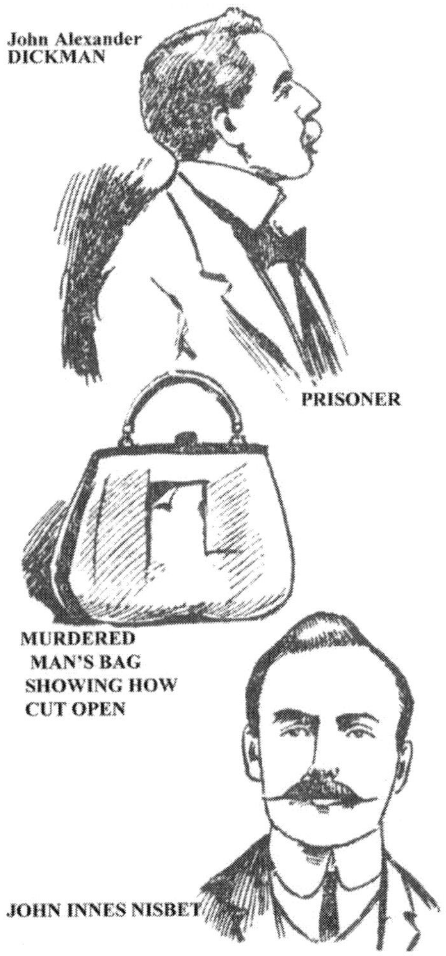

The judge then put on his black cap and, "in calm, solemn tones, vibrant with a touch of dramatic force", he declared:

> Prisoner at the bar, the patient and careful trial is now ended. The irrevocable decision has now been given and the jury have found you guilty of the crime of murder. In your hungry lust for gold you had no pity on the victim whom you slew. It is only just that the Nemesis of the law should overtake the author of the crime. The punishment is death. I do not presume to judge you. I am nothing but the minister of the law, but in passing sentence I can only do that which the law commands.

Following the sentence of death, Dickman looked all around the court and shouted:-

> "I declare to all men that I am innocent."

8-17 Artist's impression of John Dickman and Alexander Nisbet (*Daily Mail* [Hull] July 9, 1910)

Despite serious irregularities having been uncovered in the police investigation, irregularities which today would have probably led to the verdict being overturned, his appeal was ultimately dismissed by the Home Secretary, Winston Churchill. A *Northern Echo* reporter who went to see Mrs Dickman shortly after the failure of the appeal noted that she was, not surprisingly, "labouring under the emotion of a very keen disappointment". Her husband was executed by hanging at Newcastle Gaol on Tuesday August 10, 1910, the *Newcastle Evening Chronicle* reporting that he "marched to his execution as erect as a soldier, never flinching, even when the rope came into view."

Newspapers reported the macabre details of what is now regarded as a barbaric practice:-

> He was given a drop of 7 ft., and death was due to dislocation of the vertebrae of the neck. Dr William Hardcastle at the inquest stated that the rope had stretched one inch when measured after the execution.[183]

He maintained his innocence to the end.

The case and the outcome was very controversial and sharply divided opinion between those convinced of his guilt and those who believed he was innocent.

The fact that the evidence was entirely circumstantial led to widespread unease with the verdict:-

> It is impossible to read the narrative of the last moments of Dickman – executed this morning for the murder of a cashier on the North-Eastern Railway – without a haunting sense of discomfort and pardonable emotion. Many persons who have followed this sordid and dreary mystery will have asked themselves anxiously today whether they really believed Dickman was guilty or not.... The circumstances of capital punishment, however necessary they may be as a deterrent, are fulfilled with horror. ...There is a poignant pathos, a subdued anguish about this plucking forth of a fellow creature from his "friends and lovers," this keeping him in sombre seclusion, and this untimely end in the gray of the morning.
> ..Although the law has uttered its opinion in the most weighty accents, a large number of the public may be pardoned if they entertained some doubt as to Dickman's guilt. The case against him was circumstantial. The crime was committed without witnesses. ...There were compromising facts – almost damning facts – against Dickman, but despite the wonderful summing up of Mr Justice Coleridge, the verdict of the Jury, and the review of the Lord Chief Justice in the Criminal Court of Appeal, the impression was not removed from some minds that the case was inconclusive. It was felt that a man's life should not depend upon these presumptions, however strong they might be.[184]

When Frank Sanderson of Hamsterley saw the photograph of the condemned man in the newspaper, he said, "That's the man! I'd never forget him", referring to the man who had attempted to rob him in Newcastle. This does not prove that Dickman was a murderer but

[183] *Teesdale Mercury*, August 10, 1910
[184] *Daily Mail* (Hull) August 9 1910

my grandfather was convinced that this was the same man who had scared the life out of him at Newcastle Horse Fair.

There is a post-script to this dramatic story. In 1976, there was a TV programme about the murder case, in which it was concluded that the man should never have been hung. FJS, with characteristic forthrightness, and perhaps characteristic embellishment in the telling, phoned up the TV station and lectured them about their misjudgement:

> What do you know? He was a murderer! He bloody nearly murdered my father! I'm telling you, there are no two ways about it! Hanging is what they all want yet. And they want the birch back too!

We do not know what the TV Complaints Department made of this unreasonable tirade. What it does show however is that FJS was somewhat right of centre in his political views and that he can be comfortably described as a "character".

Chalk and Cheese

Frank Sanderson of Hamsterley was a church-goer and a Church Warden for many years at Hamsterley. The fact that he went to church far more frequently than Edith isn't surprising, given their different temperaments and outlook on life. Whereas he was reserved, self-contained, and a God-fearing person, Edith was in many ways the opposite, being essentially irreverent, emotional, gregarious, wilful, fun-loving and convention-breaking. To some extent, the two were the inevitable products of different families - he the son of a strict and proud father and a mother who displayed 'airs and graces', and she the daughter of more down to earth, not to say, earthy, parents, without pretentions of any kind.

Frank was blessed with an equable temperament whereas Edith had more of a roller-coaster temperament, characterised by emotional highs and lows. She was somewhat headstrong, maybe even high-strung, and liked excitement and stimulating company, and would easily become bored. She achieved pleasure from social occasions and from bucking conventions. It is likely that there was lots of laughter when she was around, although no doubt occasionally there would be tears. She appears to have inherited her small and plump physique from her mother, and her temperament from both parents: the generous nature from her father and emotional volatility from her mother.

And then there was the age difference of 15 years: despite living until the second half of the 20th Century, Frank was a classic Victorian, whereas Edith, despite her untimely death in 1922, was a child of the twentieth century. There is no doubt that she would have been perfectly at home as a young woman in the 1920s and in the 1960s. The same could be said of her daughter, Ella, with whom she shared many personality characteristics, e.g., fun-loving, impulsive, and extrovert in nature. In a letter to me in September 1998, Freda Ellis remembers "Auntie Edie" as being 'trendy' and Ella and FJS as being 'headstrong' – as was their mother.

The recollections of Freda Ellis

The contrast between Frank and Edith was mentioned in a letter sent to me by retired schoolteacher Freda Ellis née Gibson in February, 1979. I had met Freda purely by chance - she and her husband Ted Ellis were visiting old haunts and parked their car next to ours at Bedburn. We got into conversation with them and discovered a mutual interest in the

Sandersons of Hamsterley. Freda revealed that she was a friend of the family and regular visitor to Pond House. Aware of my interest in family history, Freda, who was 69 years old at the time, wrote to me shortly afterwards with memories from her childhood:-

> Whether the nostalgia I feel for times gone by is a sign of approaching old age, or a desire to get away from the complications of life as it is now, I cannot tell, but I have found myself thinking a lot about visits to Pond House, for I know that I loved going there. Sometimes your grandfather would come to Howden-le-Wear for us in the little tub trap, and these were indeed "Red Letter Days". I remember him better than your grandmother, for it was his custom to come to our house once a fortnight on Saturdays to collect rent from some property which he owned.[185] Usually, he stayed for lunch, and would exchange news with my parents before returning to Hamsterley.
>
> Auntie Edie, your grandmother, I cannot remember so well, for I would have been only twelve when she died. I picture her smoking cigarettes, which in those days was a pretty daring thing for a woman to do, and I think I was quite fascinated by this habit. From what my mother told us, she was very fond of company and may have found "Uncle" Frank rather staid, as there was a fair difference in age between them. She was, as I remember, not very tall, pleasant and attractive, and made us very welcome. She sometimes took us to Bedburn for picnics, and I fancy relatives or friends would be there too. Ella and Frank, I know, were there too. My mother must have grown up with Auntie Edie, as she was born in the "Spinning Wheel" (now the Workman's Club)[186] and lived in Hamsterley until she married my father.

Edie and Freda's mother Elizabeth Anne Pallister[187] were very good friends. At about the time that Edie married Frank Sanderson of Hamsterley, Elizabeth Ann married Joe Gibson, after which they moved to Holley Terrace, Howden-le-Wear. Evidence of the friendship is provided by an unsent and undated postcard from Edith:-

> Dear Lizzie, Only a line from Auckland to let you know I have got 12/- worth of eggs and I hope to see Joe up soon. With heaps of kind love, Yours, ES.

It turns out that there was more than a close friendship between the Stephenson and Pallister families: Edith and Elizabeth Anne were first cousins, once removed – Elizabeth Anne Pallister's grandmother was Mary Stephenson, Joseph Stephenson of Bedburn's older sister (See Fig 8-18). Freda Ellis spoke of 'Auntie' Edie' when in fact she is her first cousin twice removed – and Freda, the total stranger I met on Bedburn Bridge, is my third cousin.

This provides yet another example of the many close family ties existing in a small rural community, with almost everyone with long association with the village being related in some way.

---

[185] My grandfather owned 16 houses in Church Street, Valley Terrace and Chapel View in Howden-le-Wear.

[186] The *Spinning Wheel* was 'possibly the old meeting place of the Bedburn Textile Workers' (notes on Hamsterley, provided by Canon J.G.S. Turnbull, formerly vicar at St Helens Auckland.)

[187] Elizabeth Anne was born in 1880, the daughter of Joseph and Annie, née Williamson.

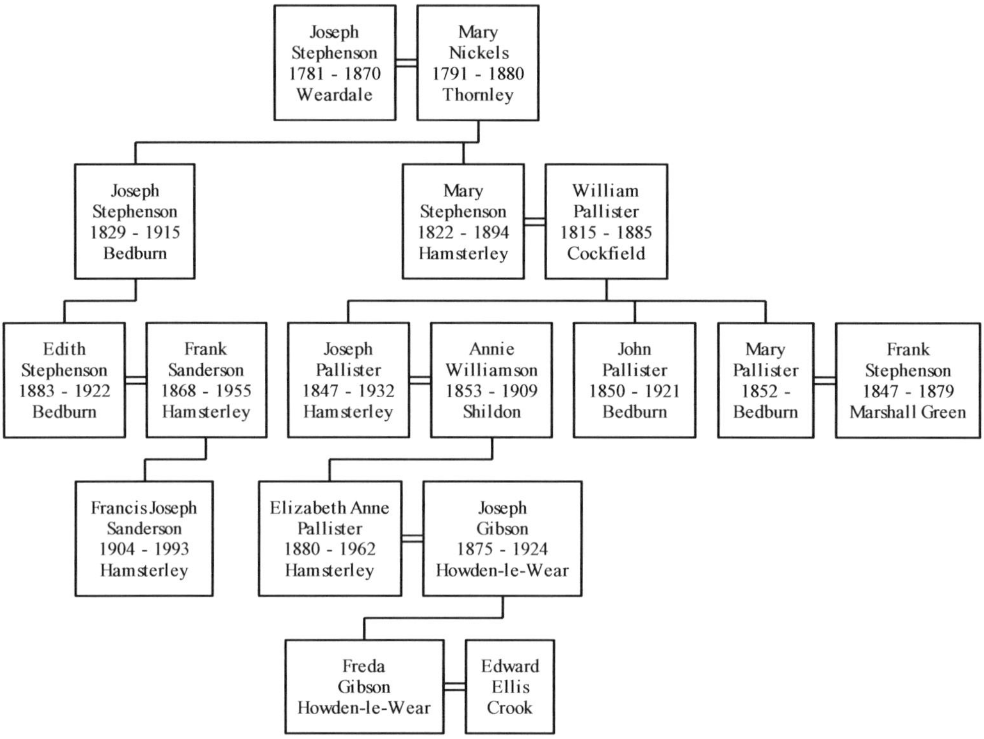

8-18 Family Connections: Elizabeth Anne Pallister and FJS's mother Edith are first cousins once removed. Frank Stephenson, from a separate family of Stephensons, is Frank Sanderson of Hamsterley's cousin.

Freda remembered Edie bringing eggs over from Hamsterley to Howden-le-Wear. In 1998, I re-contacted Freda, by then 87 years old, who wrote with further memories from her childhood and early adulthood:-

> The last time I saw your father Henry would be at Ella and Dick Atkinson's farm at West Auckland.[188] When Auntie Edie (as she was known to us) died, he must have been only 2 years old. We visited Ella and Dick periodically, but my more vivid memories are mainly of visits to Hamsterley, where we made the journey there in Uncle Frank's (Frank Sanderson of Hamsterley's) tub-trap. That was quite a high-light of our childhood days. I remember being led round the fields on the big cart-horse, games in the loft, picnics at Bedburn, and the fear of having to go at night to the loo at the end of the garden. I was rather scared of Ella and Frank, as they teased me a lot, and both were headstrong. On several occasions, Frank would take the gun from the wall threatening to shoot his father.[189]
>
> Your grandmother, Edith, my mother's dear friend seemed to us, and was of course, much younger than Frank. She was always smart, lively, kind to us, and smoked a lot, which in those days was quite uncommon. You might say nowadays she was

[188] Acrum Farm

[189] It was about this time that FJS was taken to task by Old Tom White for pointing a gun at him (See p.60).

> trendy. In retrospect, maybe she was too young for Frank. After her death, Frank came regularly to Howden to collect rent from a few houses he owned. He always had dinner (lunch) with us, but I think our visits to Hamsterley ceased after her death.

The letter confirms a few impressions I had gained: that FJS and Auntie Ella were 'headstrong', that my grandmother was trendy, and that the Hamsterley social whirl diminished with my grandmother's death in 1922.

Freda Gibson's mother had also described her cousin Edith as 'flighty'. A Victorian dictionary defines 'flighty' as 'wild' and 'fanciful', and 'flightiness' as ''capricious', itself defined as 'whimsical' and 'fanciful'. The Collins English Dictionary defines it as 1. frivolous and irresponsible; capricious; volatile. 2. mentally erratic, unstable or wandering. 3. Flirtatious; coquettish. From what I have gleaned about Edith's personality, I can imagine her to have been 'flighty' in every sense of the word, although my imagination has to work harder on the idea of her being 'flirtatious', given that she was quite short of stature and somewhat overweight.

Following a request to readers of the *Teesdale Mercury* for information about the Sanderson family, I received the following letter in 1980 from Mrs Mary Weir of The Green, Hamsterley:-

> I live opposite Pond House, now called its original name, Hamsterley House. I came from Tyneside during the War and worked at Pond House, as it was then known, for two years. A Mr Sanderson[190] used to call and he told me he used to live there. Then after I married a farmer's son[191] I worked for Mr Bill Stephenson[192] at Blackhill Top. My late mother-in-law[193] used to work for Edith Sanderson, your grandmother.... Mr Bill Stephenson's widow Mrs Doris Stephenson (née Lockerbie) still lives in the village. The last I heard about your family was Mr Frank Sanderson (FJS) coming visiting the church.
>
> Good Luck, Mary Weir.

Mary Weir died in Hamsterley in 2016.

Arthur Henderson's visit to Hamsterley

Edith Stephenson was described by her son FJS as "a red-hot conservative" who was secretary of the local Conservative and Unionist Party.

At election time, Edith would take people to the polling station by pony and trap, trusting that such generosity would ensure a vote for the Conservative candidate. Jos Coatsworth, who wrote the poem, *The Story of Little Titch*, (See p.225) was one of the few local labour people about at that time. FJS thought he was a great character, but Edith was wary of him because of his politics. Despite her natural generosity of spirit, she appears to have felt that the relatively privileged position of the tenant farmer was under threat from the gathering trade unionism and the increasingly vociferous and organised labouring class. For decades

---

[190] Frank Sanderson of Hamsterley, my grandfather

[191] Mary Adkin married George Ridley Weir, a farmer from South Bedburn (East Mayland), in 1944.

[192] Edith's nephew Bill, my first cousin once removed.

[193] Mary's mother-in-law is Isabella Olive Coatsworth who married William Weir in 1913. Olive worked as a maid for the Sandersons at Pond House during WW1.

there had been growing agitation for solidarity amongst labourers in various parts of the country, particularly in the Midlands and the South where agricultural wages were especially low. For the landowners and tenant farmers, the prospect of organised labour was frightening in the extreme as it directly challenged long-established social hierarchies, the right of bosses to set wages as they saw fit, and to hire and fire at their convenience. Much of the blame was placed on nonconformist preachers who were accused by the Anglican clergy of alienating villagers from the established church, and encouraging disaffection and insubordination against not only the clergy but against employers. In the light of this, it is easier to understand why the 'dead Labour' Jos Coatsworth should shout and curse at the parson on his way home from the pub, and why Edith Sanderson should be so hostile towards his open demonstration of disrespect for the established order.

Decades earlier, a newspaper editorial had expressed the concern of the employers, although reference to "very large wages" was a gross overstatement of the reality:-

> I hear serious complaints regarding the want of honesty and presence of laziness which (working men) often display while at work. It is an everyday remark that one can no longer get a fair day's work for a fair day's wage. The tables are completely turned. If the employer used to obtain a great deal of work for a very small wage, the workman now secures a very large wage for a modicum of work.[194]

A prominent Liberal-turned-Labour politician, Arthur Henderson was detested by Edith because he was an effective representative for the emerging labour movement. The working classes needed affordable food, and this was increasingly supplied by foreign farmers who enjoyed unfettered access to British markets (thus keeping down home prices), whereas foreign markets often imposed high tariffs on British exports. The beleaguered farmers were also fearful of the costly prospect of improved wage levels and working conditions. Given these perceptions, it was not surprising that people such as Edith Stephenson supported the Conservative and Unionist Party which represented the established order and more specifically, was advocating retaliatory tariffs for foreign produce – good news for farmers perhaps but the inevitable increase in food prices would badly affect the working class.

Arthur Henderson was born in Glasgow in 1863 but moved with his parents to Newcastle in about 1870. After becoming the agent for the Liberal MP for Barnard Castle, Sir Joseph Whitwell Pease, he moved to Darlington in 1896. He became Mayor of Darlington in 1903 and, following the death of Sir Joseph in June, he stood in the July 1903 Barnard Castle bye-election – a constituency which took in Darlington and all of Teesdale and Weardale. He had been considered to be a Liberal, but, much to the consternation of the Liberal Party, stood in the bye-election as a Labour candidate.

Mr Hubert Beaumont stood as the Liberal candidate, declaring at a meeting in May 1903:-

> I believe in the greatest good for the whole community, and will utterly decline to pledge myself in any way simply to vote for one class, whether it was the labour class, the aristocratic, or the landlord class. ... I come forward as a Liberal and Labour candidate - Liberalism embraces Labourism.[195]

[194] *Newcastle Courant*, January 29, 1869
[195] *Teesdale Mercury*, May 20, 1903

Mr Beaumont stated that he would be willing to step aside if Arthur Henderson would pledge himself to the Liberal Party – to no avail. Henderson clearly felt that the traditional paternalistic and well-meaning "radicalism" of the Liberals was not enough:-

> I am strongly of the opinion that one of the great necessities of the moment is an increase in the House of Commons of representatives from the ranks of the people (men who know the workers' grievances, and who share their aspirations and hopes). I believe that such representatives would exercise greater influence for good than men whose knowledge of the needs of the toilers has not been acquired by close personal association with them.[196]

In the third week in July, Mr Henderson held meetings in Witton-le-Wear and Hamsterley. He received a mixed reception in Hamsterley with the outspoken Edith Stephenson at the forefront as angry villagers threw sods at the shaken candidate as he fled the village in his motor car.

Mr Henderson won the bye-election by 47 votes from the Conservative and Unionist Party. If Liberalism and Labourism had combined forces, they would have had an overwhelming majority, but Henderson split the Radical vote.

The Times noted presciently that the result "may prove to be a symptom of some importance in the future development of our public life."

The *Sheffield Telegraph* got to the heart of the matter:-

> We offer the Liberal Party our most respectful condolences. That party has coquetted with labour, it has flattered labour, it has spoken smooth words to labour, it has allowed labour to pick up a few crumbs that have fallen from its ample table, and yet labour is not satisfied. Was there ever such ingratitude known? Labour actually covets more seats for itself. It refuses to act as the handmaid to Liberalism, and humbly to assist it obtain the sweets of office and the responsibilities of power. The grasping ambition on the part of labour must have wrung the very heart of Liberalism.[197]

Arthur Henderson retained the Barnard Castle seat until 1918, becoming President of the Board of Education in 1916 in succession to Joseph Albert Pease of Darlington, and co-authoring the Labour Constitution, including the famous Clause IV, in 1918. Thereafter, he was successively MP for the more working class constituencies of Widnes, Newcastle, and Burnley. He became increasingly internationalist in his outlook, to such effect that he was awarded the Nobel Peace Prize in 1935, a year before his death.[198]

8-19 Arthur Henderson

---

[196] *Teesdale Mercury,* July 8, 1903
[197] Press reactions reported in *Teesdale Mercury*, July 29, 1903.
[198] *Northern Echo*, June 17, 1998

FJS, in commenting on the harsh attitudes of his mother to labour activists, said:-

> The whole point was that at that time, the labour was trying to get a say. Until then, they had to do what they were told. Actually, it didn't make a lot of difference at that time, because they still had to do what they were bloody told! My grandfather and the parson would take a stick to you if you didn't touch your hat!

This last comment gives an indication of the conventions and social rigidities of life in a small village in those days. The Parson would have had a high status, above other professional people, and perhaps on a par with local gentry. It also shows how the relative prosperity of the more successful tenant farmers, gained during the early Victorian Golden Age of agriculture, led to many of them acting like quasi-gentry in small communities. In commenting about village schoolchildren, Pamela Horn reports:-

> If the squire or the clergyman drove past, the children were expected to curtsy or bow with suitable respect. Failure to do so could lead to severe reprimands in school the next day. For both inside school and out country children were always exhorted to "labour truly to get their own living and order themselves lowly and reverently to their betters....the word 'betters' was firmly underlined and annotated"[199]

Not all labourers were suitably deferential, as was evident in the case of Jos Coatsworth in Hamsterley (See *The Story of Little Titch*, page 225). Pamela Horn quotes the story of a boy asking his father why he should say 'Sir' to the squire "or anyone else who thought himself a step above" the farm labourers. His father replied:-

> "Sir", my boy, is only the nickname for a fool.

Agricultural labourer James Hawker (1836-1921)[200] provides another example of the disrespect that many of the labouring class held for their "betters". In his diary of life in Victorian Leicestershire, he observed:-

> If I had been born an idiot and unfit to carry a gun – though with plenty of cash – they would have called me a grand sportsman. Being born poor, I am called a poacher.

Nowadays, no-one gives a damn if you die or you don't

But despite the existence of a fixed social hierarchy, there was a great sense of community with people readily helping each other in times of need and the better off showing generosity to their less fortunate neighbours. FJS saw a stark contrast between the community values he witnessed during his childhood to those predominating in the late twentieth century:-

> My father was a conservative but he looked after the poor people. After Christmas, he would have all the kids in the village - 50 to 80 people - to the house. Each would have a handful of nuts, sweets, penny orange, and apple as a New Year's gift. If

[199] Horn, Pamela (1976) *Labouring Life in the Victorian Countryside*. Dublin, Gill & Macmillan. p.59.

[200] Jenkins, Robin P. 'Hawker, James (1836–1921)', *Oxford Dictionary of National Biography*, OUP, 2004

> anyone was ill in the village, grandmother and others would be round to help. Nowadays, no-one gives a damn if you die or you don't.

Edith's poor health

Just after the turn of the century, Edith was riding her horse side-saddle when the horse backed into a garden seat and caught its hoof in the seat. It bucked and bucked until it broke its girth, throwing Edith who landed on her back on the stone yard and hurt it quite badly. The saddle came off with her. Afterwards, she wore a special jacket for a number of years and visited Harrogate Spa for treatment. FJS recalls that she was there for several weeks seeking treatment for her "terrible" back and that when she came home, she was "never right no more".

An insight into Edith's health is gained from the messages in postcards she received between 1903 and 1918.

On November 10, 1903, friend Edie Metcalfe[201] wrote, "I hope you are a lot better by this. How does the jacket fit? Don't be long in coming to Highcliffe..."

Edith wrote to Rose Ellen Douglas in 1904, "...I think I am improving and with a little bit of care, I hope to be alright. Still the jacket on..."

A postcard from Rose to Edith on October 27, 1905 contains the message, "Would have liked to have been with you this weekend, but I can't manage it....Try not to worry."

On December 11, 1908, girl-friend Evelyn Lowson wrote, "awfully sorry to hear you are not so well, but hope you will soon be all right again."

On June 9, 1909, a month before Frenchman Louis Blériot flew from Calais to Dover in the Blériot XI, becoming the first person to fly across the English Channel in a monoplane, Edith had a card from "LW" of Butterknowle, informing her that:-

> Rose's address is 39 Windsor Terrace, Gosforth. I had a great long letter from her on Monday morning. She says she thinks they will all like well sorry you don't get as well as you should (sic). It seems very funny, doesn't it?

On 16th August, 1914, a postcard from "L" begins, "I hope you are well again..."

Despite her poor health, Edith was clearly the life and soul of the party, more than capable of raising the spirits of her friends. In 1980, almost 60 years after her untimely death, FJS spoke of his mother with great affection:-

> My mother Edith was very well liked. A smart woman, always well dressed. She was a wonderful woman, full of kindness, full of life, always laughing, and had many close friends. She had an affectionate nature and was always helping people.

Edith Stephenson was born in 1883 at Bedburn Hall Farm, the youngest child of Joseph and Eliza Stephenson. She grew up to be a lively, generous, trusting extrovert, but her *joie-de-vivre* was somewhat dampened by the recurring bouts of ill-health.

Edith's affectionate nature, thoughtfulness and generosity are evident from the messages from her friends, as demonstrated on a postcard sent to 'Edie' on July 2, 1914 from 'PS' in Middleton-in-Teesdale.

---

[201] Edie Metcalfe married Jack Swinbank, a cousin of Edith Stephenson. She died aged 81 in 1965 after breaking her leg.

> Dear Edie, Many thanks for the berries, it was very kind, when you are so busy as well. Do not trouble next week as I shall be very busy every day and I will not have time to boil them..."

It is easy to imagine 'PS' becoming concerned at the thought of being inundated with weekly supplies of berries from her generous friend in Hamsterley. The berries in question were most probably gooseberries – there was a gooseberry bush in the garden at Pond House and gooseberry jam was very popular at the time, especially with children.

8-20 Postcard from Nellie in August 1918

In August, 1918, she received 3 postcards in 2 days from Eva, Alice and Nellie who were holidaying together in Salburn-by-the Sea.

The card from Nellie, a comic card asking, 'When is the war going to end?' suggests that Edith and her three girlfriends didn't take life too seriously, despite the fact that we were still at war with Germany and her allies for another three months. The message is as follows:

> Thanks so much for your PC which we got on Sunday morning. I am very downhearted you can't come and cheer us all up as there is nothing doing amongst Sn Cs[202]. Understand. I'm fed up at the sight of them. Bow wow. Am very pleased to hear that you are coming to the party (some party, eh). We are, I believe, coming home on the 26th, so look out for the "Lassies". Am longing to be home amongst you all. Please accept my very best love and tons of kisses. Nellie."

Just at the time when the 15 year age-gap between Edith and Frank was becoming more telling, Edith became pregnant in the Spring of 1920. Because of her age and her medical history, the pregnancy and birth were overseen by Professor RP Ranken Lyle at Newcastle Medical School. My father Henry Sanderson was born in December 1920 at Jesmond. His mother was 37, his father 52, and his brother and sister, 16 and 13 respectively.

Edith was so grateful to Professor Ranken Lyle for the successful delivery of her son that she tried hard to persuade Frank to christen the baby 'Ranken', but Frank was adamant that the baby should have a family name, Henry. He won the day, making doubly sure by promptly completing the formalities at the Registry Office himself.

---

[202] It is possible that "Sn Cs" is a reference to "Saltburn Chaps" – it cannot have been "senior citizens", a descriptive term which only came into popular use later in the century.

8-21 Edith with baby Henry in 1921

Despite the joy of the new baby, Edith remained dogged by ill-health.

The Wearmouth Sisters

In 1920 FJS planned to go to America with a friend from Hamsterley, Edger Jewitt,[203] but after desperate pleas from his sickly mother, he decided stay at home, a decision for which he was ultimately thankful.

At the time FJS was going out with his third cousin[204], farmer's daughter Charlotte Violet (Lottie) Wearmouth of The Ashes Farm, Wolsingham, and Edger was close to her sister Florence Esther (Essie) . FJS and Edger perhaps would have got to know the sisters well on the summer picnic trips to Ayhope Shield during and just after the Great War (See p. 213).

8-22 Essie and Lottie Wearmouth : adventurous and fun-loving sisters. (Courtesy of Geoff Wearmouth)

In December, 1920, Edger Jewitt, together with his married sister Jane (Seers) and her two children, set sail from Southampton for New York on Cunard's *Aquitania.* He did however envisage a future with Essie and so asked FJS to keep an eye on her during his absence.

[203] FJS noted that Edger was Arnold Jewitt's uncle. He was the son of James Jewitt of East Rackwood Hill and the younger brother of Josiah, See p.196.

[204] The sisters and FJS shared great great grandparents Francis Vickers (1749-1822) and Mary Raine (1753-1833). Essie and Lottie had a brother with the family name "Frank".

Before long, Essie struck up a friendship with George Cowley from Shull, and FJS dutifully wrote and told Edger of this development. Edger wasn't pleased and, unfortunately for FJS, neither was Essie when she found out she had been betrayed. FJS recalled:-

> Edger bloody well wrote and told her what I'd said! Soon after, I saw Essie at a dance and she went mad with me, and she never spoke to me for years afterwards. Bye, she was cross with me.

It is quite possible that this episode signalled the end of FJS's relationship with Essie's sister Lottie Wearmouth, a noted dancer of the Charleston and described along with her sister Essie as "adventurous and fun-loving" by great nephew Geoff Wearmouth. It was not however the end for Edger Jewitt and Essie.

In 1923, Essie sailed on the *Aquitania* to America where she married Edger. Before long they were back in Hamsterley but in 1930 made another attempt to start a new life in America. By 1933, they were home again and 2 years after Edger's death in 1943, Essie married Frank Sanderson – not FJS but his cousin Frank of Burnigill (See p.106).

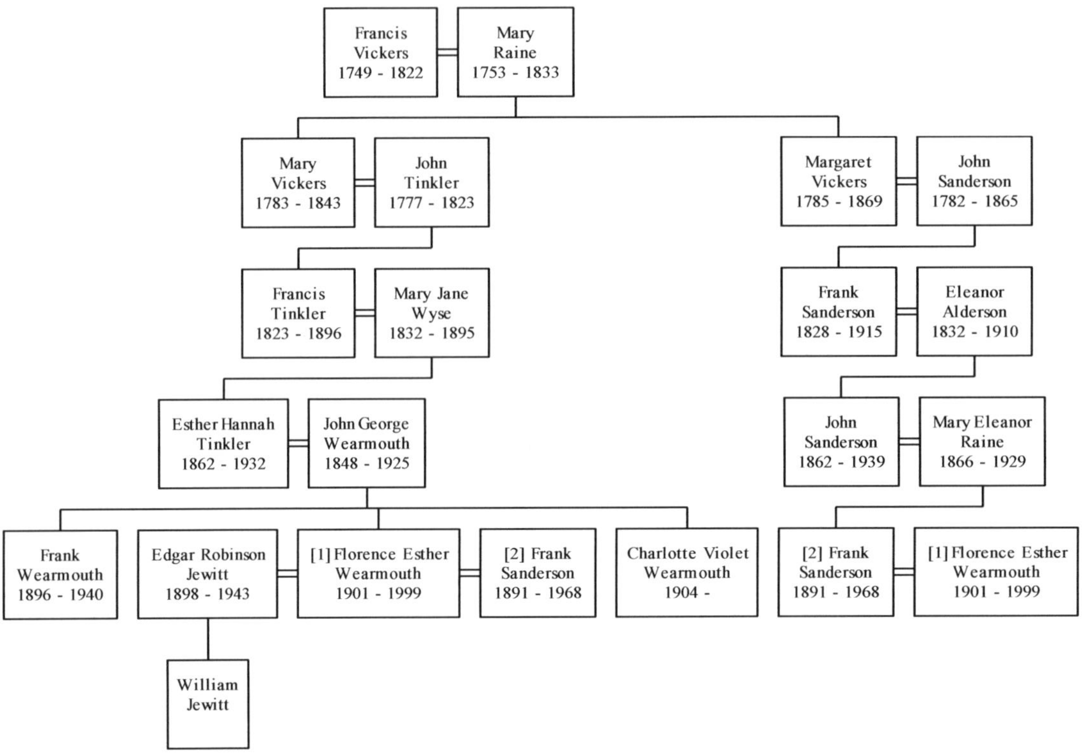

8-23 Selective Family Tree showing Vickers, Sanderson and Wearmouth links. Frank Sanderson (1891-1968) and Essie Wearmouth are third cousins. "Frank" is a family name that can be traced at least as far back as Francis Vickers of Pease Mires.

The end of an Era

Immediately after her 39th birthday on 14th June, 1922, Edith developed a severe chest infection, a condition probably made worse by her smoking habit. FJS recalled that her breathing could be heard all over the house. She became so ill that she was transferred to the Clairmont, a Maternity Hospital in Bishop Auckland, but she was back home at Pond House when she died on Tuesday, 20th June of acute pneumonia. Her husband Frank Sanderson of Hamsterley was present when she died.

The next day, the death notice appeared in the *North Star*, concluding with the poignant, "Jesu Mercy". Edith was buried in the churchyard of Hamsterley St James on Thursday, 22 June, with a shocked and heart-broken family in attendance.

8-24 Robert Patton Ranken Lyle (Professor of Obstetrics)

Edith's presence at the Clairmont can be explained by her connection with the resident Obstetrician, Professor R.P. Ranken Lyle, whose help was sought when she became ill. Originally from Coleraine, the Trinity College Dublin-educated Ranken Lyle had been appointed in 1899 as Lecturer in Midwifery and the Diseases of Women and Children at Newcastle Infirmary. In 1907, he established a Department of Gynaecology at the Infirmary and in 1908 he became the first Professor of Obstetrics and Gynaecology at the University of Durham. He was widely respected, as the following extract from a book by Derek Tacchi[205] shows:-

> He was a man of strong and affable personality, he was a first rate clinician, a competent surgeon, a popular teacher and an indefatigable pioneer.... He brought about great changes. Lyle established his discipline in the University, and became active socially in the community as a Justice of the Peace.

There was no cure for pneumonia at that time, and FJS and his sister Ella were utterly devastated by her death which signalled the end of an era in the Hamsterley branch of the Sanderson family. Ella, a clever 14 year school-girl, had not only lost her beloved mother, but she had to leave school to look after her baby brother Henry and an ageing, bewildered and dependent father. Edith's out-going and lively personality had ensured that despite her chronic ill-health, family life had been happy and life enhancing. The 18 year period from her marriage to her death had been characterised by an unusual frequency of holidays, including extended visits to the sea-side and to spa towns, short visits to friends and family, social gatherings, and concerts in the village hall. Edith had many friends and enjoyed this hectic social life alongside her duties as farmer's wife and mother. Unlike many other families at this time of general austerity, the Sandersons of Hamsterley were having fun.

---

205 Tacchi, D. (1994) *Childbirth in Newcastle Upon Tyne 1760-1990.* Whitley Bay, Bewick Press

This social whirl came to an end in 1922 and there began a period of relative withdrawal and a preoccupation with immediate family matters which meant that some of the friendships and some of the extended family ties were weakened. It is worthy of note that despite very close contact between the families prior to Edith's death, it appears that no-one from Hamsterley attended the funeral of Frank Sanderson of Nafferton in 1934. Indeed, it was not until 1980 that contact was re-established when I, and then FJS and his wife Joan, visited Jack Sanderson, the grandson of Frank Sanderson of Nafferton, at Stocksfield. I subsequently made contact with another of Frank's grandchildren, Frank Sanderson of Acomb, near Hexham, where he lived with his wife Nancy (Rogerson) until his death in 2002 at the age of 94. I visited them in 1998 and also met their daughters Sheila and Kathleen.

The Surrogate Mother

Ella was very much like her mother – generous and outgoing, certainly not a shrinking violet. Taking on the family responsibilities made her into an excellent cook as Jackie Cousins recalled from his association with the family during the 1940's, "Ella was a marvellous cook. Those Yorkshire Puddings......" In fact, Jackie recalled that his wife became really fed up with hearing about Ella's Yorkshire Puddings.

In 1926, when she was just 18 years old, Ella married Richard Thomas (Dick) Atkinson. It was the year of the first general strike in British history when the TUC voted to back the miners who were striking over proposed cuts in pay and longer working hours.

8-25 Ella and Dick at Pond House Hamsterley on their Wedding Day in August 1926.

Ella and Dick first lived in Toadpool, close to Acrum Farm in West Auckland where Dick worked for his father. Shortly after their first son Richard Maxwell was born in 1927, the family then moved a mile out of West Auckland to Low Staindrop Field House which they farmed until Dick's father died in 1947.

Given the fact that Dick and Ella had not only Max but also her brother Henry and her father to look after, it is perhaps not surprising that 10 years elapsed before they had their second child, Terry, in 1937. Terry remembered his mother as "very intelligent, articulate and numerate all her life. It took a very sharp tradesman to get anything past my mother."

Ken Wilkinson, son of Ella's cousin Gladys Wilkinson née Stephenson, has vivid memories from the 1930s and 40s of Ella, her son Max and my father Henry:-

> I first remember your Aunt Ella when living at the *Wheat Sheaf Inn* in St Helens Auckland. When I was quite small, about 4 or 5, she used to pick me up in her car and take me along to Staindrop Field House. Max was a year or two older than I but seemed to be much much older. I can remember him wearing a horror mask and chasing me around the furniture, and Aunt Ella coming into the room and giving him a chewing up. Then he would get his meccano or railway set out and we would have some real fun.
>
> I remember your father at times and he was really big like a man, probably because he would be wearing long trousers. He always seemed to be in a hurry, even if I saw him in the street he would be shooting along, that to me was Henry. I do remember being quite confused when my mother tried to explain the relationship between Max and Henry.[206]
> After tea when the nights were light, Aunt Ella would walk me down to the main road and make sure the conductor understood exactly where I had to alight.
> Later when I was in the Infants and Max in the Juniors at the old school in St Helens next to the Vicarage. It was dinner time (lunch) and I was having a fight with a kid, Tommy Heys. The whole school was standing around egging us on. At a particularly difficult time I came up for air and there in front of me was Max, waving his fist in the air and shouting, "Come on Ken knock his bloody head off!" I was so thankful for the support of a BIG (junior) boy and his mates.
> The next memory I have of Aunt Ella was several years later. I had left school at 14 and was working at The Eden garage. One of my duties was serving petrol to some of the few people who had cars and petrol coupons (it was 1943 and wartime, and England was a very drab place, especially viewed from The EDEN Garage). Aunt Ella had coupons, it was summer and she was pipping her horn. I walked over to the pump, a big smile from her and wow! She was wearing open toed sandals and her toe-nails were painted RED, well it is nothing today but in 1943 it was amazing, those were the first painted toenails I had ever seen. That was Ella, a remarkable person.

The Atkinsons farmed at North Bedburn during the latter part of the 19th Century and would have been well known to the Sanderson family who were farming in the same locality. Indeed, the Atkinsons were at Wadley Farm near Fir Tree, which was a fifteen minute walk along a footpath from Low Harperley where the Sandersons were farming. No doubt my grandfather and Terry's grandfather were acquainted as children and attended Thornley School together, all of 50 years before the two families were united through the marriage of their children.

Terry's grandfather, also Richard Thomas Atkinson, was born in Witton-le-Wear in 1871 and was a successful farmer. He was described by Jackie Cousins as "a proper stickler, all the men knew just how far to go", which means that he was respected rather than liked by the men. Jackie recalled being one of the bearers at his funeral in 1947.

---

[206] There was only a seven-year age-gap between Henry and Max who were brought up as brothers when Henry was actually Max's uncle.

8-26 Ella Atkinson née Sanderson. The painted fingernails would have matched the RED toe-nails that so amazed 14 year-old Ken Wilkinson.

Young Dick on the other hand was quiet and not as business-like as his father, but he had a strong-willed wife in Ella, and a son, Max, who appears to have taken after his grandfather. Jackie Cousins recalled that Max, intelligent, ambitious, and hard-driven, always seemed to get his own way.

After his father died, Dick took over Acrum Farm. In the late 1940s, thirty corn-stacks at the farm were burnt, the entire year's supply and a main source of income, with the fire being so fierce that the fire brigade had to hose down the houses in the adjacent hamlet of Toadpool. Jackie Cousins remembered that there were rumours that the fire might have been arson, but "nobody could pin-point anybody". Whatever the cause, it appears that the family took it very badly, and shortly afterwards, sold the farm to the Chamberlain family and moved to Essex along with Ella's father Frank Sanderson who by then was 80 years old. They lived in Colchester, not far from FJS at Great Holland Hall, Frinton-on-Sea.

Henry Sanderson who lost his mother in 1922 when he was 18 months old, turned out to be a godsend for his ageing father, providing him with company and a purpose in life. Henry was cared for by a nursemaid, Cissie Raine,[207] in the early days, but it was Ella who gave him the love and family life so necessary for a growing child.

[207] Cissie Raine's father was a stonemason, and his father farmed New Hall Farm

8-27 Sister as surrogate mother: Ella with Max and brother Henry in 1927.

FJS's view was less generous:-

What did my mother want with him - having a baby when she was 38? We (FJS and Ella) were both grown up. And when my mother died, my father had a lot on his plate with our Henry as a little baby, but he was a bit of company for my father. Ella and me were getting out a bit. I was 19 years old and you couldn't expect me to stop in the house every night. I didn't go out much in the week but I was out at weekends.

After Ella and Dick married, they had the unusual responsibility of not only raising their own baby but also raising Henry and looking after Ella's ageing father. Henry was thereafter treated as an integral member of the family, as Terry Atkinson recalled:-

> Henry and my grandfather were treated like the rest of us in the Atkinson family... My father always insisted Henry be treated the same as Max, same Xmas presents, etc. He was also allowed to drive our family car before Max.[208]

The sacrifices made by Dick in particular are obvious, and are neatly summarised by Terry:-

> Just think of the early married life my dad had, lumbered with most of my mother's family. What sort of a life for my father, a young married man? I can tell you he put up with a darned sight more than I would have done in his place.

In his teens, Henry joined the Merchant Navy, serving as an apprentice on Jedmoor MV in the late 1930s. *Jedmoor MV* was a British Cargo Motor vessel of 4,392 tons built in 1928 by William Doxford & Sons Ltd, Sunderland and owned by Moor Line Ltd, W. Runciman Shipping Co Ltd, Newcastle upon Tyne. Not enjoying the experience on *Jedmoor*, perhaps through home sickness, he persuaded his father to buy out his service in 1939. Later that year, Britain declared War on Germany.

Leaving the Merchant Navy and *Jedmoor MV* in particular was timely for Henry Sanderson. On the 16th September 1941 when on route from Santos, Brazil via Trinidad to Sydney, Cape Breton Island where she joined up with Convoy SC-42 carrying a cargo of 7,400 tons of iron ore, *Jedmoor MV* was torpedoed by U-98 and sunk. Thirty-two men were lost from a complement of 37, and 14 other ships in the convoy were sunk in what was one of the worst convoy disasters of the war.

---

[208] Not surprising that he drove the family car before Max - he was six years older.

Henry was well liked. His nephew, Terry Atkinson, described him as “kind, considerate, generous and my hero as a little boy. I always loved Uncle Henry.” His other nieces and nephews in Essex also regarded him as their favourite uncle. And Jackie Cousins who knew Henry in West Auckland during the Forties, said of him:

> Henry, I bloody well liked him. He was good to me. Bit of a dandy.[209] I remember he loved his bloody motorbike. Every Sunday, I cleaned it and he would give me two shillings.

Jackie remembered Henry crashing his bike into the back of a bus in Darlington in the mid 1940’s, and being injured to such an extent that it was “touch and go” whether he would survive.

8-12 Elizabeth Chapman

Henry married Elizabeth Chapman in 1946 at St Helens Church, and I was born at Barnard Castle later the same year. Within two years, 80 year old Frank Sanderson, the Atkinson family, and Henry Sanderson and family followed FJS to Essex. Five years later, my mother and her children returned to St Helens Auckland for good.

A grand old gentleman

I remember Frank Sanderson of Hamsterley as an elderly man down in Essex. I visited Tudor Cottage in Great Holland once or twice in the early Fifties. He was a kind, reserved and gentle old man, reserved. I remember him having quite shaky hands, signs of Parkinson's disease.

My maternal grandmother, Mary Chapman and my mother always spoke highly of him. There would have been natural respect for him because of his age alone – he was 26 years older than my maternal grandmother – but he was also a dignified and courteous person. He was invariably described as a "grand old gentleman".

[209] “Dandy” is defined in the OED as “one who dresses elegantly and fashionably”. I remember his immaculately creased trousers, highly polished shoes and smart shirt and cravat.

8-29 Frank Sanderson of Hamsterley in 1946

In the mid 1940's, just before he went to live in Essex, grandfather Sanderson used to come every Sunday from West Auckland to church at St Helens and then to Dale View Cottage for a game of cards. He would have been in his mid-seventies at the time, whereas my Grandmother Chapman would have been just over 50. Card playing can be quite competitive, but he would bring a sense of proportion to these occasions by saying to my grandmother, "Now then, Mrs Chapman, we're not playing for Raby Castle!"

Jackie Cousins liked my grandfather, describing him as "a grand old chap, a canny old fella, I cannat say nowt wrong about him." But he was also canny in the Scottish sense, i.e., like many farmers, he was careful with his money and would often get off the bus one stop early to save a penny on the fare: for example, getting the bus from St Helens to Mill Bank in West Auckland and walking the rest of the way to Acrum Farm at the other end of the village. FJS remembered:-

> My father was a bit mean, you know. He used to buy cattle in Gateshead, and he wouldn't give the drover more than half-a-crown to drive the cattle to the station and load 20 or 30 on the rail wagons. They used to 'chop' him - take one out and put a bad'n in sometimes.

No doubt "Pennies make Pounds" and "Waste not, want not" were oft-repeated by my grandfather, sentiments he undoubtedly shared with his sister Lizzie, but not with his brother John – to whom he was notably unsympathetic (See p.101).

8-30 Frank Sanderson and the author at Great Holland Hall Farm in 1948.

It seems that he resented his brother's profligacy, perhaps feeling that it had deprived him of what should have been a more substantial inheritance from his father.

Frank Sanderson of Hamsterley died in 1955 at Great Holland, Essex. He was 86 years old. He had left the North-East with his daughter Ella when she moved to Essex in the late 1940s when he was about 80. He then lived with his youngest son Henry at Tudor Cottage in Great Holland, but died at FJS's Vesey Farm, a mile along the road.
He is buried in All Saints churchyard, Great Holland, a stone's throw from Great Holland Hall.

8-31 On the beach at Frinton-on-Sea in 1949. From left: Frank Sanderson of Hamsterley, Terry Atkinson, the author wearing sunglasses, and Elizabeth Sanderson, née Chapman.

9. THE STEPHENSONS OF BEDBURN

FJS talked at length about his mother's family of Weardale sheep farmers and woodmen. His g. grandfather Joseph Stephenson senior was born in 1781 in Weardale, possibly the son of John Stephenson and Hannah née Beaston of Paddock Nook (Ludwell). The Stephensons were tenants long associated with farms on the Horsley Estate of the Hildyards, notably Billing Shield but also with nearby farms, including Ludwell, Haggate, Rose Hill, Sunderland Cleugh and Ambling Gate.

Joseph moved to Hoppyland Park in South Bedburn to work as a gardener shortly after his marriage in 1812 to Mary Nickels from Thornley. It was there that John, Ann, Mary, and Henry were born. By the late 1820s, Joseph obtained his first tenancy at Larch Hill, a long-gone hill farm a mile south of Wolsingham, and it was there in early 1829 that FJS's grandfather Joseph was born. Another son, Thomas, was born after the family had moved to Low Redford Farm in South Bedburn in the early 1830s.

In 1841, the family were farming at Low Redford on the Bedburn Beck, with the children still at home except Ann who had married John Marquis Snr in 1834 and moved to Hamsterley. In 1842, John Stephenson married Margaret Stephenson, daughter of an innkeeper and grocer from Hamsterley. In 1844, Henry Stephenson took the tenancy at West Hoppyland, and in 1847, his sister Mary married William Pallister who worked as an edge-tool maker at Bedburn Mill. The Stephenson and Pallister families were to remain in close contact until well into the twentieth century (See p.135).

9-1 Bedburn, home to the Stephenson family

Melancholy Deaths at Bedburn

By 1850, the Stephenson family had moved 1½ miles downstream to Bedburn Hall Farm. In May of that year, a new family arrived in the neighbourhood: William Harle, a 52 year-old shepherd born in Corsenside, South Northumberland, together with his wife and daughter, moved to Middle Redford to work for Robert Surtees Esq of The Grove. They would have quickly felt at home in South Bedburn where the whole community regularly came together on the great social occasions such as the clipping days at the local sheep farms (See p.185).

The Harles had been at Middle Redford for about 15 months when, on Thursday September 25th 1851, William Harle together with his wife Martha and 12 year-old William Henderson[210], the son of Margaret Henderson from Blazon Hill, set off with a horse and cart on the ten mile journey to Bishop Auckland market. Their business done, they started for home in the evening just as a storm was breaking. In the face of torrential rain, high winds, and an evening dark beyond darkness, they eventually reached the ford at Bedburn Beck near Middle Redford where they were faced with what was described with some understatement as "an impetuous stream". It was reported that the narrow ford was dangerous at all times, and that with swollen waters, was considered impassable even in daylight. William Harle, who would have had little experience of the beck in full spate during his short time in Bedburn, made the fateful decision to attempt the crossing. They didn't have a chance. The horse, cart and the three unfortunate passengers were engulfed by the raging torrent and swept away to a watery grave.

> *If not the largest the Bedburn is one of the most picturesque tributaries of the Wear - its course is never tame or its scenery insipid. Its current is always sufficiently swift and strong from the rapidity of its descent to prevent any stagnant reaches...*[211]

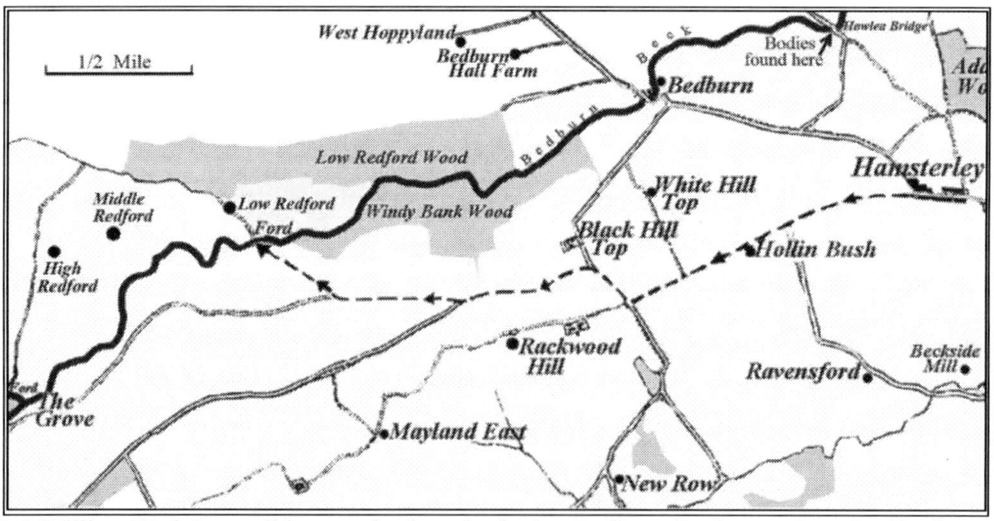

9-2 William Harle's possible route back to the ford at Bedburn Beck, near Low Redford

[210] William Henderson worked at The Grove for Robert Surtees Esq.

[211] J.P. Soutter, *A Paper on the Bedburn*, included in W. Herbert Smith's *Walks in Weardale* (1885).

Because of the stormy weather, no alarm was raised when they failed to return home that night, the assumption being that they had stayed overnight in Bishop Auckland. It was only when a saddle, and then a basket containing plates, pots and glasses belonging to Martha Harle were found by the waterside on Friday afternoon that fears were raised. Local volunteers quickly began to make a thorough search of the Bedburn Beck downstream from the ford:-

> The cart was found about 300 yards below the ford, and the mare a little further on. From the marks it seemed that the mare had got nearly to the opposite side. The body of the poor boy was next seen lying on his back, on a sand-bed about 200 yards below Howlea. His head was much cut and bruised, and blood was flowing from the wounds, apparently caused by the sharp stones and rocks in the water. On Saturday morning, about seven o'clock, Mr Stephenson[212] of Bedburn Hall found the body of William Harle in the Bed Burn, at the junction of the Harthope rivulet.[213] He was lying with his face downwards under a bush. His head was cut and bruised, and his clothes torn. On examining his pockets, some coppers (4d.) and a few trifling articles were found, and also his watch, which was standing at ten minutes to ten. About the same time, the body of the poor woman was found by Thomas Longstaff, a labourer, in the water behind a hazel bush. Her bonnet was gone, and the front of her head was much cut.[214]

The bodies were taken to Bedburn Hall where an inquest was held on Saturday afternoon before the Coroner, William Trotter Esq. A verdict of "Accidentally drowned" was returned. The Burial Register records that the unfortunate travellers were buried on September 30th in Hamsterley Churchyard where they are commemorated with memorial stones.

9-3 Memorial to William and Martha Harle.

[212] Joseph Stephenson (1829-1915), my great grandfather.
[213] The bodies had been carried over 2½ miles downstream.
[214] *Newcastle Guardian*, October 4, 1851

At the time of the tragedy, William and Martha Harle had one daughter Martha at home who was still at school. It can only be imagined the distress the young Martha would have felt as it became known over the course of the weekend what had happened to her parents. By 1861, Martha was teaching at a National Church school in Manchester with her sister Mary. Within a few years, Mary had married a clergyman and Martha, a chemist: on the face of it, good marriages for two orphans from relatively humble beginnings.

In 1861, Henry Stephenson, who had married widow Elizabeth Gardener née Proud in 1859, was still at West Hoppyland and his brother Joseph was running Bedburn Hall Farm and looking after his retired parents. The family had one servant living with them and, intriguingly, his name was William Harle.

William, aged 20, was born in Waldridge and came from a family long-established around Witton Gilbert. It has not proved possible to confirm a family link with William Harle of Corsenside, but it does appear a strange coincidence that my great grandfather Joseph Stephenson of Bedburn, aged 22 at the time, should find the drowned body of William Harle of Corsenside by the Bedburn Beck in 1851 and 10 years later be employing someone of the same, uncommon, name. Kinship between the two men named William Harle is probable, with the possibility that Joseph Stephenson and family at Bedburn Hall established links with the wider Harle family after the tragic events of 1851.

9-4 Bedburn Hall Farm, home to Joseph Stephenson and family.

Joseph of Bedburn's father, Joseph Stephenson of Weardale, was to live almost another decade, finally expiring in October 1870, aged 89 years. His widow Mary then went to live with her eldest son John in Hamsterley who had remarried in 1866 after his first wife had died in 1864. Mary Stephenson died in 1880 aged 89 years.

Joseph Stephenson of Bedburn was married twice, first to Nancy Dodds, the daughter of Matthew Dodds, an edge-tool manufacturer from Bedburn. They married at Hamsterley St James in 1863 and Nancy soon bore Joseph a son, also named Joseph. Just twelve days after the birth of their second child Mary Ann, Nancy died from heart disease (uncertified) in 1865 aged 28 years.[215] The same year, Nancy's nephew Matthew James Dodds, a half-cousin of Edith Stephenson, was born (See p.167).

Three years after the death of Nancy, 38 year-old Joseph married 28 year-old spinster Eliza 'Bedale' at Hamsterley St James.[216] Eliza's mother was Ann Simpson née Beadle, and it is her maiden name which is entered under "Father's name and Surname" on Eliza's marriage certificate, indicating that Ann is the only acknowledged parent. This confirms that Ann's husband William Simpson was not Eliza's father, but her step-father (See "The Simpsons from Pennington Farm", p.183).

Joseph Stephenson Junior's emigration

According to FJS, Joseph's son from his first marriage, also Joseph, "did something wrong" in his late teens. His wrong-doing remains a mystery but his delinquency, if that's what it was, triggered his emigration to Australia at the age of nineteen.

It may well be that he had a difficult relationship with his step-mother, Eliza. Joseph's mother Nancy died when he was 12 months old, and he was four years old when his father married Eliza - who already had a child (Sally) of about the same age as Joseph. Eliza soon had more children of her own to care for, making it quite possible that young Joseph, not to mention his sister Mary Ann, were somewhat neglected by their step-mother. Furthermore, as the eldest son, Joseph may have held a special place in his father's affections.

It is possible to speculate therefore that Eliza, who was over a decade younger than her husband, turned the wrong-doing of Joseph to her advantage by orchestrating his departure to the other side of the world. Joseph was not a beneficiary under his father's will of 1915, but it is presumed that he was given funds to help him get established in Australia.

FJS recalled:-

> Joseph emigrated before my mother (Edith Stephenson, Joseph's half-sister) was born in 1883. Out in Australia, he had a son Joseph Hamsterley Stephenson.

Joseph's Death Certificate confirmed that he had emigrated in 1882 as a 19 year-old to Victoria, probably with the Orient Line which advertised its services in the *Northern Echo*:-

> Orient Line Steam from London to Cape of Good Hope, Adelaide, Melbourne, and Sydney, every fortnight. Fares from 15 to 70 Guineas. For particulars apply to B.T. ORD, Hatter, 93 Newgate Street, Bishop Auckland.[217]

Ocean-going steamships offered a faster and less arduous passage than the old sailing ships, but the passengers would have experienced considerable discomfort at times. John

---

215 Despite the uncertified cause being recorded as "heart disease", it seems likely that the death was connected with complications arising from the birth of Mary Ann.

216 Before Eliza married Joseph Stephenson, she had a daughter Sarah (Sally) Beadle in 1864. Sally married Tom Race in 1883 and they farmed at Ravensford.

217 *Northern Echo*, Jan 4, 1882

Philipson, the former Mayor of South Melbourne who returned to his native Weardale for a visit in 1889 spoke of the terrible heat of the tropics, explaining:-

> Fancy sleeping in the cabin with the temperature at over 90 degrees, and getting up several times in a night with your body shirt wringing and the perspiration streaming down your limbs![218]

Not long after his arrival in Melbourne, Joseph worked for the railways. He married Henrietta Maggie Maher from Dublin in 1890, and as FJS recalled, they had a child, Joseph Hamsterley Stephenson, born in 1891 in Melbourne. Ultimately settling in nearby Geelong, Joseph died in 1947 of bronco-pneumonia and arteriosclerosis, aged 84 years.

A Nice Old Boy

By 1891, Joseph, Eliza and seven of their children were farming at Bedburn Hall - including 7 year old Edith, FJS's mother. As for the children of his first marriage, Joseph was by then established in Melbourne (See p.157), and Mary Ann had married Hugh Spence, a carpenter from Hamsterley, in 1884.

FJS remembered his grandfather Stephenson very well:

> My grandfather was a nice old boy. He was tall and thin, like our Tom. Always wore a frock coat. He rode a pony called Daisy – he bought it off my father. Had a white terrier called Nellie - you could hear him shout "Nellie! Nellie!" a mile away, his voice did carry.

FJS's recollections together with the photograph of Bedburn (Fig. 9-3) give us a feeling for Joseph Stephenson and the life he led over one hundred years ago. The motor car and agricultural mechanisation had yet to make their impact, although countless agricultural labourers had already emigrated to America and Australia, or migrated to the industrialised towns of northern England, or sought better paid employment in the northern coal mines. Joseph's death in 1915 coincided with the early stages of the First World War, a war which heralded fundamental changes in British society and the British way of life.

9-5 This photograph of the wood wagon and horses at Bedburn was taken in about 1900 (See front cover). It also depicts FJS's grandfather Joseph Stephenson (on the extreme right) and his son, Tom Stephenson (in shirtsleeves) who died in 1947 on Bedburn Bank (See p.164). The man in plus fours in the photograph is possibly John Walton Fogg-Elliot (1867-1933), Land Agent and owner of Bedburn Mill who lived at Bedburn Old Hall. Behind the woodwagon can be seen the legs of a young boy. The dog is Nellie, Joseph's white terrier.

[218] *Northern Echo*, June 5, 1889. An account of John Philipson's visit to Weardale appears in my book, *Life and Times in Victorian Weardale: The Letters of Francis Vickers (2012).*

John Denby, a friend from college days, visited Bedburn in September 1997 and compared the present-day scene with that depicted in the old photograph:

> Comparison of Bedburn in 1904 and in 1997 is to find things essentially the same. The house on the corner next to the pond now has an extension, but otherwise is similar except that the doorway at the right hand part of the building has been blocked up (now one dwelling it seems). This alteration is almost obscured by ivy which reaches up the wall, spreading nearly to the upper windows. Standing where the extension was is a whitebeam, while over the road a strong willow now grows next to the pond. Upgrading of the road over the years has raised the general surface I would guess. I stood next to the gate where Tom Stephenson is chatting, and was able to peer straight over the wall. I always felt warmth from this photograph, and to stand looking at the scene while listening to the echoing quack of ducks on the pond was quite special. I just needed Nellie, trotting over with wagging tail, to complete the picture.

9-6 Another photograph of the wood wagons at Bedburn, taken on the same day. Tom Stephenson is now second left by the leading wagon, his father Joseph Stephenson in the middle of the road, and on the extreme right, one of the Lowson sisters in the boater, and on her right, Edith Stephenson and her brother George. Joseph's dog Nellie is nowhere to be seen. (Courtesy of Ken Wilkinson).

FJS remembered:-

> My grandfather Joseph Stephenson had a good business with no end of sheep, cattle, and timber. At the clipping days at Bedburn Hall, all the farms from round about

> helped with the clipping. It was a great day and I remember as a boy running to Bedburn and carrying the wool from the clippers. The food was good and there was a hell of a party in the evenings, and there was always a dance in the barn. It was a great time (cf Clipping Days at Pennington Farm, p.185).

But FJS recalled that things didn't always go smoothly for the family:-

> There were six sons but instead of sticking together and doing what old Charlie Humphries' sons had done, they got married, fell out, and one was jealous of another.[219]

Having said that, FJS clearly got on well with all his uncles - he particularly liked his Uncle George (Fig 9-3), and thought it noteworthy that he had never had any rows with any of his maternal uncles. He recalled that a few members of the family - aunts, uncles, and cousins - often used to come to Hamsterley on a Saturday to do some shopping and call at Pond House for supper.

Death of Joseph Stephenson of Bedburn

Joseph Stephenson experienced considerable ill-health in his later years, and had particular trouble with his legs, "they were dead before the rest of his body", according to FJS. Eliza actually tripped over his legs when she was 69 and broke her thigh. She died in 1928 at the recorded age of 91, although she is believed to have been born in early 1840, which would have made her 88 at the time of her death.

The main news in the papers on 25 May, 1915 was about Italy's declaration of war on Austria-Hungary and about a massive train smash near Gretna Green. The report of the latter in the *Northern Echo* referred to "the most terrible disaster in the history of British railways" and the "indescribable scenes of horror". A troop train full of Scotch (sic) soldiers travelling south from Falkirk at an estimated 45 mph was in collision with another train travelling at 65 mph. There were estimates of 158 dead and missing, and 199 injured, mainly soldiers.

Joseph died on that day of "senile decay" at Bedburn Hall, aged 87. His son Henry, a woodman of Orchard House, Hamsterley, was in attendance at the time of death.

FJS maintained that his grandmother Eliza Stephenson was left "very badly off" when Joseph died, although he acknowledged that the economic situation at that time for farmers was unfavourable. He recalled:-

> I was at the sale at Bedburn Hall after my grandfather's death. Fresh calf cows were £8 a-piece, and horses only £10-15 a-piece.

Joseph left £493 10s 6d in his will, the equivalent of about £270,000 in 2013 in terms economic status:-

> I give to my son William my old violin, to my son Thomas the case containing the fox and otter and to my daughter Mary Ann Spence the set of old china.

Joseph also bequeathed a legacy of £35 to each of the following sons and daughters: William, Thomas, Henry, Samuel, Mary Ann Spence, and Edith Sanderson, with the residue going in trust to George Stephenson.

---

[219] I have been unable to identify Charlie Humphries – perhaps FJS meant "Charlie Proud"?

George Stephenson

Joseph's son George Stephenson was born in 1880 when William Gladstone was Prime Minister, and was three years older than FJS's mother Edith. Although brother Sam was younger and closer in age to Edith, there was a special bond between Edith and George. He was her 'big brother', the one she spent much time with in their childhood, with George looking out for his little sister. The photograph of five year-old George with his bucket and spade was much admired and copies were widely distributed to friends and family.

9-7 George Stephenson in 1885

Little is known about George's early life but one photograph of George with Edith is particularly noteworthy. Taken at the turn of the century, when he was 21 and Edith 18, it shows the two of them in fancy dress - an early example of 'cross-dressing'! The occasion for this unusual photo is unknown - perhaps a birthday photo or maybe they were rehearsing for a concert at the Mission Hall - but it does seem to provide confirmation of Edith's irreverence and liking for devilment.

Edith's daughter Ella was told that the Reverend Lovejoy, Vicar of St James's Church in Hamsterley, had seen the photograph at the time and had taken a very dim view of such frivolity.

9-8 Edith and George at the celebration of their 18th and 21st Birthdays respectively. The second photograph raised local eyebrows.

Rose Ellen Douglas

Schoolteacher Rose Ellen Douglas was a close friend of Edith Stephenson. In Edith's postcard collection many cards are signed "R.E.D". In due course, it became evident that the initials were those of Rose Ellen Douglas, a bridesmaid at Edith's wedding.

Rose Ellen was born in 1880 at Thornley[220]to school teachers Thomas William and Ann Elizabeth Douglas. In 1890 the Douglas family moved to Woodland where Rose's parents ran Woodland Colliery School. By 1901, their daughters Elizabeth and Rose Ellen had become Assistant Teachers at the school.

Schoolteachers were generally respected in their communities but it had not always been the case. David Souden notes that during the early Victorian era, prior to the Education Act of 1870, the schoolteacher was "commonly the most ridiculed person in the village". He continues:-

> At Wortham, George Howlett "was a specimen of a gone by day" and describing Maria Jolly, who ran the Dame School, Cobbold[221] wrote: "She required no puffing up from others, being sufficiently puffed up within herself to think herself wonderfully clever… and in one sense she was! – because anyone may teach that they do understand, but it requires a very clever person to teach that they do not understand!"[222]

Rose and Edith became friends in their teenage years and Rose's friendship with George became closer as Edith's marriage plans progressed. FJS remembered Auntie Rose often stayed at Pond House during their long courtship. George and Rose seemed destined for marriage, but they fell out and went their separate ways, only to re-ignite the flame years later and decide again to get married. Before the marriage, George had to go to hospital for minor surgery, but died on the operating table.

Rose moved to the Gosforth at about the time that George died. In 1935 Rose Ellen Douglas married widower William Tattersall in Easington. She died at West Hartlepool in 1963.

Rose's friendship with Edith may well have been influenced by the state of the former's relationship with George; cool during their falling out, flourishing during the marriage preparations when a new sister-in-law was in prospect, and finally fizzling out after George's death and Rosie moving away to Newcastle. It is also likely that Edith, dogged by ill-health, was not able to invest much effort in nurturing the friendship.

Thomas Stephenson

Edith's brother Thomas was born at Bedburn Hall in 1874. By 1901, he was working as the business manager for his father in Bedburn. A year later, he married Sunderland-born Alice Dowson Kirkup. Her father Thomas was from a long-established Hamsterley family, who for many years worked in Sunderland as a brewer before returning to Hamsterley to run the *Cross Keys* in the 1890s. Tom and Alice had three children: Gladys, Lawrence, and Edward Stephenson. Further information about Tom Stephenson and his family was

[220] Note: Thornley five miles East of Durham City, not Thornley near Tow Law.

[221] Rev Richard Cobbold wrote about village life in the 1860s

[222] Souden, D. (1991) *The Victorian Village*, London, Collins & Brown, p.25.

provided by Tom's grand-daughters, and my second cousins, Marjorie Cooper and Ena Gowland. Inspired by the Family History Day at Hamsterley School in August 2011, Marjorie wrote down her and Ena's memories of their grandfather and their father Edward:-

> Grandad Thomas Stephenson ran Bedburn Mill as a saw-mill, he had a little terrier called Trixie just like his father Joseph Stephenson had one called Nellie.
> Tom had a generator to make electricity wired up to Field House Cottage, and would walk down to the Mill each evening to switch on. He also had the phone in the cottage for the business at the Mill. As children we used to think these were very special as we were using oil lamps at home. Throughout the war, Mr. Fogg-Elliot, the owner, had furniture stored in an upper story at the Mill.
> Grandad and his workers built a Summer Chalet for Mr Fogg-Elliot and also made the furniture for it. I stayed with my grandparents for holidays quite often as a child and always remember the huge horses that pulled the wood wagons and the lovely warm smell of the stables, also the whine of the saws as they cut the wood. The way that Grandad controlled the water down the race for the mill always fascinated me. We certainly knew not to go near it when it was in full flow.

9-9 Alice and Tom Stephenson, Bedburn Mill in background

> I remember travelling on the flat cart from Butterknowle with Dad to Grandad's Mill at Bedburn for fencing posts and rails, and calling at his cousin Bill Stephenson's farm at Black Hill Top to give the horse a rest after the long pull up from the Mill. We also went to Rackwood Hill Pit for loads of coal.

> We would travel in the tub trap as a family to visit our grandparents at Bedburn, and after tea, the adults would play cards. There would also be aunts, uncles and cousins there sometimes and we children would entertain ourselves in the kitchen. Our eldest cousin Ken would lift down a side of bacon in the pantry and cut some pieces off, then fry them in an old tin lid on the open coal fire. It always tasted delicious, even though it was sometimes burned a little. Ken didn't dare use Nana's frying pan. When Dad was able to buy a car in 1941, this made visiting much easier, though it was only supposed to be used for business. Ena, Eric and I would hide under a rug on the back seat whenever we passed anyone.

9-10 Bedburn, with the Mill in the background.

Death on Redford Bank

FJS related the sad story of how his Uncle Tom Stephenson was killed on Bedburn Bank[223] on 7th January 1947 aged 73 years. On that fateful Tuesday morning, Tom was on a motor tractor pulling a wood wagon when the tractor skidded and turned on the hill. Tom jumped off the tractor and tried to put a chuck against the wheel of the wagon to stop it but the wagon went over him and killed him. The Coroner John Brown Humes reported the cause of death at the Inquest held on 17th January:-

> Rupture of the Lung due to fracture of ribs accidentally sustained upon 7th January 1947 when he was riding on a tractor and trailer hauling timber when the tractor skidded on the snow-bound road and he was thrown off and the trailer wheel passed over his body.

The following report of the inquest appeared in *The Northern Echo*:-

Son's evidence at inquest on Hamsterley man of 73

> A verdict of "Accidental death" was returned at a Hamsterley inquest yesterday on Thomas Stephenson, aged 73 years of Croft House, Hamsterley who was killed by a trailor drawn by a tractor, which his son Lawrence Stephenson (See photo overleaf), aged 41, was driving down Bedburn Lane (sic), near Hamsterley.
> It was stated that the trailer was loaded with timber from a nearby wood. Snow was falling and while the outfit was going down the bank the drawbar broke and Stephenson jumped off the tractor and was run over by the trailor. His son stated that the tractor skidded and after the drawbar broke the tractor went one way and the trailor the other. The coroner said that it was a pure accident for which no one was responsible.[224]

[223] The accident happenend on Redford Bank, not Bedburn Bank.
[224] *Northern Echo*, January 18, 1947

9-11 Lawrie Stephenson, second-right, a woodman all his life

Tom's grandson Ken Wilkinson is adamant that the accident occurred on Redford Bank. He remembers his grandmother Alice Dowson Stephenson telling him that she had seen the tractor and trailor on Redford Bank shortly after the accident. He points out that Bedburn Bank is not visible from Field House where his grandparents lived.

Although there was snow on the ground when Tom died in early January, it was in the third week of the month that the dales had their worst snowstorm of the century. Roads were blocked, buses were unable to run and trains were frequently brought to a halt. Groups of workers made heroic efforts throughout the six weeks, cutting through drifts of up to thirty feet to get roads open, but at times it was a losing battle as fresh snow soon filled them in once again. One of the worst hit villages was Woodland, which ran out of food after being isolated from the outside world for four weeks. Fifty years on, *The Teesdale Mercury* recalled the "six weeks of hardship, danger and misery for countless families:-

> A road gang....put in a superhuman effort to cut a route through to Copley. The Co-op store sent 570 loaves to Cockfield, where they were loaded onto sleighs along with a large supply of meat. PC Dixon and his team arrived back in Woodland several hours later - much to the relief of the villagers, who were able to eat heartily that night...There was a wonderful community spirit... with young people looking after the elderly and calling to ensure those in isolated houses were safe. They shared out any food they had left, and carried water to homes that were totally frozen up. A widespread outbreak of a serious form of measles made matters even worse.[225]

Tom Stephenson's son Edward, Marjorie and Ena's father, was at Butterknowle, then later at Hunwick. He was described by Marjorie as "over six feet tall, muscular and rangy with it, and very strong, and one hell of a worker. He was a very good farmer and much respected by his neighbours."

Marjorie remembered visits from FJS:-

---

[225] *Teesdale Mercury*, January 15, 1997

> Dad's cousin Frank Sanderson from Vesey Farm, Great Holland, visited us quite a few times over the years. If he was by himself he would stay overnight with us. If his wife Joan was with him they sometimes stayed at *The Eden Arms* at Rushyford. Frank visited with his two sons, Frank and Tom, when they were about 14 and 15 years old. Jim (Marjorie's brother) remembers going to the pub opposite the farm with them and Dad. Frank was telling Dad that he couldn't grow turnips to his taste down in Colchester, they just weren't sweet. So when dad's crop was harvested, he bagged some up in hessian sacks and Jim took them to the station and sent them to Frank by rail. At one time Dad and Mam visited Frank and Joan for a holiday. Dad really appreciated looking around Frank's farm, as he had been proud to show Frank his farm at Hunwick.

Marjorie also wrote of the visits of her father and the family to see his cousin Ella Atkinson at Low Staindrop Field House Farm. The families were close, and Edward's sister Gladys was a bridesmaid at the wedding of Ella and Dick at Hamsterley in August 1926. Gladys married Harold (Harry) Wilkinson in Darlington in 1931.

9-12 The Wedding of Ella Sanderson and Dick Atkinson in 1926 at Pond House: standing l to r, John George Coates Atkinson (brother, smoking a cigarette), Richard Atkinson (father), Groom with the Bride, Frank Sanderson of Hamsterley, Lizzie Stothard, and FJS. Seated from left, Dick's mother Elizabeth Hannah (Coates), Frances Muriel Rodmell, Gladys Stephenson,[226] Ella's cousin, and Eliza Stephenson, Ella's maternal grandmother. The little boy is my father, Henry Sanderson of Hamsterley, aged 5.

[226] Gladys, born 1903, is the daughter of Thomas Stephenson, the brother of Ella's mother Edith.

9-13 A trip to Blackpool in the 1950s to enjoy the sea air was captured on camera by a member of the Woodland Farmer's Discussion Group, and submitted to The *Teesdale Mercury* by Jack Forster of Butterknowle.Those pictured from the left: Jimmy Lamb, Charlie Turnbull, George Wilson, Harry Jewitt, Roland Collinson, Jonathan Hutchinson, Vickers Forster (Jack's uncle), and Sid Hurworth. Seated are Hector Lamb, "an unnamed gentleman thought to be a Ministry of Agriculture representative", Ted Stephenson, and Jack Talentire.

When Ena and Marjorie saw the photograph in the newspaper, they couldn't stop laughing. The bespectacled unnamed gentleman was not The Man from the Ministry, but The Man from the Pub, their uncle, Harry Wilkinson, landlord of the *Cross Keys* in Hamsterley and husband of Aunt Gladys née Stephenson. The Woodland Farmer's Group would hold meetings in the *Cross Keys,* and Uncle Harry, as a member of the NFU, would be invited to join them, hence his presence in the seaside photograph. Whenever Ena and Marjorie see the photograph, they still have a good chuckle about the mystery man from the ministry.

Matt Dodds, Jack Marquis, and Mary Jane Fatkin

The Dodds family were close neighbours of the Stephensons in Bedburn and had business interests in common, as well as the aforementioned family ties (See p.157). Matthew Dodds, born in 1813 in Bedburn, was an edge tool manufacturer with interests in farming and the timber business. He and his wife Mary brought up a family of 12 children, including, Ann (Nancy) Dodds, born in 1837, and Michael John Dodds, born in 1841. FJS talked about the Dodds family only in relation to his grandfather Joseph Stephenson's first marriage, to Nancy Dodds in 1863.

When he was in his mid-teens, it seems that Michael John Dodds moved to South Northumberland near Chollerford to lodge with Peter Littlefair who was originally from Hamsterley. In 1860, he married Peter's daughter Hannah at Hexham. They had their eldest child, Matthew James (Matt), in Newcastle before the family returned to Hoppyland Lodge, Bedburn. Matt was born with a club foot in 1865, the year that his Aunt Nancy Stephenson died. It is not known how close he became to his Uncle Joseph Stephenson, but in this small community they would have come into regular contact.

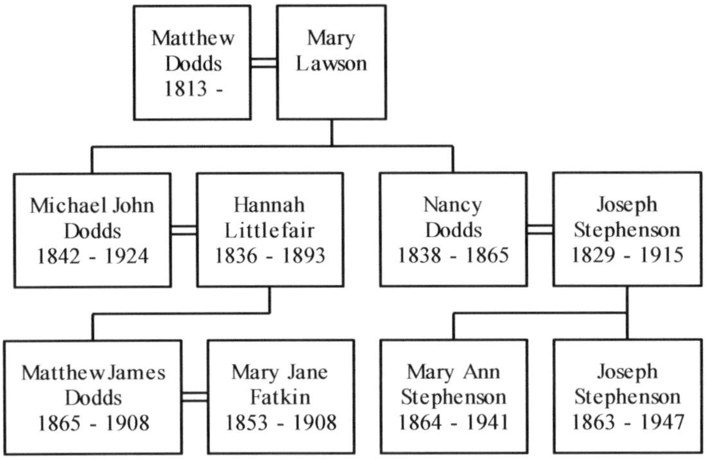

By the time of the 1881 Census, Matt was 16 year's old and living with his parents and siblings in Hamsterley, a mile up the road from Bedburn. Ten years later, he was a Woodman and living as a lodger with family friends in Cotherstone, and by 1901, 36 year's old and unmarried, he was back in Hamsterley working as a wood sawyer with his father and family – his mother had died in 1893.

9-14 Selective Dodds family tree. Joseph Stephenson of Bedburn is Matthew James Dodd's uncle through marriage to Nancy Dodds

Back in 1851, William Fatkin, a coke drawer born in Wolsingham, was newly married and living with his wife Elizabeth née Hodgson in Hamsterley. Their first child was born in 1852 and named Mary Jane, but she was to die the same year. Their next and only child was born in 1853 and was also called Mary Jane.

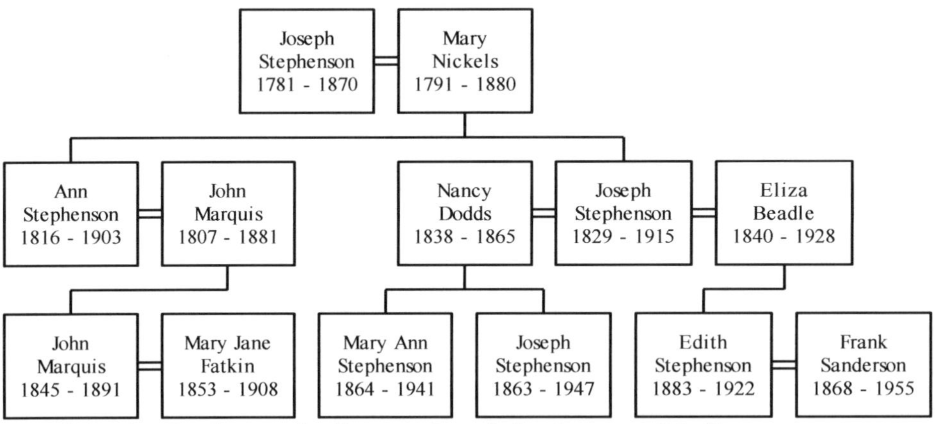

9-15 Selective Stephenson family tree. Joseph Stephenson of Bedburn is John Marquis Jnr's uncle, and Edith Stephenson is his cousin.

John Marquis, known locally as Jack, was born on September 19, 1845 into a family long-located in Hamsterley. The family was closely related to the Stephensons – his mother was Ann Stephenson, sister of Joseph Stephenson of Bedburn, making him Joseph's nephew and FJS's first cousin, once removed. In the 1860s, Jack Marquis had become an assistant grocer at his brother Joseph's shop next door to the *Cross Keys* in Hamsterley. When Joseph Marquis died at the age of 34 in 1872, Jack took over the shop, and three years later, married "the girl next door", Mary Jane Fatkin.

Robberies with Violence

Two cases involving Jack Marquis came to court in 1877 and 1880 respectively, the first concerning violent robbery and the second concerning the ill-usage of a young boy accused of attempted theft.

Like most of his male contemporaries in Hamsterley, Jack Marquis would go out most evenings for a drink, usually in Hamsterley but sometimes at a public house in a nearby village. On Tuesday, January 23, 1877, Jack and his friend from schooldays, John Dodds[227] from Bedburn, spent the evening in one of the Witton-le-Wear hostelries[228] before setting off to walk home at about 9.30 pm. They crossed Witton Bridge, walked up Crakehill Bank and were just passing Hamsterley Church on the way to the village when, out of the darkness, they were set upon by three young roughs. The two friends were knocked over and violently kicked as they cowered helplessly on the ground. They were robbed of what money they had, and their hats and a stick were stolen.

Battered and bruised, Marquis and Dodds reported the incident to the police but because it was so dark at the time, were only able to give vague descriptions of their assailants. Nevertheless, PC William Cruikshanks with the assistance of his brother Sergeant Alexander Cruikshanks and PC William Hutchinson, quickly apprehended three young men in Etherley: brothers John and Michael McEleavey, and John Sparks, alias Etherington. Subsequently, neither Jack Marquis nor John Dodds were able to identify the attackers to the presiding magistrate at Bishop Auckland Police Court. Consequently, despite the stolen property having been found at the house of the McEleaveys, the Rev George Wilkinson JP felt that there was insufficient evidence to commit the prisoners to trial and they were duly discharged.[229]

Three years later, Jack Marquis appeared much less deserving of sympathy when a child attempted to rob him of a few coppers. The child in question was 10 year-old John George Dove who was living at Dixon Carr near Hamsterley with his grandmother Jane, and step-grandfather Samuel Lamb, a farmer and butcher. When John George was 2 years old, his father Thomas had died in a pit accident[230] and his mother had quickly remarried, resulting in him going to live with his paternal grandmother Jane Lamb née Dove and her husband Samuel. In the summer of 1880, the boy visited the Marquis shop and, when Mr Marquis went into the back room, he saw an opportunity and took 5 pence from the till. Unfortunately for him, Jack Marquis returned to catch him in the act. He was doubly unfortunate when Marquis, rather than clip him round the ear and/or inform his grandparents of the deed, chose to make an example of the boy. His hands were tied and Marquis marched him through the village, accompanied by the grocer's black retriever dog which repeatedly jumped at and bit the terrified boy.

The harsh treatment of the young boy by Jack Marquis suggests a man who was finding life difficult, perhaps as a result of business worries or maybe because of an unhappy

[227] John Dodds is first cousin once removed of Matthew James Dodds.

[228] The visitors would have had the choice in Witton-le-Wear of *The Railway Hotel, The Mason's Arms,* and *The Victoria Hotel.*

[229] *Northern Echo*, January 26 1877

[230] The boy's father Thomas Dove was killed at Littleburn Colliery on February 5 1872 when a winch knocked him and a fellow worker off a hoisting bucket, causing both of them to fall to the bottom of the shaft.

marriage. Eleven years later, his despair was complete when he went out the back to the hayloft early one morning (See p.173).

On Monday, July 5, John George Dove, described as an orphan, was charged at Bishop Auckland Courthouse with stealing 5 pence (equivalent in value to less than £2 today) from Jack Marquis. The Bench, ignoring the evidence that the child had been mistreated and claims from witnesses that he had been bitten eight or nine times by the dog, declared that Mr Marquis had only being doing his duty and sentenced the orphan to be whipped with a birch rod. The boy's grandfather was referred to another court in connection with the alleged attacks by the dog.[231]

Up until 1879, the birch was usually administered in prison, but it is likely that John Dove was birched by a policeman either at the courthouse or at a nearby police station. For ten year-olds, "the birch" consisted of birch twigs bound together with a total length of 40 inches and a weight of 9 ounces (cf adult birch weight of 12 ounces).[232] Procedures varied from place to place:-

> The method most commonly adopted is to bend the boy over a low bench or table. His hands, and sometimes his feet also, are held by police officers. This is done in order to ensure that he shall not move. In some Police Forces one constable takes the boy on his back, drawing the boy's hands down over his shoulders; another constable holds the boy's feet, drawing his legs round the sides of the first constable; the first constable then leans forward, and the birch is applied (to the bare buttocks) by a third.[233]

It was not until 1948 that corporal punishment was abolished by statute on mainland Britain.

Samuel Lamb met a sad end when he was driving home to Dixon Carr from Shildon on Friday, 4th November, 1887. Between Toft Hill and Hamsterley, sixty-three years-old Samuel was getting off the cart when he lost his balance and fell head first to the ground. With his master lying motionless, the lad who was with him ran to the nearest farmhouse for assistance and in the meantime, the Rev Graham-Barton, the Baptist Minister from Hamsterley who had been preaching at Toft Hill, came upon the scene and found that Mr Lamb's neck had been dislocated and that "life was extinct". Dr Williamson of Witton Park certified the death and the body was conveyed home to "the sorrowing widow".[234]

Mary Jane's Terrifying Accident

By 1881, Jack Marquis was well established as a grocer, draper and small farmer in Hamsterley, and Mary Jane's parents were living next door with a lodger, PC James Thompson (See next page). In 1884, Mary Jane's father William Fatkin died and her mother continued to live next door.

On Monday, January 10, 1887, Mary Jane was the victim of a terrifying accident in her own home. At the weekend, there had been severe snowstorms in the area, leaving many

---

231 *Northern Echo*, July 6, 1880

232 Farrell, C. *Judicial and corporal punishment in Britain*, (Corpun.com).

233 Cadogan Report (1938) *Report of the Departmental Committee on Corporal Punishment*, HMSO, Cmd. 5684.

234 *Northern Echo*, November 7,1887

roads blocked, but Dr Browning Patterson of Butterknowle was able with some difficulty to make the 3-mile journey by trap to his surgery in Hamsterley. He arrived in the afternoon, alighted from the trap, and left the driver to walk the horse about. It was reported:

> In turning, the animal hit its foot, causing it to plunge across the road into the gutter. It then backed across the road, driving the trap against a stone wall, overturning it, and breaking off the shaft. The driver was thrown out on the road. Thus liberated, the horse ran at a furious rate down the village, the shafts dangling at its feet. The door of Mr John Marquis was standing open, and the horse ran into the house, knocking Mrs Marquis down and breaking her leg. The animal was secured, and Mrs Marquis attended to by the doctor.[235]

Given the circumstances of Mary Jane's accident, it is assumed that Dr Patterson waived his usual fee for treating her injuries.

9-16 The Marquis shop is on left. Jack and Mary Jane lived next door, and the runaway horse entered the house through the door to the right of the archway.

PC James Thompson

PC Thompson, a lodger with the Marquis family, would for the most part have found his working life as the village "pollus" to be fairly straightforward, providing a reassuring presence for villagers, dealing with poachers, and keeping the peace when faced with rowdy drunks emerging from the local public houses (See p.187). But there would also be the occasional incidents of high drama, as was the case in October 1884 when he was threatened

[235] *Teesdale Mercury*, January 12, 1887

with a loaded revolver by John Taylorson, a desperate man on the run after trying to cut his wife's throat.[236]

John Taylorson, a 73 year-old carpenter from Chester-le-Street who had recently lost his first wife, married widow Mary Ann Noble née Egdell, in Chester-le-Street in 1883. The marriage was disastrous from the start with Mary Ann subject to what we would call domestic violence and what the court then described as "ill-usage". Within six months of the marriage, Mary Ann fled Chester-le-Street and sought sanctuary in Hamsterley with her Aunt Margaret Spence née Anderson. Margaret had moved from Chester-le-Street to South Bedburn in about 1840 to take a position as farm servant at The Grove, and in 1850, she married Mark Spence at Hamsterley St James. By 1881, the widowed Margaret was living in Hamsterley with her niece Sarah Stephenson née Spence - whose husband Joseph was an inmate at Bishop Auckland Workhouse at the time.

In the months after her arrival in Hamsterley, Mary Ann Taylorson was subject to frequent threats from her husband which caused her to apply to Chester-le-Street magistrates for a protection order against him. In spite of this, at noon on Monday, 6th October, an agitated John Taylorson arrived at Hamsterley demanding that Mary Ann return home with him. When she refused, Taylorson knocked her into a corner and produced a cord with a noose attached to a stick, presumably with the intention of looping the noose around her neck and dragging her back to Chester-le-Street. When thwarted by Mary Ann and her aunt seizing the rope, he took a knife "in appearance like those used by shoemakers" from his pocket. He then seized his wife by the hair and threw her down, knelt upon her and attempted to cut her throat, but mercifully with the back of the knife rather than the sharp edge.[237]

In response to Margaret Spence's cries for help, Sarah Stephenson entered the room and grabbed Taylorson's hand. In the melée, Sarah's finger was cut and Mary Ann suffered cuts to her head and arm and her face was bruised. The local blacksmith Michael Henderson who lived just across the road, heard the screams and ran into the house, knocked over Taylorson and gripped him by the throat, thus allowing Mary Ann and Sarah to escape. Taylorson then wrestled free and, after much cursing and violent threats, left the house and walked off in the direction of Witton-le-Wear.

PC Thompson was quickly on the scene. Together with John Egglestone, a game-watcher, the constable chased Taylorson over the fields. When they caught up with him near the river, he produced a loaded revolver and threatened that he would shoot the first man who came near him. He then waded across the Wear and headed into Witton-le-Wear where he was cornered by his pursuers. A stand-off was ended when a man crept up behind him and "with a heavy blow, felled him to the ground". PC Thompson arrested the desperate and bedraggled man and took him by train to Bishop Auckland where he was held in custody.

Three weeks later John Taylorson appeared at Durham Autumn Assizes charged with attempted murder. He was found guilty of unlawfully wounding his wife and sentenced to two months imprisonment, a sentence which, in view of the evidence, would be considered lenient by modern standards. The incident caused the "utmost excitement" locally.

---

236 *Newcastle Courant*, October 10, 1884

237 *Leeds Times*, October 11, 1884

9-17 Hamsterley Post Office. The post-master was Anthony Stephenson, and John Jopling Stephenson took over after his father's death in 1888 (Courtesy of Joey Brown Humes).

Tragic Death of Jack Marquis

By 1891 Jack and Mary Jane Marquis had two lodgers, and next door PC Thompson had been replaced by PC George Applegarth[238] as Elizabeth Fatkin's lodger.

On the morning of Friday May 22nd 1891, Jack left his grocer's shop and went out the back to his hayloft. Soon afterwards, neighbour William Coatsworth[239] was attracted by the agitated behaviour of Mr Marquis's dog. He shouted at the dog, "Where's Jack?" The dog came to him, then turned and ran in the direction of the gate leading to the hayloft. Coatsworth followed but the dog wouldn't go through the gate, but instead ran off down the village. Hearing another dog barking in the hayshed, he approached and saw the dog racing about in the hay. He called out "Jack, what are you doing?" just before seeing the lifeless body of Jack Marquis hanging from a beam by a rope which was wrapped seven times around his neck. When he was cut down, he face turned black.

At the inquest, Elizabeth Fatkin née Hodgson, Mr Marquis's mother-in-law, explained that he had been rather low recently and had been drinking heavily all week. Coroner Thomas Dean returned a verdict that the 45-year-old deceased had committed suicide whilst temporarily insane.[240] He left an estate which included seven properties in Hamsterley to Mary Jane.

What made life so intolerable for Jack Marquis? Apart from business worries, it is possible that he felt trapped in an unhappy marriage and that Mary Jane's affection was

---

238 In April, 1891, George's brother, Sergeant Thomas Applegarth, was shot and nearly killed in Spennymoor by John Hardy, alias "Sailor Jack" (*North East Daily Gazette*, April 15, 1891)

239 William Coatsworth was one of Hamsterely's most colourful characters (See p.187)

240 *Newcastle Courant*, May 30, 1891

focused on her mother next door. Perhaps a tendency to depression was exacerbated by drink. Jack had been drinking heavily and Mary Jane also liked a drink, so perhaps alcohol played a part as it was alleged to have done during a dramatic trial concerned with the death of Mary Jane 17 years later.

Mary Jane's Second Marriage

After the death of her husband, Mary Jane moved in with her mother and John Robson took over the grocer's shop next door. By 1901, she and her 73 year old mother were supplementing their private means with lodgers. Three years later in 1904 her mother died and Mary Jane, by this time just turned 50 years old, was left very much on her own with a property portfolio to sustain her in her old age but no doubt feeling a great sense of loss and loneliness.

A near neighbour in Hamsterley at this time, someone who had known Mary Jane since childhood, was the aforementioned bachelor Matt Dodds. He was 11 years her junior and from a respectable chapel-going family. Both parties may have imagined marriage as an attractive prospect. From Mary Jane's perspective Matt was a relatively young bachelor who could offer companionship and would be able to look after her in old age. For Matt, Mary Jane was a childless widow with private means who would be a companion and housekeeper, and who would ultimately provide him with a pension. On 24 June 1905, within a year of her mother's death, 51year-old Mary Jane Marquis[241] married Matthew James Dodds at Bishop Auckland Register Office, no doubt both hoping for a shared life of happiness.

In the event, the couple were ill-matched from the outset and endured a stormy relationship at the house she had shared with her mother, as noted in 1908 by several neighbours and acquaintances in the close-knit and gossipy village.

Looking back at this ill-fated marriage, it is not hard to see how it would have created problems for the two of them. Matt was a long-time bachelor, 40 years old and likely to be quite independent and set in his ways. Moreover, his disability will have caused him much difficulty and was probably a source of significant unhappiness in his life. Mary Jane, tragically widowed, without children, and so recently having lost her mother, may have been full of regrets and even bitterness about the cruel blows that life had inflicted upon her, diminishing her ability to start afresh with a second husband.

Mary Jane's Puzzling Death[242]

Less than 3 years after the marriage, shortly after 4 pm on Thursday, 20 February 1908, Matt Dodds summoned next-door neighbour Sarah Jane Wade[243] née Wild (wife of farmer George Appleton Wade) to his house, claiming that his wife had burnt to death. Sarah Jane, accompanied by the Dodds family housekeeper Dorothy Hodgson, found Mary Jane lying dead on the hearth, grasping a burnt-out cinder, and her clothes alight despite there being no fire in the grate. The immediate assumption was that, perhaps the worse for drink, she had

---

[241] Mary Jane's age on the Marriage Certificate was given as 45 years.

[242] Transcriptions of newspaper accounts and other useful documents were provided to me by Mrs Joy Walker of Crook. Joy, descended from the Dodds family of Bedburn, published a prize-winning account of the case in 2001 in *Readers' Digest.*

[243] On September 25 1906, Sarah Jane's eight year-old son William was run over and killed in Hamsterley by a motor-car driven by Mr Charles T Fogg-Elliot, Private Secretary of Lord Barnard.

tripped and fallen into the fire and burnt to death. When the news emerged, the local paper described Matt and Mary Jane as "well respected in the neighbourhood as Dodds is a member of the Non-conformist Church and Mary had private means."

At the hastily-arranged Coroner's inquest a day after the death, at which key witnesses were not called to give evidence and in the absence of a post-mortem, Matt Dodds explained that he had left the house at 2 pm to work in his father's joinery shop and had returned home at 4 pm to find his wife dead on the hearth, badly burnt. Although the jury's verdict was "of a non-conclusive character", the assumption was that Mary Jane had somehow died from burns, and she was duly buried in Hamsterley churchyard. Nevertheless, Coroner John Thomas Proud asked the police to make further enquiries.

Matt Dodds Charged with Murder

After the funeral, rumours and stories began to circulate in the village. It was well known that Matt and Mary Jane had a tempestuous relationship and that Matt had been witnessed on several occasions being violent towards her and had been heard making threats. The Coroner became so suspicious that, with the approval of the Home Office, he ordered the exhumation of Mary Jane's body on 10th March, 18 days after she had died. The 3 doctors who carried out the post-mortem were all agreed that she had been strangled, most probably with her own shawl. They could not tell whether she had been burnt before or after she had died.

Matt Dodds was arrested and charged with his wife's wilful murder, a development that caused a sensation in the Bishop Auckland district. At his arraignment at Bishop Auckland Magistrates Court on Tuesday 24th March, 1908, the local press described him thus: "He is a man about 45 years of age, thick-set, broad-chested and with a shaggy dark brown beard."[244] He also had a club-foot rendering his right leg useless, and he needed a caliper, described as an "iron foot", and two sticks to enable him to walk.

The Sensational Trial

Matt Dodds was placed on trial at Durham Assizes on Monday June 29th before Mr Justice (Sir William) Grantham, charged with the wilful murder of his wife, Mary Jane Dodds at Hamsterley. From the outset, Mr Dodds steadfastly maintained his innocence, declaring, "I didn't dee it, that's all".[245]

Several witnesses spoke of shouting coming from the Dodds' house after about 2.30 pm on the day she died. William Waistell from Podge Hole Farm and Jane Braithwaite, a servant at the *Cross Keys*, came into Robson's shop next door to the Dodds' house and drew attention to the shouting and screaming. Mr Waistell had heard Mary Jane shouting, "Oh, behave; give over." George Marr, a shop assistant at Robson's, heard Mary Jane exclaim several times, "Oh dear, Oh dear, dinnat dee it!" He also testified that at about 2.30 pm, he had heard the side door being bolted and that afterwards, all was quiet. Elizabeth Ann Marquis, a neighbour and niece of Mary Jane, stated that she had seen someone pull the blinds down at 2.15 pm. It was explained in court that none of the witnesses had investigated the shouting as quarrelling between the couple was a common occurrence.

---

[244] At his trial, *The Durham Advertiser* described Matt Dodds as a "powerful and intelligent-looking man".

[245] *The Auckland Times*, July 3, 1908 covered the trial in great detail, and served as a major source of information.

The Rev John Holliday, Vicar of Hamsterley, told the court that he had seen Matt Dodds leaving his house and heading down the village towards his father's workshop at about 2.45-50pm. Another witness, Garthwaite Wilkinson, who was emptying ashpits, thought that Mr Dodds had left his house at about 2.40pm.

9-18 Matt and Mary Jane Dodds lived in the house to the right of the archway. To the left is Robson's shop which was then next door to, and now part of, the *Cross Keys* (extreme left).

Other witnesses gave evidence about the quarrelling and the verbal and physical abuse. Alice Dowson Stephenson, wife of Thomas Stephenson[246] (the landlord of the *Cross Keys* and half-cousin to Matt Dodds), stated that the couple had been frequent visitors to the pub and were often quarrelling. She had once seen Dodds kick Mary Jane from the archway of the gate to the footpath. Other witnesses had seen Dodds hit his wife with a sweeping brush and heard him threaten to kill her, "make her mincemeat", and to "strike her brains out". The prosecuting barrister argued that Matt treated his wife with great cruelty, whilst acknowledging that "it does not follow of course that he intended to carry out the threats".

A number of witnesses spoke of the evidence of ill-treatment. George Marr testified that he had seen Mary Jane with teeth knocked out, and with black eyes on several occasions. Mary Jane had complained to him and he had heard Mr Dodds make threats against her. Elizabeth Ann Marquis reported seeing her with black eyes, a swollen neck and other bruising. Sarah Jane Wade, the first to see the body after Mr Dodds, described the "miserable life" they had shared, and told of seeing Mary Jane with cut lips, teeth knocked out and black eyes, and on one occasion had seen her struck on the head and made senseless by Mr Dodds. Jane Braithwaite described occasions when she had seen Mary Jane with black and blue marks on her arm and with swollen lips. A neighbour, Mary Hannah Blackett, witnessed threats and beatings, and had seen Mary Jane being put out of the house on occasions. PC Thomas Lowe recounted being called to the house a few weeks earlier

[246] Thomas Stephenson is my great uncle.

when Mary Jane was locked out of the house. She complained about being beaten by her husband but the constable told her that there was nothing he could do, and that she should consult a solicitor.

9-19 Alice Dowson Stephenson née Kirkup and Tom Stephenson at the *Cross Keys* in 1910. With them are their children Gladys and Lawrence (Courtesy of Frank Davey of Ontario).

With this strong evidence that he treated his wife badly, together with the medical evidence, the prosecution alleged that he strangled Mary Jane to death, and in order to cover his tracks, placed the body in the fender and set fire to it. A possible motive was that he would benefit from her last Will in which all her estate, including 7 cottages in the village, was left to him.

There had been three Wills: the first Will of January 1907 written out by Rev John Holliday, the vicar of Hamsterley, left all of her estate to her husband; the second, witnessed in August 1907, left only £40 to her husband and the rest to her cousin, Margaret Jane (Meggie) Pattison; the final Will which was hand-written by Matt Dodds in the month before she died, was a copy of the first will which made him the sole beneficiary. There was however no evidence that Mary Jane had been coerced into signing the final Will, with witness William Henderson, the village blacksmith, stating that she signed the Will without demur.[247]

Despite Meggie Pattison being cut out of the third Will, her evidence at the trial was not prejudicial to Matt Dodds. Asked about the quarrelling, she stated that one was as bad as the other, that when she visited them, Matt was very kind to Mary Jane, but she had heard that they quarrelled in her absence.

Matt Dodds' defence was that he was not present when Mary Jane burned to death, and that she fell onto the fire when the worse for drink. Witnesses testified about her drinking.

[247] William was the son of Michael Henderson who had come to the rescue of Mary Ann Taylorson in 1884 (See p.172)

George Marr stated that he had never seen Mary Jane completely drunk but that when quarrelling with her husband, she was very often under the influence of drink. Alice Dowson Stephenson said that she would describe Mary Jane as a woman who took drink rather than a drunken woman. Mary Hannah Blackett told the court that she had seen Mary Jane the worse for drink.

Jane Braithwaite testified that on the day of Mary Jane's death, she had supplied her with a gill (2 pints) of beer at 8.30 in the morning, and at about 1.40pm with a shillings worth of whiskey.

Matt Dodds was called to the witness stand. He said it was the first trouble he'd ever been in, that his wife's lost teeth, cut lips and bruising had been caused by various falls, and as to him kicking her, she had attacked him and he pushed her away. Regarding her being locked out of the house, he stated that she was in the habit of going out when she'd been drinking. He went to bed early because of having to be up by 4.45.am to go to work at Seven Sisters Colliery, Cockfield, and when awakened by her knocking, he got up and let her in. The quarrelling was attributed to her drinking, her constant nagging and her taunting him about his disability. His wife called him "awful names", he said. Sarah Jane Wade confirmed that Mary Jane taunted her husband about his club foot.

9-20 The Hanging Judge:
Mr Justice Grantham

Verdict of "Guilty"

In his summing up, the judge remarked on the conduct of Matt Dodds:-

> It does seem to be about as heartless as it is possible to imagine. Let us assume he was innocent: what would be the conduct of an innocent man having lost his wife by the painful death of burning? Do you think he would have simply gone to somebody and said 'My wife's been found dead'; not asked for anyone to go for a doctor, or telegraphed for one? He never did anything. When the people come there he does not even go to the room but stands at the door – exactly the same when the doctor does come when telegraphed for. He does nothing, never assists. But, there was something he did and said which was very significant; it was the great anxiety he had…that the inquest should be held the next day – as soon as possible. … Why should he be so anxious about the inquest? You would have thought there (would be) every desire to find out everything that had occurred. There is no doubt it was a great advantage to him having it the next day because the enquiry was rushed in a way it ought not to have been.

As reported, the above comments were extremely damaging to Dodds in that Mr Justice Grantham is strongly suggesting his guilt: he says, "There is no doubt that (an early inquest) was a great advantage to him…", rather than, "If he was guilty, there is no doubt…" It is worthy of note that Mr Justice Grantham was regarded at the time as a controversial figure, notorious for incendiary speeches and partial judgements. In 1911, an indiscreet speech to the grand jury in Liverpool led to him being rebuked by the Prime Minister, Herbert Asquith.[248]

Under this strong steer from the judge, the jury in due course returned the verdict of "Guilty". When asked if he had anything to say, the prisoner replied in a firm clear voice, "Well, I am not guilty, sir." He remained unmoved as Mr Justice Grantham donned the black cap and declared:-

> It is not for me to aggravate the painful position in which you must feel placed at the present time, nor is it necessary for me to go into any causes which may have induced you to do this. I have only to perform the duty cast upon me and that is to pass upon you sentence of death. You will be taken from this place to prison and thence to a place of execution and you will be there hanged by the neck until dead and your body will be buried in the precincts of the gaol. May God have mercy on your soul.

Execution after Appeal Fails

His appeal, the very first capital case before the newly established Criminal Court of Appeal under the Criminal Appeal Act, on the grounds that the learned judge had misdirected the jury, was accompanied by a petition containing almost 2000 signatures to the Home Secretary asking for the sentence to be commuted to life imprisonment. Why did so many people in Hamsterley and the surrounding district sign the petition? It seems that there was genuine local sympathy for Matt Dodds in his terrible predicament, and a desperate wish by the community to believe in his protestations of innocence. It was probably also a sign of an emerging public unease about the penalty of death when even slight doubt remained about the verdict (See p.133).

Unfortunately for Matt Dodds, the Secretary of State "failed to discover any sufficient ground to justify him advising His Majesty to interfere with the due course of the law."

Matt Dodds maintained his innocence to the end in several letters to family and friends, claiming that Mary Jane's death was "an accident in some form or other".

He wrote to his father and brother:-

> Do keep your heart and don't fret about me. As I told you before, I am quite innocent and nothing to be afraid of to meet death. I will be far better off when I reach Heaven City, when all trouble and sorrow will then be over and to be with those who have gone before and enjoy the pleasure for evermore. And never for one moment think me anything else but innocent. If I hadn't been, I would have confessed to you like a man before I parted from this world…"

In conclusion, he wrote:-

> Well dear father, put your trust in the One above and you will find in Him a great help and comfort for the remainder of your years…shortly after you receive this letter I will have been launched out of time into eternity to be with God and His redeemed One, around His Throne to sing His praises.
>
> From your innocent and true son,

---

[248] Hansard, HC 5ser, Vol 22, Col 366

MATTHEW JAMES DODDS[249]

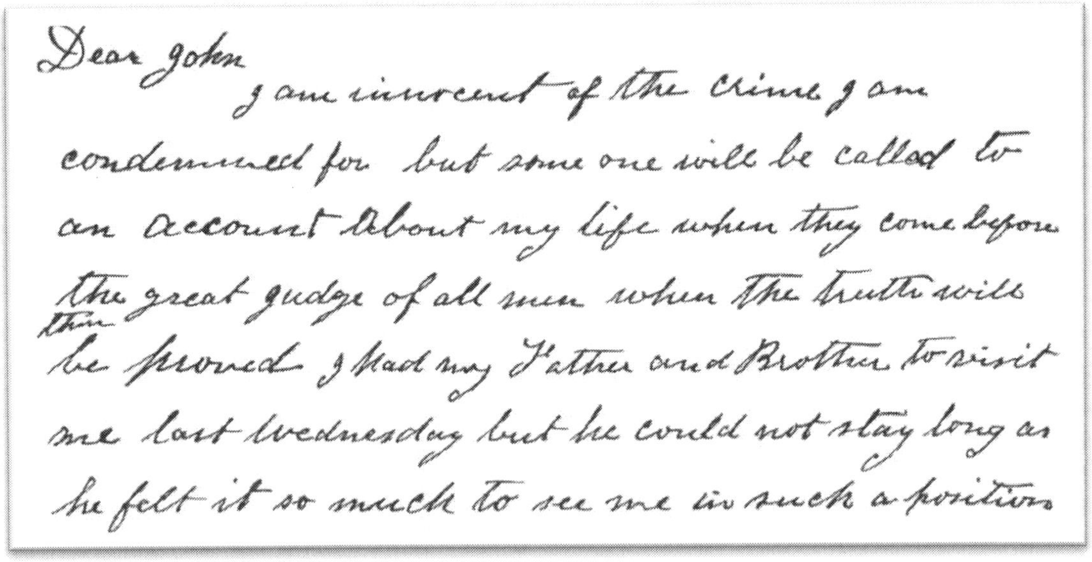

Dear John
I am innocent of the crime I am condemned for but some one will be called to an account about my life when they come before the great judge of all men when the truth will then be proved I had my Father and Brother to visit me last Wednesday but he could not stay long as he felt it so much to see me in such a position

9-21 Extract from a letter dated August 3rd, 1908, written by Matt Dodds in his condemned cell to John Heads, a blacksmith at Seven Sisters Colliery, Cockfield. Matt's father was so distressed that he only stayed for 15 minutes on his last visit.

The *Durham Advertiser* noted:-

> The morning of Dodds' last day on earth broke dull and lowering, and rain fell in the early part. This cleared off about half past eight, however, but the sky still remained grey and overcast, as if in sympathy with the tragic act which was to be performed."[250]

The execution was carried out by Henry Pierrepoint, assisted by his brother Thomas, at Durham Gaol at 9 am on Wednesday August 5th 1908:-

> Dodds was wearing the suit in which he was tried, and his beard appeared to have grown considerably longer. Arrived at the execution-house, Dodds was placed upon the folding doors, across which planks had been placed, so that the two warders who had assisted him in his last walk might still continue to support him. The younger Pierrepoint adjusted the ankle strap, placed the cap over the condemned man's head, whilst the elder adjusted the noose. The executioner then pulled the lever, and Dodds shot out of sight. The drop was a seven foot one, and the rope hung with hardly a tremor

Matt Dodds never spoke a word, remaining cool and collected to the very end. [251]

---

[249] The letter was reproduced in *The Auckland Times*, August 7, 1908
[250] *Durham Advertiser,* August 7, 1908
[251] *Durham Advertiser,* August 7, 1908

Postscript

In the back section of the graveyard of the Baptist Chapel in Hamsterley is a memorial stone with the following inscription:

> In loving memory of John Robt son of Michael J and Hannah DODDS of Hamsterley who d 17 Feb 1891 aged 24 years. Also Annie and Nancy their daus who died in infancy. Also the above-named Hannah DODDS who d 15 Nov 1893 aged 58 years. Also of the above-named Michael John DODDS who d 29 Dec 1924 aged 83 years.

Not surprisingly, Matt Dodds is not acknowledged on this Christian memorial stone. Having been subject to capital punishment as a convicted murderer, his body was buried in unconsecrated ground within Durham Gaol. The details on the stone reveal that his mother thankfully didn't have to endure the tragedy that ensued, unlike Matt's father who lived a further 16 years after his son's death, carrying the grim family legacy within this small community.

In Matt Dodds' Last Will and Testament, he directed his executors (his father and brother George) "to erect a tombstone to the memory of my late wife" in the graveyard of the chapel. The Executors appear not to have honoured this request – they had an unshakeable belief in Matt's innocence, and most probably an accompanying view that Mary Jane was the cause of all his trouble.

Viewing the evidence today, the case against Matt Dodds appears strong. There was evidence of a stormy relationship and of his serial physical ill-treatment of Mary Jane. There was evidence of shouting and screaming coming from the house on the afternoon of her death, and there was strong medical opinion that Mary Jane had been strangled. If she had been strangled, there was every indication that the perpetrator must have been her husband, Matt Dodds. On the other hand, forensic techniques were fairly rudimentary in those days, and a modern defence barrister may have been able to advance a more convincing theory supporting the accidental death of an inebriated woman. Alternatively, Matt Dodds might have been persuaded to admit to manslaughter on the grounds of diminished responsibility, triggered by the cumulative effects of the taunts of a drunken scold over a prolonged period of time.

It was suggested in court that because Mary Jane owned substantial property in the village and had made her husband the sole beneficiary in her Last Will and Testament, Matt Dodds had a clear motive for the murder. However, the evidence suggests a crime of passion rather than a premeditated act, one violent row too many followed by a clumsy attempt by Matt Dodds to conceal his responsibility for Mary Jane's death.[252]

Nobody alive remembers the tragic events of over 100 years ago, but an oft-repeated macabre riddle in Hamsterley about Mary Jane Dodds ensures that the sad tale will not be forgotten:-

Mary Jane Dodds was married twice, buried twice and both her husbands were hung.

[252] I am grateful for helpful comments from Frank Davey of Ontario, the great nephew of Alice Dowson Stephenson née Kirkup, one of the key witnesses at Matt Dodds' trial.

9-22 Hamsterley in 1910. Note the un-made road surface. (Courtesy of Joey Brown Humes)

10. THE SIMPSONS OF PENNINGTON

"My grandmother was a Simpson from Pennington,
a big sheep farm up on the moors near Woodland"

Although FJS was incorrect in describing his grandmother as a Simpson, Eliza Beadle was brought up in the Simpson household at Pennington from the age of four. Her mother Ann Beadle was born in Ettersgill, Upper Teesdale, in 1821 into a large family of lead miners. By 1841, Ann (Nancy) was helping her mother Jane Beadle on the smallholding at Bank Top, Ettersgill. Along with several brothers and sisters, also present was a one-year old baby girl, "n.k. Beadle" (name not known). Eliza Beadle was born in 1840, so her age corresponds with that of the unnamed baby at Ettersgill. Before she married, Ann Beadle had another child, Sarah, in 1843.

William Simpson was born at Palletstone House, Langleydale, in 1812, the eldest son of farmer Edward Simpson and his wife Sarah (Talentire). In 1841, William was farming at Pennington Farm, and it is possible that Ann Beadle was employed by William as a farm servant prior to their marriage at Hamsterley St James in August 1844. Thereafter Eliza, undoubtedly an illegitimate child of Ann Beadle and father unknown, was brought up at Pennington Farm.

Pennington farm consisted of over 400 acres of rough pastures and wood, and access to almost 3000 acres of moorland where thousands of sheep and a small number of cattle and horses were reared. It was owned by the Surtees family who used nearby Redford Grove as a summer retreat.

Here nature's wild beauties are seen to perfection,
They strike the beholder in every direction,
Enhancing the pleasure on closer inspection,
Enrapturing our souls as we stroll by the Grove.[253]

10-1 Crosyer Surtees

Crosyer Surtees of Redford Grove, a particularly disreputable member of the family, married his cousin Jane Surtees in 1769. He treated her badly and they separated in 1800, a few years after he had entered into an adulterous relationship with "a local farm lass" Jane Shaw, who bore him three illegitimate children at Pennington – Crosyer Surtees Shaw,[254] George Surtees Shaw, and Robert Surtees Shaw. Crosyer, "a designing, artful man, a bad character", was unlamented when he died in the cold waters of Linburn Beck:-

[253] From *The Grove: a Song*, by Richard Watson, published in *The Teesdale Mercury*, August 8, 1888.

[254] Crosyer junior's illegitimacy appears to have excluded him from the gentry: he settled in Swaledale, first becoming a schoolmaster, then a labourer and in later life, a gardener.

> He lived out the end of his days with (Jane) in Pennington Rake, an isolated farm on the moors above the forest… Crosyer's days ended quite suddenly. In (December) 1803, he was returning very drunk from a banquet with Lord Barnard in Raby Castle. On the moors, his horse failed to negotiate a stream properly. He tumbled from the saddle, fell into the water and froze to death.[255]

At Pennington, William and Ann Simpson raised a large family and enjoyed considerable success with the farm. During her childhood, Eliza Beadle took her step-father's name, being described in both 1851 and 1861 as 'Eliza Simpson'. But when she married Joseph Stephenson of Bedburn in 1868, she was described as 'Eliza Bedale' (sic). Like her mother before her, Eliza had a child, Sarah, before she was married: Sarah's name was also given as "Bedale" when she married farmer Thomas Race at Hamsterley in 1883.

Eliza's half-sister Elizabeth Simpson married farmer's son Joseph Swinbank of Woodland at Barnard Castle Wesleyan Chapel, apparently without the approval of their parents. On the morning of February 18th 1871, Joseph arrived at Pennington Farm, gathered up 18 year-old Elizabeth and galloped off to Barnard Castle with her on the back of his horse. Witnesses at the wedding in the Wesleyan Chapel were Elizabeth's sister Emma and her husband George Littlefair of Mayland Hall. At the time of the 1871 Census two months later, Joseph and Elizabeth were reconciled with the Simpson family and living at Pennington Farm,

Joseph Swinbank was born in 1848 at Baldersdale (Hauxwell Country) and, according to his grandson, Bill Swinbank of Carabooda, WA, worked down the pit where the Swinbanks received royalties on the coal on East Fold Garth Farm, Woodland. In 1881, he was described as a Farm Bailiff, living at Woodland with his 28 year old wife, Elizabeth, and children. The family moved to Highcliffe Farm near Winston in the 1890's, then finally to Greystone near Caldwell. His obituary in 1924 noted:-

> He was well-known as an agriculturalist, and he took an active interest in public affairs, having been a member of the Teesdale Board of Guardians and the Barnard Castle Rural Council for 35 years, and also a member of the Winston Parish Council. He was closely identified with Wesleyan Methodism, having been a steward of Winston Chapel for many years.[256]

Highway Robbery

William Simpson senior, like most other farmers at the time, was a frequent patron of the local hostelries. On one occasion, Monday, April 25th, 1870, he visited a public house near Etherley and in the late evening, somewhat the worse for drink, he set off for Diddridge Farm where he had recently set up his newly-married son Edward. On the way, he was robbed of 28 shillings in silver. William told the magistrates at Bishop Auckland Police Court that he had been "attacked, knocked down and brutally ill-treated on the high road" in such a manner that his face still showed the effects of the blows. Knowing the assailant, he reported the offence to the police, who quickly apprehended John Caile, a pitman from Etherley, who was charged with robbery with violence.[257] Caile was bailed to appear at

[255] *Northern Echo,* February 6, 2008
[256] *Teesdale Mercury*, December 24, 1924
[257] *Northern Echo*, May 10, 1870

Durham Quarter Sessions in July, at which time he was sentenced to 18 months imprisonment with hard labour.[258]

Clippings Days at Pennyton[259]

From days unnumber'd hath the custom been
To shear, in summer months, the loaded sheep,
And keep the jocund feast: so still remains
The festival among the rustic race.[260]

William Simpson senior died in 1876 aged 64 and left an estate to Ann of circa £2000: in terms of the relative economic power, today's equivalent value would be about £2.5M. Ann, known as "Annie" by family and friends, continued farming at Pennington with her youngest sons, William and John. Despite a reduced acreage, Pennington remained an exceptional sheep farm and the sheep clipping days were memorable occasions, as recorded by the celebrated Teesdale poet Richard Watson. In July 1883, he reported his visit the previous month to a clipping day at Pennington in the form of a letter to *The Teesdale Mercury*:-

> DEAR SIR,-Having been invited to attend the sheep shearing at Pennyton Farm, on the 28th ult., I resolved to go, knowing that I would meet with several of my old Teesdale friends. Having wrought a shift in the pit, it was late in the afternoon before I could bend my steps to the said farm. Proceeding northwards, I soon reached Black Ling Hole, a picturesque place in the Bedburn valley, near a mile west of the "Grove", the late residence of H. Surtees, Esq. Here the wild beauties of nature are seen in every direction. It was a pleasant day, the sun was shining brightly, casting its slanting rays into the thick plantations on both sides of the valley like burnished gold. From the fern-fringed rocks by the little cascade, the wild rabbits peered forth, scampering back into their burrows whenever my presence was detected, reminding me of the beautiful lines of Burns to the mouse:
>
> I'm truly sorry man's dominion
> Has broken nature's social union,
> And justifies that ill opinion
> Which makes thee startle
> At me, thy poor earth-born companion,
> And fellow mortal![261]
>
> As I gazed on the varied beauties around me, my ears were sweetly regaled with the music of the feathered tribes above my head, mingled with the bleating of sheep in the distance, and the roar of the little brook as it leaped into the dark pool below.

---

258 *Newcastle Courant*, July 15, 1870

259 Pennyton is a local phonetic spelling of "Pennington"

260 Extract from *"Sheep Shearing"*, a poem published in *The Ladies Cabinet of Fashion, Music and Romance*, July 1, 1849

261 From *To a Mouse, on Turning Her Up in Her Nest with the Plough:* Published in 1785 by Robbie Burns.

10-2 "The roar of the little brook as it leapt into the dark pool below". Black Ling Hole on the Spurlswood Beck. (Courtesy of Tom Hutchinson)

No wonder Black Ling Hole has become of late frequented by tourists, picnic parties, and other pleasure seekers. Talk of poetry! Here is food to inspire any musing lover of nature. I felt her influence, and was just taking out my pencil when I was roused from my reverie by the approach of two horsemen. "Hillo (sic), is that you," said they, "We were afraid you were not coming," as they warmly shook hands with me. They were Mr Hankey, and Mr Simpson of Pennyton. I put up my pencil and proceeded with them up a winding path, and soon reached the old farm house, where I was kindly welcomed by Mrs Simpson, the mistress, in the broad vernacular of Upper Teesdale, her native place (Map on page 197 shows Richard Watson's route from Copley to Pennington).

After partaking of ample refreshment, I went to the scene of the clipping operation. It far exceeded my anticipations: upwards of a hundred of both sexes were busily employed, nearly two thousand sheep having to undergo the divesting operation. On low benches, forming a large semi-circle, sat the shearers. While some were engaged in bringing in sheep, others with tar-pans stood ready to mark the newly shorn ones. Near a huge pyramid of wool several merry laughing rustic beauties were wrapping the fleeces. Their cheerful voices mingling with the noise of the clippers, the barking of dogs, and the bleating of sheep, had a strange though pleasing sound to the ear. On every side hands were held out to greet mine, and I felt myself at home among warm-hearted friends. The whole scene would have made a splendid picture of rural life, fit for our highest galleries of art. Great praise is due to Mrs Simpson for the able way in which everything was conducted for the pleasure and comfort of her guests. A splendid dinner was provided. At the head of the table sat WJ Garbutt, Esq., land

> agent. I noticed amongst those present, Mr Walker, Langleydale; Mr (Joseph) Allinson, Egglesburn; Mr Hunter, yeoman, Hamsterley; Mr (John) Hankey; Mr (Thomas) Alderson, Middle End; Mr Hutchinson, Hope House; Mr W Coatsworth, Hamsterley; Mr J Blacket, Woodland, Mr Potts, Hoppyland Park; George Spence, Esq., Hamsterley; George Littlefair, Esq., Mayland Hall; Miss Spence, Hamsterley; Miss Robinson, Wolsingham; Miss (Jane) Longstaff, Woodland, &c. By eight o'clock in the evening the shearing was ended; the rest of the time, till night's dark shadows began to fall, was filled up with songs, recitations, &c. when the party began to disperse, each one pleased with the enjoyments of a sheep shearing on a large scale. – I am yours truly,

RICHARD WATSON, Copley Lane Head, Woodland, Cockfield, July 19th, 1883[262]

The Teesdale Poet paints a vivid picture of a Victorian clipping day. Amidst the sounds of the cheerful voices of more than a hundred helpers, barking dogs and the bleating of two thousand sheep, the shearers worked on low benches in a semi-circle, whilst others stood by pans of hot tar to mark the clipped sheep. One by one, a huge pile of fleeces was being wrapped by "several merry laughing rustic beauties". Richard Watson clearly enjoyed himself: as a celebrated working-class poet and entertainer, he received a special invitation from the Simpsons and when he had not arrived by late afternoon, William Simpson junior accompanied by John Hankey from Ayhope Shield set out on horseback to search for him and they met him at Black Ling Hole Waterfall. On arrival at the farm, he was welcomed by the hostess, my great great grandmother Annie Simpson, "in the broad vernacular of Upper Teesdale" and warmly greeted by his many friends at Pennington that day. With the shearing completed, the gathering enjoyed a "splendid dinner" followed by song and recitations late into the evening, no doubt greatly enhanced by the enthusiastic participation of Richard Watson himself.

Three months later, William Coatsworth, who had attended the clipping day at Pennington, held a public auction of cattle, sheep and horses at the *Cross Keys*, Hamsterley. Included in the sale were: 20 fat sheep, different sorts; 14 half-bred ewes and shearlings, for tupping; 70 half-bred tup lambs, 2 Leicester tups, 3 Leicester tup lambs, 70 Scotch Ewes, for tupping; 80 three-years-old Scotch wethers, nearly fat; 40 Scotch wether lambs. The notice of the sale stated that "Most of the sheep are from Pennington, one of the soundest sheep walks in the North."[263]

William Coatsworth, like his kinsman Jos (See p.223) was a colourful character. From a Teesdale family, he was born at St John's Chapel and first worked as a leadminer in Weardale. Later he farmed in Hunderthwaite before moving to Hamsterley in the 1870s where he became an auctioneer of livestock and a notable village character.

In May 1880, he was charged at Bishop Auckland Police Court with assaulting PC Thompson in Hamsterley.[264] The constable stated that he saw Coatsworth leave the *Cross Keys* and then heard him using strong and abusive language on the street. He ordered him to go home, but shortly afterwards, the defendant, clearly somewhat the worse for drink, followed him into Jack Marquis's shop and began haranguing him and allegedly hitting him

---

[262] *Teesdale Mercury*, July 25, 1883

[263] *Teedale Mercury*, October 10, 1883

[264] PC James Thompson was lodging with William and Elizabeth Fatkin who lived next door to their daughter Mary Jane and her husband Jack Marquis (See p.170)

with a stick. In court, Coatsworth strenuously denied the charge and called a number of witnesses to support his claim that he did not have a stick with him at the time. Faced with conflicting testimony, the magistrates chose not to give the benefit of the doubt to PC Thompson and discharged the defendant.[265]

In October 1883, he was charged with practising as an auctioneer without a license. The Excise Officer, Mr William Gibson who was stationed in Wolsingham, explained that he had attended a sheep and lamb sale at Hamsterley on Sept 12th where Mr Coatsworth acted as auctioneer and sold two lots of lambs. When he asked to see the auctioneer's license, the defendant claimed to have forwarded the money for the license to the collector in Sunderland on the previous day, but it had not arrived. It transpired however that, far from being "in the post", the license application was not taken out until a month later. As this was the second offence committed by William Coatsworth, a heavy fine of £25 was imposed; in default, three months imprisonment.[266]

By 1891, William was described in the census as a "Casterrater", i.e., a castrator of livestock – and a month after the census, he was the one who found the body of Jack Marquis in the hayloft. By 1901, his much more impressive title was "Veterinary Surgeon", although whether he had a license for this exalted position is doubtful.

William Coatsworth died in Hamsterley in 1904 at the age of 72.

10-3 Victorian Clipping Day: Sheep in the pens in the background, the shepherd's wife providing refreshment, a heap of fleeces in the foreground, and a few shearers - a much smaller scale than at Pennington Farm.[267]

[265] *Northern Echo*, May 21, 1880
[266] *York Herald*, October 23, 1883
[267] *Illustrated London News,* July 18, 1846

The Teesdale Bard returns to Pennington

On Thursday July 3 the following year, Richard Watson paid another visit to a clipping day at Pennington:-

> PENNINGTON SHEEP SHEARING.
>
> Another year has passed away since I gave, in the Mercury, an account of Pennington Sheep Shearing, and the same busy time has again come round. Having been invited to be present on the interesting occasion, I bent my steps, on Thursday morning, the 3rd inst., to the old farmhouse on the moor. The weather was hot and sultry, the sun blazing from a clear sky, and I keenly felt his oppressive influence; but, after passing the Woodland Coke Ovens, and diverging from the dusty road, I felt some relief by walking in the green fields, my olfactory nerves being gratified by the fragrance of clover, hyacinths, and other wild flowers, which enhanced the pleasure of my journey.
>
> Yet, when I reached Black Ling Hole, I was in a state of perspiration almost as bad as a smelter or iron puddler in the midst of his hot occupation. Owing to the long drought the brook had dwindled down to a slender rill, as clear I should think, as the brook of which Elijah drank when the streams of Israel were almost dried up, in the reign of wicked Ahab. I sat down to rest beneath a shady tree, and was beginning to feel tolerably comfortable when, glancing on the ground, I saw myriads of busy ants moving about in all directions, no doubt enjoying the heat and sunshine to me so oppressive; and I quickly rose from my seat, fearing that they might soon direct their attentions to myself.
>
> Continuing my course northward, I soon arrived at Pennington farmhouse, where I was kindly welcomed by Mrs Simpson, the worthy mistress. After a short rest, I went to the scene of the clipping operations. All were as busy as bees on a summer day; the voices of the clippers, markers, and those bringing in the sheep, with the loud barking of dogs, making a din not easily forgotten. Several of my old Teesdale friends were present, and gave vent to their satisfaction by a loud cheer when I made my appearance. However, two old patriarchs I missed from the throng, namely, Mr G. Richardson (late of Stotley), my much respected friend and godfather, who has since succumbed to this relentless hand of death, leaving Teesdale to lament the loss of one of her best men. The other friend missing was Mr Dougald Carmichael, late of Neighbour Moor House. Never shall I forget the evening when two musicians and myself went from Little Eggleshope Mine Shop, bent on a convivial night at his dwelling. When approaching Cloudy Beck we discovered his house in flames; large tongues of fire shot up from the thatched roof, illuminating the surrounding wilderness. When we arrived at the burning building, the old man was pacing round his desolate home, saving what he could from the devouring element. "This is a sad job, chiels,"[268] said he, as we came near "nae music the nicht but the crackling o' the fire; but we mun ae put up wie disappointment when we canna mend it." He is still living, and looks quite hale, I am told, considering his great age.[269]

---

[268] Chiel (which rhymes with "peel") is a Scots term for "young man".

[269] Dougal Carmichael died in 1888 at Redford aged 89 and is buried in Hamsterley Churchyard.

An excellent dinner was provided by the worthy hostess; T. Garbutt., Esq., at the head or the table, doing the carving business. Toward evening dark clouds began to hover near, and vivid flashes of lightning, accompanied by loud peals of thunder, brought the clipping to a hasty close, to be resumed next day. However, a very pleasant day was experienced by all present, consisting of both sexes, and we think great credit is due to Mrs Simpson for her hospitality, and for the admirable way in which all the details were carried out.

RICHARD WATSON[270]

Copley Lane End, Woodland,

The "two old patriarchs" referred to by Richard Watson were George Richardson of Stotley Farm and Dougal Carmichael of Neighbour Moor.

George Richardson was a Teesdale-born farmer who died at the age of 75, a week after the clipping day and a few days before Richard's report was published. He was a noted breeder of black-faced sheep: in the notice of an auction of his sheep in 1877 at Middleton, it was stated that:-

The Auctioneer wishes to call special attention to the above class of sheep, as they are from a good sound heath; and Mr Richardson having so frequently taken first honours at almost all the agricultural shows in this northern district with his black-faced sheep, the above sale may be regarded by Graziers and intending purchasers an opportunity seldom to be met with.[271]

10-4 Wood Carving of Richard Watson by Phil Townsend (www.sculptedart.co.uk)

[270] *Teesdale Mercury*, July 16, 1884
[271] *Teesdale Mercury,* April 4, 1877

Richard Watson greatly admired his 'godfather' George,[272] as evidenced by an elegy published in *The Mercury*, two verses of which follow:-

Ye neighbouring moors, clad with brown ling.
From whence the becking red grouse spring,
Where oft he went, his sheep to tend,
Near lone Hope House and Middle End,
No more your dark, bleak wilds he'll tread,
He's gone, - George Richardson is dead.

A friend of mine, too: my rough muse
Could joy still in his breast infuse;
He like a parent look'd on me,
My godfather indeed was he,
I saw him laid in his last bed,
My friend George Richardson is dead.[273]

RICHARD WATSON
Woodland, July 19th, 1884

Argyll-born shepherd Dougald Carmichael was 85 years old and despite spending many years in County Durham, still spoke with a strong Scots dialect. No doubt he would have always dealt with the "sad jobs" of life by stoically reminding himself that "we mun ae put up wie disappointment when we canna mend it." He died in 1888 at Redford aged 89 years, and, although he was not accorded an elegy for posterity, he does have a memorial stone in Hamsterley Churchyard where he was buried.

10-5 Henry King Spark, the Bard's benefactor (detail from a painting by William Rathwell, Darlington Borough Art Collection)

A Hard Life and an Agonising Death

Richard Watson was never suited to the hard physical labour he had to endure throughout his life. Turned 50 when he wrote of his visits to Pennington, he was then living at Copley Lane Head and working at Woodland Pit. Soon afterwards, he moved to Baldersdale to work at Hury Reservoir, then to the whinstone quarries of Messrs Ord & Maddion near Middleton-in-Teesdale, and finally and fatefully to work as a labourer in the erection of Holwick Hall for Mr Cosmo Bonsor, the Conservative MP for Wimbledon. It was at Holwick in 1890 that he sustained a crushing injury to his toe. Several months of agonising suffering followed. After his toe and then his foot had been amputated, a fund was raised to send him to Edinburgh Infirmary for the best treatment available. Two days after his leg was amputated, his suffering was over:-

> ...after the operation, (he) was conscious, cheerful, and resigned. At the moment of death he kissed his wife, and, with radiant face, pointed to visions in the air, and said, "See, see!" But only he could see them. Were they not the visions of his life—the

[272] George Richardson was Richard's uncle through marriage.
[273] *Teesdale Mercury,* July 23, 1884

> Angels who had guided him through suffering to perfection, and now led him to his Father's Home? So passed away the Poet.[274]

The Northern Echo reported thus:-

> Sad, very sad, are the circumstances of the death of Richard Watson, the Teesdale Poet. His life indeed was sad…with true poetic gifts, and loving his native hills and woods as only a poet could, his career has been one long struggle with terrible poverty." Since his accident, now nine months ago, he has been bedfast…and suffered great agony and depression of mind." The newspaper printed the last words he wrote – to his benefactor Henry King Spark[275]:-

> Blythe summer now is on the wane;
> The beauties of its genial reign
> Have all been lost to me.
> Green fields, green woods, and shady bowers,
> Clear rippling streams and lovely flowers,
> Alas! I cannot see.
> I often from my window look
> On a green mead close by;
> Though but a poor restricted view
> 'Tis pleasant to my eye,
> It charms me; it warms me,
> And gives my mind relief;
> It lightens and brightens
> My load of woe and grief.[276]

The poet's body was brought back from Edinburgh for burial at Middleton-in-Teesdale, "that little pastoral town, so picturesque and quaint, nestling in the embrace of the hills, and lulled by the meandering Tees."[277] An appreciation in the *Mercury* noted:-

> Richard Watson, the Bard of Teesdale, was buried at Middleton-in-Teesdale on Wednesday last….. Like most men with anything in them worth having he inherited his genius from his mother (Rebecca), who belonged to the good old Walton family of Weardale. At ten years of age he wrote verses and pricked music to the wondering delight of his mother, who encouraged her boy with tender deeds of love, and assuring words of hope. This, the happy time of his life, was the forerunner of the hardships that followed it. The early death of his father, and the necessities of a large family, drove Richard, at an early age, into the lead mines, and, when this employment failed him, he tramped and starved, and laboured alternately.
>
> To deplore their loss he leaves a widow and children, and, to extend his fame, a large number of poems, many of them being of a higher order than those already published in three volumes issued during the last twenty years, and which are now out of print,

[274] *Teesdale Mercury*, October 14, 1891

[275] Henry King Spark was a radical coal merchant and owner of the *Darlington & Stockton Times* who waged a battle with the Pease family for political power in South Durham in the 1860s.

[276] *Northern Echo*, October 5, 1891

[277] *Ibid.*

and only obtainable at enhanced prices. Such in brief is the life of Richard Watson, the Bard of Teesdale. He was physically unequal to hard manual labour, and that which fell to him was hard, grinding, and crushing. Latterly, under the care of a friend, his labours and anxieties were much eased, and there was a prospect of relieving him altogether from manual labour, and giving full freedom and scope to his literary powers. He possessed engineering skill and scientific knowledge, but the poet's vocation was his, and all else was distasteful to him.

A vein of religion runs through his writings, and his reliance was more on providence than in himself. "Consider the lilies of the field how they grow; they toil not neither do they spin," was not to him a mere sentiment, as with most people, but a divine reality....Burns could have revelled in prosperity, but be was a poet, and must suffer, and be poor, and our own Bard of Teesdale might have forced his way through paths of worldly success, but he, too, must be a sacrifice, and take what might fall upon him, and it was a cruel share. Poor mother! You little knew when you encouraged your boy's muse that you were lending an impetus to a career that would be so hard, so rugged, and so sorrowful! "Ah, ah," says Mr Worldly-wise, "it was a sad case of misdirected talent." But, Sir, it is to misdirected talent such as Richard Watson's in the past, as well as in the present, that you owe the pleasant life you cherish and enjoy. All poets, great and small, are, according to their degree, teachers and pioneers. Richard Watson, hungry, ragged, and despised, yet ever singing the songs that purify, exalt, and ennoble, has fulfilled his mission, and gone to his reward. It was his wish that his poor maimed body should rest in the churchyard so sacred to him in his native dale, and it was a consolation to him under his sufferings, and, in the hour of death, to know that the friend upon whom he relied would see his wish fulfilled, and honour and respect were paid by all classes of the people of Middleton and the dales to the memory of the poet.

The Rev. John Milner, the Rector, was accompanied to the Church gates by the Rev. W. R. Bell, Vicar of Laithkirk, an old friend of the poet, where they lovingly received the corpse. The principal bearer was Mr Charles Parsons, who, in other ways, has been very generous and attentive to the bereaved family in their hour of need. It is also pleasing to notice that our brethren of the press have wakened up to a recognition of the poet, which hitherto has mainly devolved upon ourselves.

The funeral procession was led by Mr Spark and Mr Granger, the coffin, borne by hand, and piled with wreaths, followed. Next it was the poet's widow, his four daughters, two sons-in-law, his sisters (Mrs Hunt, Mrs Anderson, and Mrs Martha Littlefair), his niece (Miss Rebecca Hunt), and nephews (Mr John Hunt and Mr Joseph Hunt), his cousin (Miss Watson), and other relatives.

It was a striking and suggestive sight to see that large and imposing funeral, consisting of all classes, from far and near, in honour of the poor, sorrow-stricken, neglected poet. The little town itself had a subdued aspect, and there was a general feeling that a great loss had been sustained. [278]

---

[278] *Teesdale Mercury*. October 14, 1891. Unattributed but undoubtedly written by William Morley Egglestone – he attributes the Teesdale Poet's genius to his Weardale genes…

10-6 Middleton-in-Teesdale: "The little pastoral town, so picturesque and quaint, nestling in the embrace of the hills, and lulled by the meandering Tees"

Weardale's Salute to the Teesdale Bard

Richard Watson was a proud Teesdale man who was appreciated beyond his native dale, not least in Weardale where William Morley Egglestone sold many copies of his books of poetry. WME was a great admirer of the Teesdale Bard and 10 years after his death, wrote a warm and fulsome tribute to him which was published in the *Newcastle Weekly Courant* and reprinted in the *Teesdale Mercury.*[279] He began:-

> As the Teesdale Bard has gone from amongst us and hung up his harp, it is a pleasure to keep green the memory of one who from the very depth of his heart sung the song of his native dale.
>
> He thus sung of himself:-
>
> From Nature's self my muse doth spring,
> Though roughly clad, to her I'll cling;
> And where the Tees rolls meandering
> The woods among,
> I'll tune my mountain lyre and sing
> My rustic song.

[279] *Teesdale Mercury,* April 20, 1898

He noted that Richard Watson's style resembled that of Robbie Burns and that "when soaring on the wings of his Muse he was oblivious to the cares and troubles of the world."

10-7 William Morley Egglestone

William Morley Egglestone concluded by reproducing the epitaph written by the Teesdale Bard a few days before his death:-

Ye lovers of the muse draw near,
And o'er this green grave drop a tear;
He - named the Teesdale Bard - lies here
In death's domain.
Who'll tune your native lyre to cheer
Your hearts again?
The beauties of his native Tees,
The rocks, and dells, and stately trees,
And cat'racts grand: such scenes as these
His soul admired.
They were his sermons, and with ease
His muse inspired.
A poor, hard-working rustic bard,
His lot indeed was crook'd and hard:
Of comforts wealth bestows, debarred;
A load of woes,
To suffering worth 'tis the reward
This world bestows.

William Simpson and Mary Hankey

Perhaps it was at a clipping day that William Simpson junior developed a romantic attachment to Mary Hankey of nearby Ayhope Shield Farm (See next chapter).

And the kind hospitable mistress now
Hastes to prepare the well-provided feast.
The table's set, and all acquaintance come
To share the healthful food and smiling ale.
The shearers put aside the fleecing-blade
And join in cheerful chat. The young and strong
In rural pastime spend the joyous hours…
In feats well pleasing to the rustic throng.[280]

[280] Extract from *"Sheep Shearing"*, a poem published in *The Ladies Cabinet of Fashion, Music and Romance*, July 1, 1849

At the clipping days the hard work was followed by singing and dancing in the evenings, providing an ideal opportunity for the eligible young men of the neighbourhood to become better acquainted with the local "rustic beauties". William and Mary had one child, Mary, just before they were married in December 1884 at Wolsingham.

Physically and temperamentally, William and Mary were quite different. Somewhat portly by middle age, and like his sisters Eliza and Elizabeth, William was diminutive and quick-tempered. Mary on the other hand was very tall and thin, known locally as "Lanky Hankey". And the photograph suggests a rather taciturn lady.

After Annie Simpson died in 1885, her son William continued farming at Pennington and brother John moved to East Rackwood Hill Farm, Hamsterley, with his new wife, Mary née Foster from Laithkirk. In 1901, William and Mary were at Pennington Farm with 6 children: Mary, John Ernest, Elizabeth Euphemia, Emma Eliza, Margaret Maria, and William Siwood. The family chose "Siwood" as a middle name for William, born in 1897. This is an unusual name: could it be that the Simpsons were honouring, or indicating a link with, the Surtees family who owned Pennington Farm? Originally the Surtees family were called "Siward", a name of Anglo-Viking origin, but acquired the name Surtees when they settled by the River Tees at Dinsdale near Darlington. A familial link with the Surtees family is plausible given that many of the Simpsons were land-owning gentry.

10-8 William Simpson and MaryHankey, with their daughter Euphemia

In the summer of 1901, Pennington Farm and East Rackwood Hill Farm were advertised to let, with both properties available from Spring, 1902. William Simpson and family then moved to Richmond, North Yorkshire, Charles Proud (see p.227) took the tenancy at Pennington, and James Jewitt farmed at East Rackwood Hill. Following James' death in 1905 at the age of 50, son Josiah Jewitt took over the running of the farm.

11. AYHOPE SHIELD AND THE MEETING OF THE GRAINS

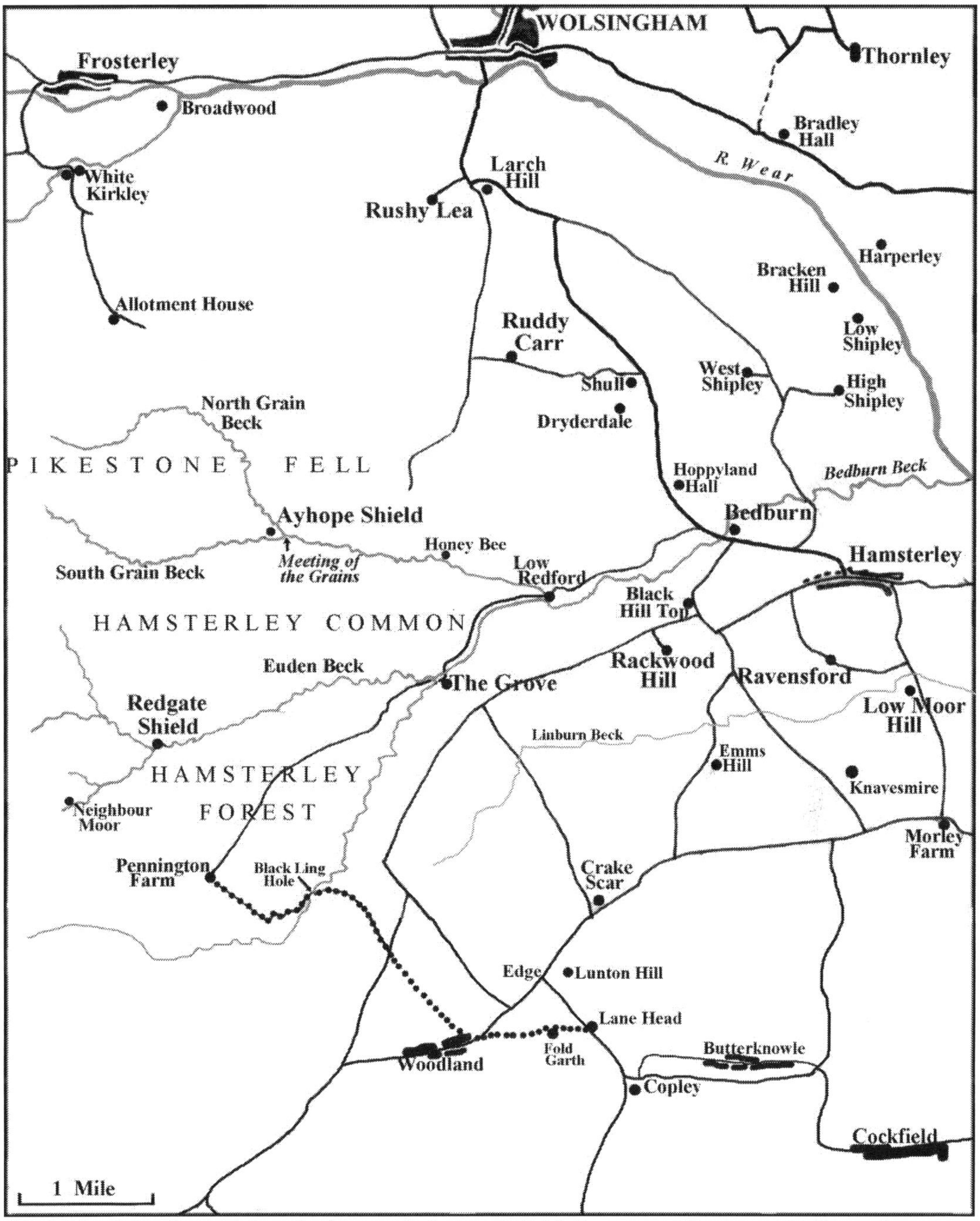

11-1 The Meeting of the Grains at Ayhope Shield Farm on Pikestone Fell can be seen centre left on the map. Ayhope Shield sheep farm is now derelict, a pile of stones. In the south-west corner of the map is Pennington Farm where g.grandmother Eliza Simpson née Beadle was raised. Also shown is Richard Watson's route to Pennington from Lane Head (See p.185).

"Ape Shield – it's where the Hankeys come from"

When FJS spoke of his picnic trips during WW1 to "Ape Shield" (See p.213), he was referring to Ayhope Shield, and he knew the Hankey family had farmed there even though they had moved to West Shipley Farm before he was born. Ayhope Shield is situated on the lower reaches of Pikestone Fell at the northern edge of Hamsterley Common, 4 miles due West of Hamsterley, on a spur at the confluence of the North Grain Beck and the South Grain Beck, known as Meeting of the Grains. The Meeting of the Grains marks the beginning of Ayhope Beck, a tributary of Bedburn Beck which itself is a tributary of the River Wear.

There have been many variations of the name over the years: since 1700, in addition to Ayhope Shield, Eileen Perkins née Hankey, a descendant of the 19th Century tenants of Ayhope Shield, found: Eape Shel, Aip Sheal, Eapeshell, Hapeshield, ApeShil, Haiphope Shield, Hayhope Shield, and Ape Shield. Other variants are Ayrehope Shield and Rapesheeld[281] The "shield" part comes from "shieling", a rough, sometimes temporary hut or shelter used by people tending cattle on high or remote ground.

Along with nearby Ruddy Carr, Ayhope Shield was farmed in the early part of the twentieth century by Tom Sanderson of Broomley and before that for several generations by the Hankey family, and before that, the Watsons.

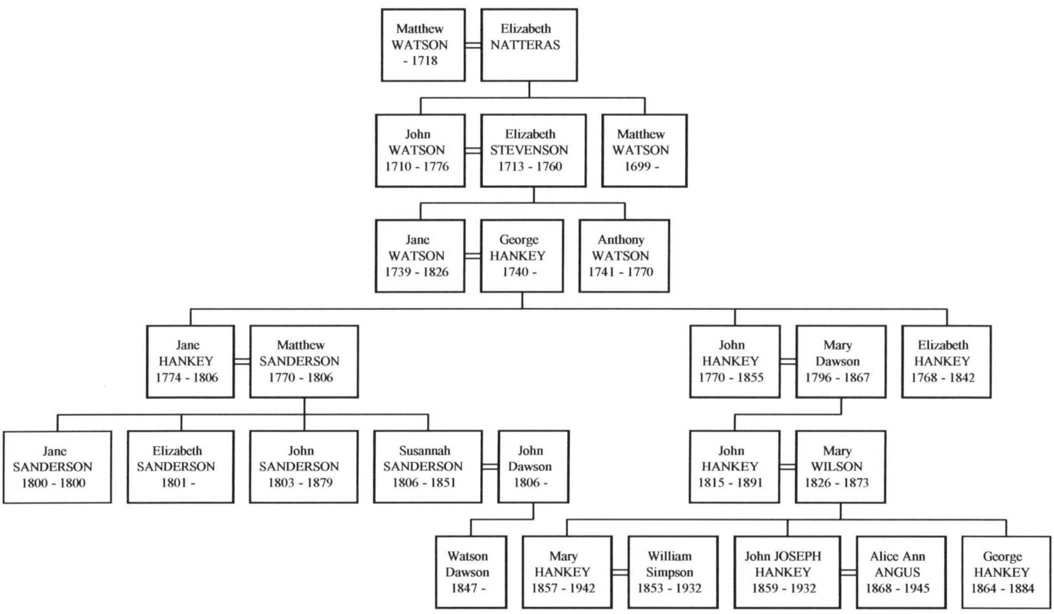

Figure 11-2 The Watson and Hankey families of Ayhope Shield. It is likely that Susannah Sanderson, and perhaps her sisters and brother, spent time there after their parents died in 1806 (See p.200).

The Watsons farmed Ayhope Shield from at least the 1690s. Matthew Watson Snr (b circa 1670) was followed by his sons Matthew Jnr and John as tenants. By the 1760s, John Watson was farming Ayhope Shield with his son Anthony.

---

281 Surtees, H.C. (1929) *History of the Parish of Wolsingham.*

Weardale winters were frequently severe in the old days, but an entry in the burial register at Wolsingham in mid-summer 1768 shows that harsh weather was not just a feature of the winter months. The register records that on 27 June of that year:-

> A poor old woman and a girl about 10 years of age, both belonging to Newcastle, found dead on the south common a little West from Pikestone, supposed to have perished on the 14th of this month which said day was so stormy and the cold so severe as to kill a great many horses and sheep.

It was noted that neither coroner nor jury was summoned, suggesting no suspicious circumstances, although the sad case does arouse curiosity. How was it known that they were from Newcastle, were they known in the parish, where were they travelling to and from, and had they been reported missing? As to who found the two unfortunate travellers, one possibility is that it was Anthony Watson from nearby Ayhope Shield as he scoured the fell in search of sheep that had gone missing after the storm. The remote place where the victims were found is about 1½ miles from the equally remote Ayhope Shield.

After Anthony Watson's death in 1770, it seems that 60 year-old John Watson was joined at the farm by his daughter Jane and her husband George Hankey who had been farming at nearby Crow's Nest, Hamsterley. When John Watson died in 1776, George Hankey assumed the tenancy.

George Hankey took part with other parishioners in the Riding of the Bounds of Wolsingham Parish in September, 1796.[282] The purpose of the Riding the Bounds was to inspect the boundary markers and reaffirm the parish boundaries so that landowners, tenants, and other interested parties knew exactly who owned the land. The account of the 1796 ride on the second day begins:-

> Beginning at the outer corner of Mr Jasper Harrison's out Allotment, formerly Greenthorn Currack. From thence crossing the road leading to Redford through Hart Soulings and down the bank to the meeting of the North and South Grain Burns under Ape Shield. NB, at the meeting of the Burns, the Rev William Wilson read a prayer. J Nicholson with the rest of the company sang old 100 Psalm.

The Canons of the Third Prebend

In medieval times, Ayhope Shield, along with Sacristan Heugh, was owned by the Sacrist at Durham Cathedral.[283] They were described as "two compliamentary (sic) halves of the same manor", which may indicate that there was seasonal migration between the two farms. Eileen Perkins' father farmed at Fulforth Farm and their land adjoined Sacriston Heugh, and she wonders if her ancestors at Ayhope Shield walked stock the long journey (about 15 miles as the crow flies) between the Sacrist's two properties and whether they crossed the land at Fulforth. It is possible that Sacriston Heugh provided a staging post, with the ultimate destination being the market at Newcastle, a further 12 miles away.

In the 18th and 19th centuries, Ayhope Shield was the property of the Dean and Chapter of Durham Cathedral and the rent from the farm was allocated to the Canon of the Third

---

282 From information held at Durham County Records Office, accessed by Eileen Perkins née Hankey.

283 *Durham Cathedral Priory as a Landowner and Landlord 1290-1540.*

Prebend in the cathedral. On October 10, 1789, George Hankey paid £10.16s. for one year's rent for Ayhope Shield and Allotments to the executors of the late Dr Chaytor.

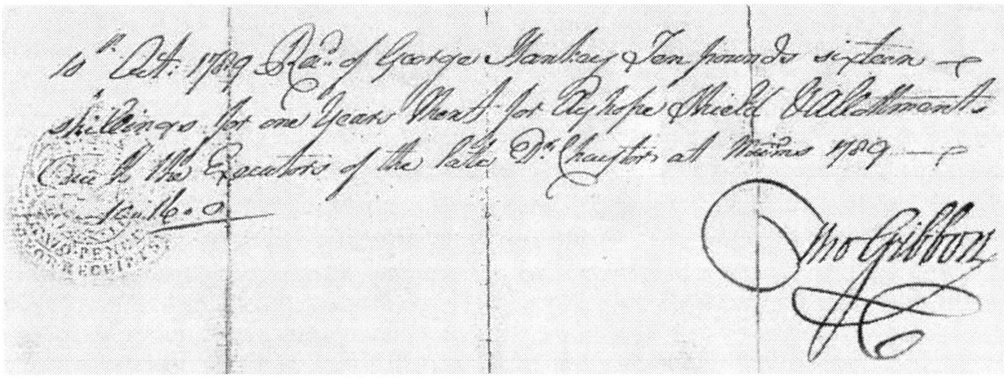

11-3 Rent Receipt for Ayhope Shield, 1789

10th Oct 1789 Recd of George Hankey Ten Pounds sixteen
shillings for one Years Rent for Ayhope Shield & Allot(t)ments
Due to the Executors of the late Dr Chaytor at Micms[284] 1789
10.16.0 Thomas Gibbon

Ordained in 1754, Dr Henry Chaytor LLD became vicar of Catterick and Croft before his appointment as Canon of the Third Prebend in 1782, at which point he received the rent from Ayhope Shield. He died in 1789[285], and the 1789 rent from the farm was assigned to his estate. Subsequent Third Prebends continued to receive the income from Ayhope Shield which remained at £10.16s until at least 1832. When George Hankey died in1805, his wife Jane held the tenancy for several years and was succeeded by her son John Hankey Snr (1770- 1855). With his mother now in old age, John employed a housekeeper, and it was not long before he and Mary Dawson entered into a 'common-law' relationship. In 1815, when John was 45 and Mary just 19, John Hankey Jnr was born at Ayhope Shield. Although they never married, it was to be a life-long union between John and Mary.

John Hankey Snr's sister Jane married Matthew Sanderson in 1799, and they farmed at Harrowbank in the parish of Stanhope, a short distance from Guy's Close where Matthew's sister Jane farmed with her husband James Vickers. Their first child Jane Sanderson was born on 8th February 1800. Next came Elizabeth in 1801, then John in 1803, and finally Susannah in 1806. Tragically, within a few weeks of Susannah's birth, the children were orphans. Matthew Sanderson died on April 19th at the age of 36 and less than two weeks later, 31 years-old Jane, most likely stricken with the same illness, died on May Day.[286]

So within the space of a fortnight, the four Sanderson children had become orphans, a fact which would have helped refocus family members' attention away from the sadness of loss and more towards how they might secure the futures of the fatherless and now motherless infants.

---

[284] "Micms", with a loop above the "m" is shorthand for "Michaelmas", falling on September 29th.

[285] *Gentleman's Magazine*, 1789, lix (1), 577.

[286] Thomas Sanderson of Snapegate died on May 3, 1806, almost certainly the victim of the same illness that took his brother and sister-in-law. Six days after his death, his daughter Mary was born, and within the month, his widow Elizabeth née Robson was dead.

11-4 The Sanderson family as imagined on the hills above Stanhope shortly before the death of Matthew and Jane in 1806. Baby Susannah in her mother's arms, and from left, John aged 3, Elizabeth aged 5 and Jane aged 6years.

The guiding principles had long been understood:-

> Plato says that "Orphans should be placed under the care of public guardians. Men should have a fear of the loneliness of orphans and of the souls of their departed parents. A man should love the unfortunate orphan of whom he is guardian as if he were his own child. He should be as careful and as diligent in the management of the orphan's property as of his own or even more careful still"[287]

At the beginning of the nineteenth century, when children were orphaned, a court could appoint guardians who might also have to provide a bond to the court as a guarantee that they would conscientiously carry out their duties. The bond was equal to or double the value of the estate to be administered.[288]

The terms of the guardianship of the Sanderson orphans are detailed in the probate records:-

> Whereas Matthew Sanderson, late of the Parish of Stanhope in the County and Diocese of Durham, Farmer, died in the month of April last past, leaving behind him Jane Sanderson, his widow him surviving, who is also since dead, and also Jane Sanderson, Elizabeth Sanderson, John Sanderson and Susannah Sanderson, his natural and lawful only children and the only persons interested in the distribution of his personal estate. And whereas the said children are now in their infancy, to wit the said Jane Sanderson of the age of six years and upwards, Elizabeth Sanderson the age of five years and upwards, John Sanderson of the age of three years and upwards, and Susannah Sanderson under the age of one year, and therefore by law incapable of electing a Guardian or doing any legal act whatsoever in their own names. And whereas Jane Vickers, wife of James Vickers, Farmer of Stanhope aforesaid and Elizabeth Wier, wife of William Wier, Farmer of Newland Side[289] in the Parish of Stanhope aforesaid are the natural and lawful Aunts and next of kin of the said infants.

[287] *The Catholic Encyclopaedia*, Vol XI

[288] Herber, Mark D (1997) *Ancestral Trails: The Complete Guide to British Genealogy and Family History*, London, Sutton Publishing/SOG, p.193.

[289] William Wier farmed at Broadwood which was just south of the River Wear near Frosterley

Now know all Men by these Presents that we the above-named Jane Vickers and Elizabeth Wier, by and with the consent and approbation of the said James Vickers and William Wier, our said husbands....do herby accept of the Curation and Guardianship of Jane Sanderson, Elizabeth Sanderson, John Sanderson and Susannah Sanderson...during their respective Minorities, and more especially to obtain and take upon ourselves Letters of Administration of....the Goods, Chattels and Credits of the said Matthew Sanderson deceased, for the use and benefit of the said infants during their Minorities...
In Witness thereof we have hereunto set our hands and seals this fourteenth day of October in the Year of our Lord one thousand eight hundred and six.
Signed Sealed and Delivered
The marks of Jane Vickers and Elizabeth Wier, followed by the signatures of James Vickers and William Wier.[290]

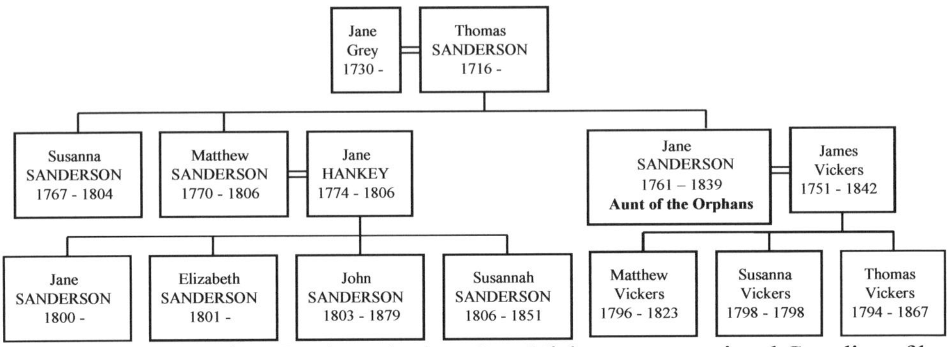

Figure 11-5 Matthew Sanderson's sister Jane Vickers was appointed Guardian of her nephew and nieces.

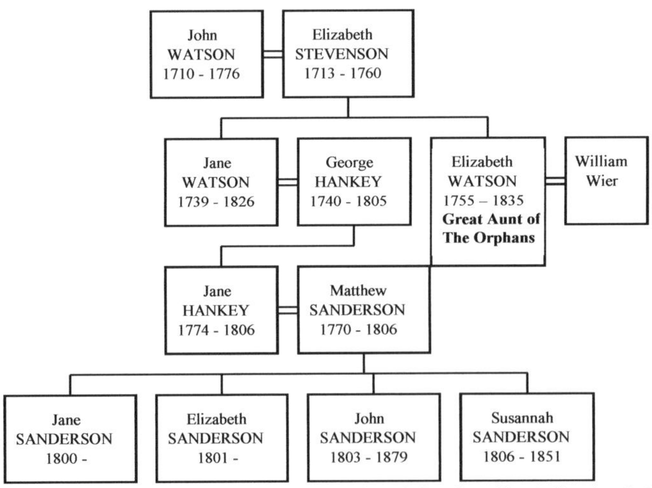

Figure 11-6 From Jane Hankey's side of the family, Elizabeth Wier née Watson was appointed as Guardian.

[290] *Acceptance of Guardianship*, October 14, 1806 (DPRI/3/1806/A126/3-5, Durham University Library).

The next-of-kin identified to act as guardians were Aunt Jane Vickers née Sanderson, and Great Aunt Elizabeth Wier née Watson. Because their husbands held the assets, they together with worthy family friends James Wall and John Pearson, were "held and firmly bound unto the … Lord Bishop of Durham ….in the Penal Sum of Three Hundred Pounds of good and lawful money" to ensure that the terms of the guardianship were properly observed. The Guardians' Oath was as follows:-

> The oath of each of you is that you will well and truly execute and perform the Duty and Office of a Tutor or Guardian to Jane Sanderson, Elizabeth Sanderson, John Sanderson, and Susannah Sanderson, Infants, that you will religiously and virtuously educate and bring up and allow sufficient Meat, Drink, Clothes and Learning and all other necessaries suitable to the Quality and Estate during their Minority. That you will manage and improve their Estate with all care, diligence and industry, and make a true and just account thereof when you shall be lawfully called. So help you God.[291]

In the event of failure to meet the obligations to the children, the penal sum of £300 would be forfeited.

Precisely how and where the orphans were raised is not known, but it is assumed that Jane Vickers and Elizabeth Wier, with the active support of other family members, ensured that they had a good upbringing. The Vickers family living adjacent to Harrowbank at Guy's Close are likely to have provided immediate care for the orphans, but both the Vickers and Wier families had teenage children at home who would have been able to provide much-needed support and companionship.

The Hankey family at Ayhope Shield will have played a part in their upbringing, as can be deduced from a letter sent by Richard Glass to John Hankey Snr in 1828.

The Letter from Richard Glass

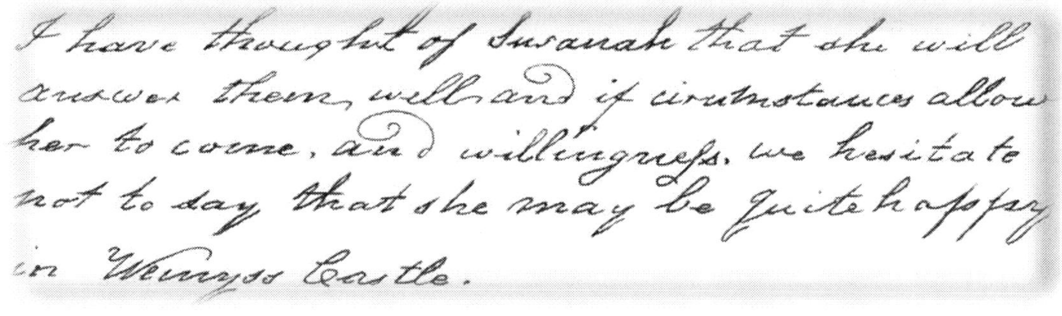
I have thought of Susanah that she will answer them, well and if circumstances allow her to come, and willingness, we hesitate not to say that she may be quite happy in Wemyss Castle.

11-7 Richard Glass wrote to John Hankey Snr in 1828 about Susannah Sanderson.

By the time Richard Glass and his family moved to South Bedburn in 1817, it appears that 11 year-old Susannah Sanderson was at Ayhope Shield, working as a dairy maid for her uncle John Hankey.

Richard Glass was born in c.1776 at Wooler in Northumberland. In 1810, he married Ann Taylor from Whittingham, a few miles south of Wooler and worked as an agricultural

[291] Administration Bond, 23 December 1806, penal sum £300, (DPRI/3/1806/A127) Durham University Library.

labourer and shepherd in North Northumberland for the next seven years. By the time he moved to South Bedburn, he had four children, including seven year-old Alison and five year-old Jane.

Richard and his family were living near Ayhope Shield from 1817 to the latter part of 1825 when Richard moved to the County of Fife to work as a shepherd at Wemyss Castle. William Glass, perhaps a brother or cousin of Richard, worked as a shepherd at Wemyss and married local girl Agnes Smart, and it is likely that he recruited Richard to take his place at Wemyss when he (William) moved to Jedburgh in 1825. Richard quickly established himself in Fife and in 1828 his help was enlisted to recruit a new dairy maid for the Estate when the incumbent got married. His first thought was to write to John Hankey at Ayhope Shield, enquiring about the availability of Susannah Sanderson for the position:-

> Wemyss Castle
> 30th January, 1828
> Dear Friend,
>
> I take this opportunity of writing you, stating that we are all well, and hoping these my few lines will have the fortune to find you all well. I have to state also that our Dairy Maid has got married and as I have been requested by both the Captain and his Lady to endeavour to get one from the South Country. I have thought of Susannah that she will answer them well, and if circumstances allow her to come, and willingness, we hesitate not to say that she may be quite happy in Wemyss Castle. She will have the charge of 3 or four Cows, and the rest of her work is in the house. The wage of the last one was 7£ but the Lady has told me that for 1£ or 2 more, she will not differ, and that her passage either in the Steam boat or upon the Coach will be paid from Newcastle to Wemyss Castle. My Captain and his Lady are very honourable, they have got but one child. They have a nurse for the child, a Ladies' Maid, a Chamber Maid, a Cook and Kitchen Maid, his and her personal Laundry Maids, a Butler, a Footman, 2 Grooms. But although we have these given on account of the place, yet we have no desire of wishing her to come against the will of any of you. Please give my respects to all my old acquaintances, and let me know how Thos.Gibben and his wife are doing, and also about Thomas Price. Aly and Jane send their best respects to Susannah and all, and would be quite happy if she would come. The Captain & her Ladyship are to set off for London on Monday and will not return until May Day. Let me know if Jane Scott is still with Squire Surtees. Let me know how the markets are, and the news of the place.
>
> Sir,
> I am
> With due respect
> Yours truly
> Richard Glass
> NB, She will have to be in place here at Mayday if she be coming
> Write me an answer immediately whither or not she will come.
> Direct To Richard Glass, shepherd
> Wemyss Castle
> County of Fife

The content of the letter from Richard to John Hankey suggests that the two families had got to know each other well during the eight or so years that the Glass family was in South Bedburn (the South Country). The life of a shepherd was quite solitary for the most part but there would be ample opportunity for socialising at market days and at clipping days (see p.185), so the fact that he made quite a few friends in the area suggests that Richard was sociable and outgoing in nature. To have established such close links with the Hankey family, the Glass family must have lived near to the remote farm at Ayhope Shield. Hamsterley baptismal records confirm that Richard and Ann were living at Redgate Shield when three of their children were baptised. This sheep farm was just over a mile from Ayhope Shield, across Hamsterley Common (See map on page 197).

11-8 Ayhope Shield in circa 1828 - as it was when Richard Glass lived nearby. In the foreground is a footbridge over the South Grain Beck which would have been used by visitors from Redgate Shield, Pennington Farm and The Grove. (Courtesy of Eileen Perkins née Hankey)

Squire Surtees is mentioned in the letter. Robert Surtees (1782-1857) owned The Grove, a hunting lodge in Hamsterley Forest about 1½ miles from Ayhope Shield and less than two miles along Euden Beck from Redgate Shield. Richard enquires about Jane Scott who would have worked at The Grove for Robert Surtees when Richard was working in the neighbourhood. He also wants to know how Thomas Gibben and his wife are doing, and Thomas Price.

11-9 The Grove, hunting lodge of the Surtees Family

A rent receipt from Ayhope Shield (See p.200) reveals that in 1789, a Thomas Gibbon collected the rent from Ayhope Shield for the Canon of the Third Prebend at Durham Cathedral - for the estate of the recently deceased Rev Dr Chaytor. This Thomas Gibbon, whose family originated from the Hamsterley area, was buried in October 1796 at Durham St Oswalds: perhaps there is a family connection with Thomas Gibben (sic) mentioned in the 1828 letter.

Who Thomas Price was is uncertain, but it is possible if unlikely that he is related to Rev Dr Robert Price and may have come to know Ayhope Shield when the Rev Dr was Canon of the Third Prebend 1794-1804.

Richard Glass conveys Aly (Alison) and Jane's best respects in particular to Susannah. Alison and Jane were 7 and 9 years of age respectively when they moved from Northumberland to Redgate Shield, and Susannah Sanderson, aged 11 at the time, may have befriended them when they first arrived in the locality, helping them settle in to the unfamiliar surroundings. It was not long after the birth of Ann Glass at Redgate Shield in the Spring of 1825 that the Glass family moved to Wemyss Castle.

The Captain and his Lady

Richard writes of "My Captain and his Lady". The Captain was James Erskine Wemyss (1789-1854). After a distinguished naval career, he retired in 1814 and returned to Wemyss Castle with the rank of Captain. He replaced his ailing father as Member of Parliament for Fifeshire in 1820 and inherited extensive Fifeshire estates when his father died two years later. In 1850, four years before his death, he was made a Rear-Admiral.

In 1826, not long after the Glass family moved to Wemyss, James Wemyss married Lady Emma Hay, daughter of William, 17th Earl of Erroll. In the letter of 1828, Richard notes that the Captain and his wife "have but one child". Frances Harriet Wemyss was born in 1827, a few months before the letter was written.

The tone of the letter indicates that Richard is more than happy with his position at Wemyss Castle, describing the Captain and his Lady as "very honourable" and no doubt pleased that they have entrusted him with finding a new dairymaid. He hints at their generosity when mentioning the likely wage that Susannah would receive, and he lists the numerous staff to reassure her that there would be many others to share the duties of working at such a large estate.

Captain James Wemyss would have been a popular figure amongst the estate workers. His obituary noted that he had a reputation as a formidable electioneer whose speeches and addresses were "those of a jolly mariner, rough, homespun, full of a sort of ready raillery, blunt, off hand and ready witted, such as were sure to draw cheers from a crowd".[292] Certainly the Glass family held both James and Lady Emma in high regard, demonstrating this by naming their first child, who was born at Wemyss a year after Lady Emma's arrival, Emma Wemyss Glass. It is assumed that for an estate worker to use family names in this way would have required the approval of the Wemyss family.

The Newcastle-Edinburgh Steamboat

Richard Glass indicates that Susannah's passage would be paid from Newcastle to Wemyss Castle, either by coach or by steamboat. In the 1820s a steamboat service between Newcastle and Edinburgh was established and offered an alternative to the cramped and uncomfortable coach journey. Several coaches connected Newcastle to Edinburgh, some covering the whole distance from the *Turf Hotel* Coach Office in Newcastle, with numerous stops at places such as Morpeth, Alnwick, Berwick and Dunbar. A daily evening coach from Newcastle arrived at Edinburgh at noon the following day, 15 hours after departure.

SAFE AND EXPEDITIOUS CONVEYANCE
Between NEWCASTLE & EDINBURGH
FOR GOODS AND PASSENGERS

That superb and powerful Steam-Packet the ARDINCAPLE, John Cunningham, Commander, will COMMENCE RUNNING between Newcastle and the Chain Pier at Newhaven, on MONDAY, the 21st APRIL, and continue to leave Newcastle every Monday and Friday Morning, at six o'Clock precisely, and the Chain Pier, Newhaven, every Wednesday Morning and Saturday Evening, at six o'Clock precisely.

Passengers have the Option of providing their own Refreshments, or of being supplied by the Steward at moderate Rates.

Apply to:

JOSEPH SHIELD, 50, Quayside and Folly Wharf, Newcastle, or ANDREW GREIG, Agent, Chain Pier, Newhaven.

Figure 11-10 Advertisement in the *Newcastle Courant* on April 5, 1828

At this time, there was not yet a rail connection, so the alternative suggested by Richard Glass was the steamboat, an increasingly popular means of travel. In 1828, the Steam Packet *Ardincaple* began a new service between Newcastle and Edinburgh, the route offering passengers spectacular views of the Northumberland coast, including Bamburgh Castle and Holy Island.

[292] *Fifeshire Journal*, April 6, 1854

But when the weather was bad, the steamboat journey could be perilous. In September, 1833, the *Ardincaple* sailed from Leith harbour bound for Newcastle. After she'd rounded St Abb's Head, the wind became a gale "such as had not been seen upon this coast for upwards of thirty years". Near Bamburgh Castle, Captain McLeod and four passengers were swept overboard and perished. The stricken steamboat was eventually towed by a fishing boat to Hartley Baits, just north of Whitley Bay. It was reported that "all the sailors behaved well with the exception of one sailor, who was drunk the whole time"[293]

At the 1841 Census, Richard is 65 and living at Bullock Shade, Wemyss Castle. He is a widower with three of his children still at home: 18 year-old Durham-born Mary, and his two children born at Wemyss Castle, Emma Wemyss (13) and Isabella (10). Alison and Jane, Susannah's childhood friends, are both married.

The Joannah Simpson Letter

John Hankey received a letter in October 1845 from his cousin Joannah Simpson née Welsh who lived in Monkwearmouth with her husband William Simpson, a butcher and small farmer with no known connection with the Pennington Simpsons. The letter was written from Ash Place[294] where the Simpsons farmed five acres right next to the Newcastle turnpike road.

> Ash Place, Oct 5th, 1845
> Dear Cousin,
> I am much obliged to you for your kind invitation to your place but thank God I am a good deal better and I hope you are all well. You did not let me know who Sanderson has married, nor where he is living. Give my kind love to him and Susan (Susannah) when you see him. We have had very bad weather, our corn was flat down to the ground but we have got it all in. Ann Welsh[295] and Adamson was over at Hannah and they came to see us. Hannah has shifted to Shields but I have not been there since. I am sorry that brother Robert (Welsh) thinks of going to Americay at his time of life[296]. We have not been over to see John and William (Welsh).[297] We have a cow and that confines us more at home. We will be glad to see any of you when you can spare the time to come.
> It has been very wet weather last week and several ships lost. There was 3 ships lost at our harbour mouth on Friday last.
> I am Yours Truly, J.H. Simpson

In the letter, in which Wolsingham-born Joannah was responding to John Hankey's invitation for her to visit Ayhope Shield, she observes, "You did not let me know who Sanderson has married, nor where he is living. Give my kind love to him and Susan when you see them."[298]

---

[293] *Newcastle Courant*, September 7, 1833

[294] Ash Place, Monkwearmouth was owned by William Simpson. In the 1880s, the widowed Joannah built houses and a hospital (now Monkwearmouth Hospital) on the land: the still-existing Joannah Street and Elizabeth Street were named after mother and daughter respectively.

[295] Probably the wife of George Welsh, Wolsingham farmer, b 1786

[296] Robert Welsh was about 65 years old, hence his sister's regret at him wishing to emigrate.

[297] John and William are brothers of Johanna.

[298] I received a copy of Joannah's letter, dated October 5th, 1845, from Eileen Perkins née Hankey.

11-11 Street in Monkwearmouth named after Joannah Simpson.

"Susan" is Susannah Sanderson, by this time Susannah Dawson. It is not known whether Susannah accepted the job at Wemyss Castle in 1828, but she was living at Ayhope Shield with her Uncle John Hankey in 1840 when she married John Dawson, a joiner from Brignall, a small village 3 miles south of Barnard Castle. They lived at Brignall and had a son Watson Dawson in 1847. Susannah died in 1851 at the age of 44 years.

"Sanderson" is Susannah's brother John Sanderson, and Joannah is keen to know about his marriage and where he is living. John Sanderson was close to his sister and was most probably raised with her at Ayhope Shield, initially working for his uncle on the farm before finding farming work in the South Bedburn area.

In April 1845, six months before Joannah's letter was written, John married Mary Featherstone at Hamsterley. The witnesses were Susannah and her husband John Dawson, together with Richard and Elizabeth Lowson, brother and sister from Crane Row, South Bedburn.

John and Mary lived at Pooltree, a farm about 2½ miles from Ayhope Shield. After Mary died in 1847, John married farmer's daughter Elizabeth Snaith at Hamsterley. Thereafter, John worked in the Hamsterley and Bedburn district as an agricultural labourer and woodman, always within two or three miles of Ayhope Shield. He died in 1879.

In 1826, John's sister Elizabeth married Fleming Wilson, a lead ore smelter and small farmer from Newlandside, at Stanhope St Thomas.

Joannah reveals that "It has been very wet weather last week and several ships lost. There was 3 ships lost at our harbour mouth on Friday last." A *Newcastle Courant* report elaborates:-

> Sunderland, Oct. 3 – Yesterday evening, *The Maraboo*, Robinson, sailed from this port for London, coal laden. Soon afterwards the wind rose high and the sea became very heavy, during which the vessel sprung a leak. She kept out to sea all night, but this morning she drove on to the bar near the entrance of the harbour, the wind being about E.N.E., and very stormy. Great fears were entertained for the safety of the crew. Rockets were fired to convey a line from the shore to the ship, which miscarried. The crew were taken from on board by the life-boat, and brought to land in safety. The vessel has become a wreck. Part of her materials have been saved.
>
> *The Rose*, Watts, of Whitby, having lost her mainyard and boom, drove behind the south pier, and has become a wreck – crew still on board.
>
> Oct 5 – The crew of *The Rose*, of Whitby, were hauled on to the pier with ropes, and were all saved – the vessel is a total wreck.

> *The Friends*, Pyle[299], of Yarmouth, a new vessel on her first voyage, in endeavouring to enter the harbour, during the storm on the evening of the third instant, drove behind the north pier, and remained until the next tide, when she was got off and towed onto the harbour. Her keel is broken, stern-post split, stanchions, bulwarks, and covering boards destroyed, combings broken, iron beam bent, &c.
> A boat was driven on shore near Ryhope, three miles south of this port – name on the stern, *Jeune St Vincent*, of Baden. On the 4th instant, the brig *Romulus*, of Wisbech, on being hauled off the slipway, where she had been under repairs, fell over on her starboard side, below the bridge, in which state she now lies. Efforts are being made to get her raised. The amount of damage the vessel has received in consequence has not been ascertained.
> Oct 6 – The *Romulus* has been got upright – she is not much damaged.[300]

After John Hankey Snr's death in 1855, John Hankey junior assumed the tenancy at Ayhope Shield and married Mary Wilson a few months later. They had several children, including Mary, George and John Joseph. George, believed to have had learning difficulties, was devoted to his big sister Mary. He was 20 years old when she married Willie Simpson in 1884 and left Ayhope Shield for Pennington Farm, 2½ miles away. George became distressed at his sister's absence and went out looking for her: he was found drowned in the South Grain Beck.

John Joseph took over at Ayhope Shield when his father died in 1891:-

> There died last week at Ape Shield Farm, near Wolsingham, a well-known Weardale farmer, Mr John Hankey, who has farmed the little farm lying among the fells between Wolsingham and the Grove now for many years; in fact, he has lived there all his life – 75 years – and his father before him. Ape Shield Farm is surrounded by moorland on every side. The Pikestone Moors are on the west, north, and east of it, and the moors belonging Mr Surtees of the Grove on the (south). It is like an oasis in the desert.[301]

John Hankey junior was a sheep farmer of note and a breeder of champion sheep dogs. For example he won first prize in the "Cur dogs, smooth" category at Wolsingham Agricultural Show in 1875 when the Vickers family from Stanhope also picked up most of the prizes for cattle. Francis Vickers of Belle Vue won first prize in the "Cur dogs, rough" category and second prize for a Moor tup lamb. His father Joseph Vickers and brothers John (Mown Meadows) and William (Howl John) were also prize-winners.[302]

John Joseph Hankey continued farming at Ayhope Shield for another four years after his father's death, during which time he married farmer's daughter Alice Ann Angus. In 1895, the family left Ayhope Shield, as explained by Eileen Perkins:-

> I first heard Ayhope Shield mentioned when I was a tiny girl. It always seemed to have been a special place to my family even though my grandparents left in 1894/5 and only three or four of their twelve children were born there. My grandmother,

[299] Pyle, Robinson, and Watts, were the captains of the three wrecked ships
[300] *Newcastle Courant*, October 10, 1845
[301] *Newcastle Courant*, February 7, 1891
[302] *Northern Echo*, September 8, 1875

who went to Ayhope Shield as a 21 year-old bride and only lived there for five or six years, said that some of the happiest days of her life were spent there. They were always having visitors and they could watch people coming over the fell long before they reached the farm.[303] The family moved to West Shipley where my father was born, but my grandfather retained the tenancy of Ayhope Shield for a number of years, and at least until 1902.[304]

11-12 A Sheep Washing Day in the 1840's, just as it would have been at South Grain Beck, Ayhope Shield.[305]

Ayhope Shield was sub-let to John Brunskill of East Fold Garth Farm, Woodland, in 1896, but it was not in continuous occupation after the departure of John Joseph Hankey. In the early twentieth century the tenancy was held by Tom Sanderson of Broomley Farm, who also kept sheep at nearby Ruddy Carr. Tom and his shepherds would lodge at the farm when occasion demanded.

---

[303] On November 11, 1895, a *Northern Echo* correspondent rated Ayhope Shield as "one of the lonliest homesteads in England". The most isolated place was judged to be a game watcher's house in Skiddaw Forest.

[304] Personal communication from Eileen Perkins née Hankey.

[305] *Illustrated London News*, July 18, 1846

11-13 This watercolour of Ayhope Shield was painted by Tom Bellerby on September 10 1926. The buildings subsequently fell into ruin until a walkers' shelter was constructed on the site in the 1980s. Now there's just a pile of stones. (Image courtesy of Eileen Perkins née Hankey).

11-14 Ella and Frank Sanderson in 1916 at Pond House, Hamsterley: they enjoyed summer picnics at Ayhope Shield.

Picnics at the Meeting of the Grains

The Sanderson children from Hamsterley, including Frank and Ella, accompanied by Uncle John's children and the Stephenson cousins used to go to Ayhope Shield every summer with lots of other young people from the village for a picnic:-[306]

> When I was a lad, there was a lot of cherry trees, beautiful cherry trees, and all the lads and lasses of the village had a picnic there once a year. The girls would take the grub and the lads used to take the pony and traps. We couldn't get the ponies and traps right there, we used to have to fasten them behind a stone wall. And we'd have a whole day on the moor on a Sunday afternoon, and we'd eat cherries till we were bad. And there was a little river and we used to have a swim – it was deep enough to have a swim in. We were right on the heather.

It is difficult to think of a more idyllic experience than described by FJS. It conjures up images of the warm sun of a beautiful summer's day, miles from civilisation, breath-taking views eastwards over Hamsterley Common towards Bedburn, with the sight and sound of the children playing, the sky-larks singing, the bees buzzing and the butterflies dancing over the heather, and the trickle of the stream at the Meeting of the Grains.

FJS's memories of this idyllic activity of childhood are from the time of the First World War. There could not be a greater contrast between such summers by a sleepy beck on the heather-clad moors and the abominable events occurring in northern France and Flanders. Indeed, two of Uncle John's children – John (Jackie) and Edgar - were seriously wounded in the fighting and Aunt Lizzie's son, Ralph Edward Stothard, lost a leg.

My direct paternal family were more fortunate in avoiding the Great War: My grandfather Frank Sanderson of Hamsterley was 46 when the war began, his son Frank (FJS) was only 14 by the time the war ended, and my father Henry was not born until 1920. My maternal family were less fortunate: my grandmother Mary Elizabeth Dunn's first husband Wylam Blenkin was killed, her second husband Moses Chapman (my grandfather) was wounded,[307] and she lost her brother Thomas Dunn.

Visits to Ayhope Shield and the Meeting of the Grains

Having heard FJS's account of carefree days at Ayhope Shield, I was determined to pay a visit one day. The opportunity came in August, 1997. On the "Glorious Twelfth", a beautiful summer's afternoon with the temperature at 25 C, Patricia and I hired mountain bikes in Hamsterley Forest and headed off to the spot at the edge of the forest where the village children had tethered the ponies more than eighty years ago. There we left our bikes, climbed the style and made our way to Ayhope Shield which was about one-and-a-

---

[306] Uncle Frank and Auntie Ella were the children of Frank and Edith Sanderson née Stephenson. Uncle Frank, born at Bedburn Hall Farm in 1904, told me in 1980 about the trips to Ayhope Shield. Uncle John was Frank senior's brother.

[307] Moses Chapman was Best Man when Wylam married Mary Elizabeth. Moses and Wylam went to Flanders together where Wylam was killed in action. Thereafter, Moses married Mary Elizabeth who had two young children, Bobby and Freda, from her brief marriage to Wylam. Mary Elizabeth had two children with Moses, Fred and Elizabeth (author's mother).

half miles away across the purple heather of Hamsterley Common. As we walked along the narrow and barely visible path, the stillness was only broken by the baa-ing of a solitary sheep and the dancing of peacock and fritillary butterflies above the heather. We became aware of the Shield when we were about a mile away. It was an oasis of green rising westwards, starkly contrasting with the heather-covered moors in which it nestled. As we came nearer, we made out the ruin of the farm - what had been a building sufficient to provide accommodation for a shepherd and his family had become a ruin.

As we descended along a track from the moorland, I understood why FJS had retained the childhood memory of his visits to Ayhope Shield. It is a special place, and more than lived up to the romantic image created in my mind by my uncle's recollections. Patricia too was captivated, by its peacefulness, its isolation, the feeling of it being a haven in a potentially hostile environment. It was most definitely a haven in the sense that the scattering of old oak, birch and rowan trees on the banks of the South Grain Beck provided welcome shade from the baking sunshine. We sat in cooling shade on the lush meadow grass by the stream and had a picnic whilst considering FJS's recollections in the light of our direct experience of the place itself.

There is no doubt that his memory did justice to the events of long ago. The ponies and traps were fastened 'some distance from the farm' as he had said, and at the same spot where we left our bikes. It is also possible that, nearby, there was a deeper stretch of the stream which enabled the children to swim, as FJS had recalled. However, at the Meeting of the Grains the streams are about six feet wide and shallow enough to be fordable at almost any point, which suggests that wading, splashing and sitting in the water were more likely activities than swimming. Fishing was not mentioned by my uncle but the considerable numbers of small fish in the stream makes it possible that some of the children brought along jam-jars and fishing nets. And finally, we found no evidence of the 'beautiful cherry trees', but we were soon to learn that FJS's memory had not been faulty. At the time, we assumed that either the trees were nearby but unnoticed during our visit or that perhaps the trees had died in one of the many harsh winters since that time.

It was a truly memorable trip to Ayhope Shield. After retrieving our bikes, we set off back to the hire shop in the forest via an old drovers' road over Ayhope Beck[308]. Just beyond the bridge over the beck, at a place called Honeybee, was Metcalfe's House, a ruined inn where we paused and tried to imagine how it was those many years ago when local farm workers, including members of the Sanderson family,[309] travellers, and drovers would slake their thirsts in this remote place. We were back at the shop within 3 hours. It is recommended to anyone as an easily manageable and enjoyable 'expedition': for members of the Sanderson family, it will have particular resonance, as it has for members of the Hankey family.

John Denby took up the recommendation and visited Ayhope Shield about a month after our visit, having read my account of the special afternoon experienced by Patricia and myself. He too relished the experience as is evident from his account of the visit:

> It would be about two o'clock, under a blue sky, when I left the Visitor's Centre in Hamsterley Forest. It was perfect walking weather, bright conditions with a cool

[308] This was an old track from Barnard Castle to Newcastle, passing over Ayhope Beck

[309] Thomas Sanderson of Broomley owned Honeybee Farm in the early part of the twentieth century.

breeze coming off the hills to the west. A variety of broadleaves[310] flanked the track, lovely birdsong coming from their midst, and from the understorey of broom, gorse and bracken. Impending autumn was indicated by the drab colour of the birch trees and the thinning canopies of rowan and sycamore. Beneath these trees flowed the shallow, rock-strewn Bedburn Beck, with here and there shafts of sunlight across the water giving a deep copper colour to the smooth-stoned bed.

11-15 Meeting of the Grains. The South Grain Beck is on the left, the ruins of the farmhouse are on the hillside 200 yards away.

Near the confluence of this stream and Ayhope Beck are grand oaks, and in the almost still air above the water flitted midges amongst floating seeds of willow-herb. A stout wooden bridge over the Ayhope gave a view upstream, its bed shelving appreciably. In a clearing nearby stood the work of some local sculptor. Six carved 'totems' were accurately set in the ground in a triangular shape in order to reveal the faces of three figures. 'Man', 'Son', and 'Father' could be distinguished clearly from three different points.

The walk on the track alongside Ayhope Beck was initially an area of conifers, with alder at the streamside, the walker all the while accompanied by small birds, gently twittering. Then came a phalanx of magnificent Scots Pine. The sunshine brought out lovely shades of orange in their mighty trunks - standing so very tall and proud - while highlighted too, but thankfully far less in number, was the deathly grey colour

[310] Willow, hawthorn, rowan, whitebeam, larch, oak, birch, sycamore, alder

of the trunks of trees which are dying. The Scots Pine thinned, revealing a clear felled area where habitat piles of grey brash were the only remains of the forest. From here was a view ahead to the open moor, heather there still clothing the land with a faint purple. A rush of goose pimples came with the thought of soon arriving at this special place concerning the Sanderson family, the 'Meeting of the Grains'.

I arrived soon afterwards at Melcalfe's House, an old inn now quite ruined, but bearing the lovely name Honeybee. Then a ford over the beck - a very clear stream with good-sized rocks - led on and upwards to the very edge of Hamsterley Forest. The final two hundred yards of woodland was again Scots Pine. Behind me was the lowing of cattle on the intake land of Redford Farm, around me the seeping of woodland birds, above the gently swaying crowns of these great trees, and ahead.... a six foot wall over which the bright afternoon light beckoned me to stride the style and... presumably... see Ayhope Shield beyond....

.....and there it lay, pretty well the picture described by Frank in his account of 12th August. I stood astride that wall, eagerly taking in the scene before me, and with a feeling of real content. I imagined the Sanderson brood tripping through the heather to Ayhope Shield which, on this day, was a wedge of green pasture framed by stone walls beyond which swelled the gentle slopes of purple moorland. I set off on the final stretch, along a firm path with its silvery hint of gritstone, and beneath my boots the wonderful crackling of the dead roots of heather. Numerous grouse, often in groups of a dozen or more, were startled to flight, their wings beating hard...... but there cries of "Go back... go back!" went unheeded as, with increasing anticipation, my eyes took in more and more detail of that green swathe ahead. Way ahead, on the western horizon, was the low peak of Five Peaks, with Pawlaw Pike just to the south of there. Closer to was the lovely tree the rowan, its shiny red berries complemented by the deep-green-turning-crimson of its decaying leaves................. and then, I was there.......... the 'Meeting of the Grains'.

I'll never forget that spot on that gentle late summer's day. It is very special, and it lived up in full measure to the homely picture painted by Frank. With his photograph of Patricia in my hand I found from where it had been taken, a spreading alder just over my left shoulder. It is not alone, the streams at the 'Meeting of the Grains' host to several of these moisture-loving trees. I found where Pat had posed - she looking across the stream with nonchalant air - and sat down there too... in order to eat a pretty late lunch. Dry bread, cheese and weak tea was a feast to a hungry (but otherwise very satisfied) man. From the south, the sun soothed, massaging the back as no doubt it did with Pat, and just below so did the beck, a gurgle of gently cascading water where the Grains meet and a clear pool beyond. On the bed of this pool was a strong sandy colour in some of the smooth stones while water at the surface shivered slightly, looking like the beaten metal of medieval armour.

I lingered there a good while before deciding to make full use of the warm sunshine and prospects of a lovely evening by taking the footpath up North Grain Beck to the moortops. However, before heading off, a little more snooping around paid dividends. I found the foundations of the farm, studied some neat dry stone walling which at one time had been sheep enclosure, came across a scattering of what I take to be coprinus comatus (shaggy ink cap) and, two hundred yards from the 'Meeting', and along South Grain Beck, several cherry trees! It was the deep crimson leaves which first attracted, and there they stood, gnarled and twisted, but not now bearing the fruit which FJS must have enjoyed so much. The joy of this discovery made light of passage along the little-used and indistinct path through rough heather which was my way along North Grain Beck. From alongside this stream can be seen remains of several buildings and/or enclosures, associated I suspect with quarrying, and perhaps mining, as well as hill farming. Spoil is most evident in an area of quarrying near Doctor's Gate, and a road from there, directly north to Wolsingham, would have been the transport route. These quarries are on the moor just north of Metcalfe's House which must have seen some hard drinking in its time!

My late afternoon stroll across these moors, now walking eastwards towards Cabin Hill, and Hoppyland Farm above Bedburn, was a treat. Apart from nature's creature comforts - the haunting sounds of red grouse, the piping of pipits, and the buzz of bees in the heather - it was quiet, with gentle winds wafting over a peaceful scene. Bright new flowers were appearing on new shoots of heather, revitalised after a burning, and where the heather was thin, the vibrant green of crowberry leaves shone. At Cabin Hill there is a large pond, legacy of quarrying. There, an iridescent blue dragon-fly buried itself amongst reeds at the water's edge, making noise like a helicopter as it winged its way, clattering against the maze of hard stems. From there, looking north-eastwards, is Dryderdale, a building at the heart of West Moor Plantation, and further, on the stretch of hills north of the Wear, Tow Law perches. It was at Cabin Hill that I chose a memento of the day's walk, a twisted dead root of heather which now adorns the windowsill at my house. I think it is at home, looking as it does for several miles up the Aire valley - and to our heather moors in the distance.

The track led downhill towards Hoppyland, alongside West Moor Plantation where there is a lovely line of beech trees at point 208 (0.5. 92 Barnard Castle). Not so permanent as these magnificent trees, but just as attractive, was a collection of fly agaric - but, sadly, no elves were about. A quiet 'B' road took me to Bedburn again, leaving a mile walk along the beck back to the Visitor's Centre. Grand it was too, midges dancing in the shafts of evening sunlight, and the odd jay screeching. The beck here is quite narrow and at times runs over a bed of solid rock. Occasional deep clefts in this rock, worn by the swift-flowing waters, put me in mind of the Strid in Wharfedale.

Before driving off - to take a fried fish at Frosterley *en route* to Edmondbyers Youth Hostel - I sat at a picnic bench, drinking weak, and by now cool, tea, reflecting on what had been a fruitful and really satisfying day. Thanks for leading me there Frank!

12. AN ENGLISHMAN THROUGH AND THROUGH

The history books tell us that 1904 was an eventful year. In Britain, Charles Rolls and Henry Royce signed an agreement to build motor cars, The Automobile Association was founded, London's first electric underground train was introduced, James Barrie's Peter Pan opened, and the explorer Sir Henry Morton Stanley died. Conflict and disaster was much in evidence elsewhere: the Russian governor general of Finland was assassinated, Japanese forces defeated the Russians and sank their fleet in China, France severed diplomatic links with the Vatican, two British trawlers were sunk off Dogger Bank by the Russian Baltic fleet, Norway declared independence from Sweden, the Prime Minister of Greece was assassinated outside the Greek Parliament, and in St Petersburg, the Czar's troops shot dead over 500 strikers on 22 January (Bloody Sunday). In New York, a paddle-steamer, the *General Slocum*, caught fire, resulting in the deaths of about 1000 people, and in Lahore, India, an earthquake claimed 10,000 lives.

12-1 Francis Joseph Sanderson with sister Ella in 1911. You can see the mischief lurking behind these seemingly innocent faces.

Francis Joseph Sanderson (FJS), the inspiration for this book, was born at Bedburn Hall Farm, the home of his mother's family, on August 16, 1904. Like his younger sister Ella, FJS was doted on by his mother. One postcard reveals a mother's pet name for her young son; in November 1912, Edith, staying with friends in Darlington, wrote to 8 year-old Frank, describing him puzzlingly as "Tomsie", and signing it, "Your Ma Mie"

His life was in many ways quite typical of a farmer's son of that time – up at 6 o'clock every morning, helping out on the farm from an early age, attending the village school (Hamsterley School between August 1909 and July 1914), then travelling to schools further afield on horseback (first Wolsingham Grammar School and then Barnard Castle School), but always wishing he was back at the farm.

The Impractical Lady Eleanor

FJS and family lived next door to his paternal grandparents, Frank Sanderson and Eleanor née Alderson. Eleanor died in 1910 when FJS was just six years old but he remembered her well, not least because of a number of traumatic experiences at her hands.

Eleanor Alderson was born at Billy Row, Crook, on July 1, 1832, the year that Sir Walter Scott and social reformer Jeremy Bentham died. Billy Row is about 4 miles north-east of High Shipley where she was living with her parents William and Eleanor Alderson when she married Frank Sanderson of Low Harperley in 1855

Eleanor's father, my g.g. grandfather William born in 1789 near Brancepeth, came from a family of farmers and maltsters. William married Eleanor Snowdon in 1816 at Witton-le-Wear and had six children, of which Eleanor was the youngest. Eleanor senior died on 14 January 1854, the same year in which the Light Brigade was wiped out in the Crimea and a year before daughters Eleanor and Ann were married at Hamsterley Church in a double wedding (See p.73). There is a heartfelt epitaph on her gravestone in the churchyard of Hamsterley St James:-

> Sleep on dear Mother and take your rest
> For God has called when he thought best
> The loss is great that we sustain
> In Heaven we hope to meet again.

After Eleanor senior's death, William retired from farming and went to live with his daughter Jane and her husband John Kirton Nattress[311] who was farming 160 acres at Walmire, Croft. William died at Walmire on Friday, 2 February, 1866, aged 77 years. The Death Certificate gives the cause of death as "Found Drowned". He is buried in Croft Churchyard. The Inquest merely confirmed that he had been drowned.

FJS knew his grandmother well enough. He remembered her as a "lady", someone with airs and graces, who was not at all practical, perhaps decidedly unworldly, "She was a lady and she acted a lady –and mind you, she was a funny, funny woman", recalled Frank, and he didn't mean that she was amusing.

He was in daily contact with her and, although he knew her as well as any child of that age could know a grandparent, there is no doubt that he learned much more about her from stories recounted after her death, which he had either been told or had overheard.

It is undoubtedly the case that Frank's view that his grandmother had limitations as a parent was a reflection of a more widely held view in the family. It could be that her husband and her surviving children were so traumatised by the death of several infants, particularly William Henry (See p.113), that they attached some responsibility to their eccentric and impractical mother for the deaths.

"She had all those babies and killed them", observed FJS, attributing this to haplessness rather than anything more sinister. She lost five children in infancy, and, although infant mortality was relatively high at that time, such an attrition rate was unusual for a comfortably-off rural farming family. Frank seemed to think that the survival rate might have been higher had his grandmother been more practical.

Warming the bedclothes

FJS told the story of his first home-coming in early September, 1904:-

> I nearly died. She nearly killed me. I was born at Bedburn and three weeks later, me mother brought us home to Hamsterley. And me grandmother had put all the bedclothes in the oven, and had got them red hot. Well, I screamed and screamed! She had them bloody red hot! If she'd had to look after me....

The sentence was left unfinished but there was no mistaking his meaning. FJS's grandmother must have been excited by the prospect of her new grandchild arriving home,

[311] John Kirton Nattress was one of the witnesses at the double wedding involving Eleanor Alderson and her sister in 1855.

Edith having given birth at her parents' home at Bedburn Hall Farm, a mile down the road. What better way to welcome the baby back to Hamsterley than to have warm and cosy bedclothes prepared? However, Eleanor appears to have misjudged how warm they were after a spell in the oven – perhaps understandable when you think of the likely toughness of the hands of a farmer's wife compared with the delicate and sensitive skin of a baby. FJS must have been told the story of the bedclothes as he was only weeks old at the time - despite the traumatic nature of the experience, he will have had no direct memory of it.

Head-first in the watter!

FJS remembered the time his grandmother applied first-aid after he'd been knocked over by a bull in 1908, telling the story with patent incredulity:-

> I could take you to the very spot in the yard at Pond House. I was 4 years old when a bull knocked me down, and it cut me head and I was bleeding, bleeding bad. And me father picked me up and carried us into the house through the backdoor and into the scullery. They were stone floors, you know, and the maid was washing the floor. And me grandmother, she got hold of us and dipped us in the watter (sic) the maid had been washing the floor with! Head first! Head-first in!!

It must have been terrifying for four year-old Frank, first to be knocked over by a bull, blood pouring from his head, and then to be nearly drowned in a bucket of filthy water.

These stories suggest a well-rehearsed family view of Grandmother Eleanor as an unwittingly dangerous person, haplessly and effortlessly causing domestic mayhem. At this distance, the image conjured is somewhat amusing, but one can imagine the kind of opinions voiced out of earshot of 'Lady Eleanor' over one hundred years ago, and not just by the immediate family. The deaths of five children together with reports of other mishaps would also have set tongues wagging in the parish and beyond. It is difficult now not to feel some affection and sympathy for this eccentric woman who was undoubtedly viewed as a 'character' in her day.

12-2 "Lady" Eleanor Sanderson and Queen Victoria.
Eleanor is wearing her Golden Wedding brooch.

The only surviving photograph of her does give a clue to her personality – FJS's description of her as a lady is supported by the regal, Queen Victoria-like demeanour of Eleanor. Indeed, she bears more than a passing resemblance to the great lady!

Eleanor died on October 20th, 1910 at Hamsterley, aged 78 years. The GRO informant was Frank, her son, who was present at the death, which was due to "Valvular disease of Heart Syncope", i.e., a heart attack. In the same year, Tolstoy, Florence Nightingale and Edward VII died, the latter being succeeded on the throne by George V.

Some of her most treasured personal possessions were bequeathed to her daughter Lizzie, including her Golden Wedding brooch, her armchair, and her mahogany chest of drawers.

The biggest dunce that ever went to school

12-3 General Sir John Moore KB 1761-1809

FJS had vivid and mixed memories of his school-days. His time at Hamsterley School was pleasant enough but things changed when he went to Wolsingham Grammar School, riding the six miles on a horse, from Hamsterley down to Bedburn, then up Shull Bank past Ruddy Carr, and then down the steep Wear Bank to Wolsingham. He recalled that "one of the blooming teachers used to thump me", treatment which caused him to freeze with anxiety, unable to learn anything.

Matters didn't improve when he moved to Barnard Castle School in 1916:-

> It was useless. I couldn't do anything. I bloody hated it. Detested it. I was never any good. I was the biggest dunce that ever went to school. Anything they tried to teach me, I couldn't do it. As soon as I left school, I could do it. I think it was nerves. I just couldn't bring it out, and that's all about it. Yet I can still tell you poetry, (for example) *The Burial of Sir John Moore*.

At this point, FJS launched into a faultless rendition of Charles Wolfe's poem about the Scottish General best known for his military training reforms and for his death in 1809 at the Battle of Corunna in which he defeated a French army under Marshall Soult during the Peninsula War:-

Not a drum was heard, not a funeral note,
As his corse to the rampart we hurried;
Not a soldier discharged his farewell shot
O'er the grave where our hero we buried.

….and ending seven verses later with:-

Slowly and sadly we laid him down,
From the field of his fame fresh and gory;
We carved not a line, and we raised not a stone,
But we left him alone with his glory.

12-4 FJS (on his mother's left), wearing Wolsingham Grammar School uniform, 1914.

So FJS had obviously learned some things at school but generally hated the experience, much preferring the young farmer's life. He had an instinctive competitive nature, and so the combination of brutal teachers and more studious classmates brought him only pain and humiliation. He is a classic example of a non-academic boy with a good business sense, attuned to the requirements, the practicalities of farming. As he recalled with a mixture of anguish and pride:-

> If they'd let me go to the cattle market every week and send a few bullocks home, bought a few beasts for my father, I might have worked better at school. But I couldn't do it. I was a waste of time. And as soon as I got left school, all those clever ones at school, I smothered them, and I meant to! I showed them! And I was buying and selling beast when they were still at their father's tail ends.

It is clear that FJS was driven by a fierce "I'll show them" competitive spirit that was fuelled by his comparative failure at school, and which helps to explain his success as a farmer. He attributed his poor performance at school to 'nerves', indicating a proneness to anxiety, which may in turn explain his reputed volatility. It is interesting to note that Freda Ellis recalls both FJS and Auntie Ella as 'headstrong' as adolescents, suggesting a temperamental inheritance from their maternal grandmother, Eliza.

The Old Man from Bedburn Lane

An 'old man' (in his mid-fifties when FJS knew him) Joseph Walton Coatsworth was born in 1861 in Hunderthwaite, a small village a mile south of Romaldkirk. He was a highly intelligent, subversive and irreverent character who never flinched from speaking his mind, and who had radical views about the rights of the working man. He was a great showman and his behaviour must have been at times entertaining, sometimes annoying but mainly shocking to many of the villagers. FJS explained:-

> There was an old pitman lived down Bedburn Lane, an old chap called Jos Coatsworth. When I first knew him, he used to work at the pit and he used to get drunk before he got home and had a wash, and he would stand outside the vicarage and shout and curse at the parson, swearing like a trooper. Black he was! Before he'd even had a wash!

This conjures up an amusing image but it is doubtful that the Rev John Holliday was amused. Jos, whose father was a leadminer originally from predominately dissenting Upper Weardale, would have had a built-in disrespect for the establishment Anglican clergy.

FJS continued his description of the "old man" from Bedburn Lane:-

> And he'd walk round with his hands in his pockets, and he was a dead labour man. By gum, a red hot labour man, but he had a great influence on my life, that man.

For a person to have his hands in his pockets seems to have been deeply frowned upon, presumably because it was seen as disrespectful, perhaps indicative of shiftiness and laziness. This together with his noisily expressed "dead labour" politics had an unsettling effect on FJS's mother Edith, a staunch Tory. But as Frank acknowledged, Jos Coatsworth's effect on him was ultimately positive, triggering his spiritual awakening and establishing his life-long faith in God.

He recalled the scary event which changed his life:-

> I went to school at Hamsterley till I was 10 and was friendly with a little boy from Shull called Jack Cowley[312]. There was a Friday afternoon holiday from school and so he invited me to go and have tea at Shull, about half way between Hamsterley and Wolsingham on the other side of Bedburn.
> My mother had me scared to death of Jos Coatsworth at that time. She hated the sight of him. He lived on Bedburn Lane, and I didn't want to walk home past his cottage on my own. I had an uncle or two at Bedburn and so I thought, well, I'll get to Bedburn and meet them in the Pub, and they can walk home with me to Hamsterley. But we played and played and it got a bit late and I was late leaving Shull. I ran all the way to Bedburn as fast as I could but my uncles had gone. And so I had to walk up Bedburn Lane, this lonely road, past Jos Coatsworth's little cottage and it was now pitch dark and I was frightened, very very frightened. So I prayed to God that He'd send my father to meet me. And before I got to Jos Coatsworth's house, father's dog came to me and my father wasn't very far behind.

When FJS said it was "pitch dark", he meant it. Moonless nights would have been much darker then as there would have been little lighting in the village, let alone on Bedburn Lane. Horace Walpole the essayist had spoken of moonless nights being "dark beyond all darkness" in the middle of the 18th Century, and nothing much had changed since then.

With his prayers having been answered, FJS developed a lifelong faith in God:-

> That incident had a tremendous influence on my life. When I want anything, I ask God and I get it. I ask for a bit of help and God always helps me. I think that through life, if you want a bit of help, and you do the thing that's right, and you ask God, He listens to what you say. And it's surprising the things that come off that you haven't got a <u>clue</u> - you just wouldn't <u>dream</u> it would happen but it does happen. You think, "I'd like that", and just suddenly, it's there. I'm thankful. I thank Him every time. I haven't done anything. Everything I've got is through Him. Don't worry about that, there's no two ways about it!

---

[312] A newspaper report of January, 1981 featured Bill Cowley, Jack's brother. The family came to Hamsterley in 1900 when Jack's father began work on the Shull and Dryderdale estate on the edge of Pikestone Fell, north of Hamsterley.

12-5 The Hamsterley Poet: Jos Coatsworth on his cart.

Despite the shocking behaviour of Jos Coatsworth and Edith Sanderson's unremitting antagonism towards him, and FJS's initial fear of the man, he developed great respect for him:-

> He swore like a trooper – like I do! But actually he believed in God and he wouldn't hurt a hair on your head. He thought a lot about me, that old man, before he died, and I thought a lot about him. Bye, he was a great character.

The Story of Little Titch

In April, 1980, FJS told me the following story about the life and death of a pig in Hamsterley towards the end of The Great War. At that time, FJS was an impressionable teenager and the events and the characters involved obviously had a lasting effect on him. The witness of the actual events and author of the poem which describes the events was none other than Jos Coatsworth, the larger than life character who had put the fear of God into FJS when he walked home in the dark along Bedburn Lane.

FJS remembered Jos having a beautiful horse – "he always kept a good pony" - and that he knew "every mortal thing about Bobby Burns" - not only could he quote Robbie Burns extensively, but he also took the part of Burns on Burns' Night. And he would often put pen to paper to describe notable events in village life through poetry.

Hamsterley, like any village, would have had its characters at that time - the gossip, the drunkard, the scrounger, the snob, the idiot, the bully, the poet, the never-grumbling and the always grumbling. As David Souden pointed out:-

> In a small and close-knit community, every foible and eccentricity was known and discussed, every particularity of feature or expression drew comment.[313]

A number of such characters were described by my uncle as he provided the explanation of a poem concerning a deformed little pig, the only survivor from a litter of twelve. The events in question took place on a small farm in the village which had recently been purchased by Mr Andrew Wilson, a prosperous man who owned Wilson's Forge at Bishop Auckland where he was making a lot of money during the First World War.

The Unpopular Farm Manager (Baron von Scheissen)

Mr Beaver who managed the farm for Andrew Wilson was the principle character of the story, apart from the deformed pig, known as Little Titch. My uncle described Beaver as "a bit of a lunatic", as exemplified on one occasion, after 14 year-old FJS had fallen from a trolley bus and broken his knee-cap (See p.231):-

> Mr Beaver was the foreman chap, the manager of Wilson's farm. He was a bit of a lunatic really. He was! A bloody lunatic! I once had a broken kneecap and he got us on a woodwagon and took us home, and he said, "You know, this iodine, it'll mend anything!" I had a broken kneecap, smashed my knee, and he said iodine'll mend anything! He put iodine on my knee, and of course it had no effect at all.

12-6 Baron von Scheissen, aka Mr Beaver

Mr Beaver was self-important and not popular with the farm workers. We were at war with Germany at the time and Jos Coatsworth thought that "Baron von Scheissen" was a perfectly good nickname for the unpopular farm manager - "scheissen" is a colloquial German word not to be used in polite company. Particularly in small communities, there was a well-developed sense of hierarchy, and anyone who got above themselves or who behaved in a high-handed way towards employees, tended to be criticised, e.g., "Baron von Scheissen, he thinks he's summat and he's nowt"!

FJS continued with the story:-

> First of all, Mr Wilson had a lot of pigs, and he had a sow that had a litter of twelve pigs. And this Beaver, Mr Beaver, decided that he was going to bring them up on Nestlés condensed milk. And he kept giving them condensed milk until they all died but one. And it was allowed to run about the farm for two or three years. It was deformed and it had a great big hump on its back, and it was a terrible thing to look at. Terrible! It was no good to sell, and it was no good to eat.

Little Titch and Peggy

The deformed pig shared a field with a stylish mare:-

> Jos had a very stylish mare, a mare called *Peggy*, and she could nearly touch her chin, she was a high stepper. She was about twenty year old and they tried for years to get

[313] Souden, David (1991) *The Victorian Village*. Collins & Brown p.22

her to breed. And they got her in foal by a horse called *Highland Prince*. And she was running in the field with her foal opposite where Jos Coatsworth lived, and he saw *Peggy* kill this pig, which had got where *Peggy* thought was her part of the field. Then up came Beaver and he saw what had happened and so he took out his pocket knife and stuck the pig.

12-7 Harry Relph, aka *Little Titch*

Observing these dramatic scenes from his cottage window down Bedburn Lane, Jos began to formulate a poem:-

FJS noted, "Jos christened the pig 'Little Titch' and christened old Beaver 'Baron von Schiessen'." And in case I doubted his account, he added:-

Now this is absolutely true because I saw the pyramid of condensed milk tins myself, and I knew the pig myself. So I know this, it's an absolute true story.

It is easy understand why the deformed pig was named 'Little Titch'. This was the stage name of Harry Relph (1869-1928) from Cudham in Kent, an international music hall star who was only four feet tall and with five fingers and a thumb on each hand and six toes on each foot.

The Rest of the Cast

Another character mentioned in the poem is 'Butcher Proud', John Proud, the son of Charlie Proud and the nephew of John Thomas Proud, the ubiquitous solicitor and Coroner at Bishop Auckland. John, born in 1898, was "not a butcher really, but a farmer", according to FJS. His father Charlie farmed first with his father William at Binchester Hall before moving to Low Shipley after his father's death in 1889. In 1902, he moved to Pennington Farm after William Simpson Junior had moved to Richmond (See p.196). Charlie, described by FJS as "daft as a brush", was married to Hannah Hall of Monkfield who had a family connection with the Sandersons – Margaret Hall née Sanderson, was her aunt and FJS's great aunt. Every New Year's Day, FJS's father Frank and his wife Edith would visit Charlie and Hannah at Pennington for "frumenty", which is a kind of porridge made from hulled wheat boiled with milk, sweetened, and spiced.

Butcher Proud's brother William farmed for many years at Pennington. At the outbreak of the First World War, he joined the Coldstream Guards, was wounded several times and was awarded the DCM. In March 1928, he was found dead with gunshot wounds at The Green, Hamsterley, where he lived with his widowed mother Hannah.

"Gibson's" is a reference to Gibson Teasdale, who had become landlord of the *Cross Keys* in 1910. Gibson was a common first name in the Teasdale family – in the 1911 Census, there are seven "Gibson Teasdales" listed in County Durham and Northumberland.

Apart from Mr Beaver, Mr Wilson had several men working for him, including FJS's cousin Norman Stephenson, and another lad, West Auckland-born Sid Robinson, both mentioned in the poem. Sid is mysteriously named 'George Robey', the name of a music hall comedian.

Sir George Robey (1869-1954) was a near-contemporary of my grandfather Frank Sanderson (1868-1955). Born George Edward Wade, he became a famous music hall comedian known for many years as *"The Prime Minister of Mirth"*. The explanation for Sid Robinson being nicknamed George Robey could be that he bore some physical resemblance to the comedian whose most famous character was "the collarless cleric with a red nose, the startled and heavy black eyebrows, the indignant stare, the ribald smile."[314] Or perhaps his sense of humour or mannerisms reminded Jos Coatsworth of George Robey.

12-8 Sir George Robey

Imagine the scene in the meadow. The deformed little pig hobbles into view foraging for food. For a while, Peggy and the pig were unaware of each other. Their paths had crossed on other occasions but they generally adopted an air of mutual indifference. The foal however was at first curious and then alarmed by this strange creature. She moved towards her mother for protection. Peggy, sensing the foal's alarm, turned and saw the pig a few feet away.

Her strong maternal instinct, coupled with the surprise at this intrusion, stung Peggy into aggressive action. She reared, snorted, and within an instant, was upon the squealing pig. She sank her teeth into Little Titch's hump and with a twitch of her powerful neck, threw him a dozen feet in the air.

If the pig was alive in the air, it was certainly too feeble to survive the impact with the ground. Then Baron von Scheissen saw the lifeless creature, took out his pocket knife and stuck it in the pig. Chuckling as he recalled the tale, FJS exclaimed:-

> Just think of it! You can just imagine a bloody old German coming and sticking him with his knife!

With some relish, FJS then recited the poem he'd first heard when he was a young lad.

---

[314] Quoted from *Encyclopaedia Britannica*

The Life and Death of Little Titch

Come listen and you shall here a story I will tell
concerning Little Titch as he walked round Wilson's Well.

He was a curious little brute, with hair and hump and snout.
And not possessed of robust health, was allowed to roam about.

Peggy was a stately mare, with offspring by her side,
a foal by Highland Prince, which was her joy and pride.

Now seeing Titchy on the grass she claimed was her domain,
She thought she'd play a trick on him by causing him some pain.

She seized him by the hump and threw him in the air,
His soul went up, his body down, a bundle of despair.

Up came Baron von Scheissen and stuck him with his knife.
Twice that day poor Little Titch was deprived of its life.

Oh Norman go and boil the pot, for he must scalded be,
And I will wager all I've got we'll have some pork for tea.

And slip to Butcher Proud, who lives across the green,
He will come and dress him up, so very neat and clean.

And take this note to Gibson's, for we must drink his luck,
and if you look slippy, you can have his little pluck.

They roasted, boiled and stewed him till they thought it was enough,
but Titchy, tender when alive, when dead, was damn tough.

So George Roby seized the lot and threw him in the ditch,
and that is all I chance to know concerning Little Titch.

Jos Coatsworth
Hamsterley

12-9 Peggy threw Little Titch a dozen feet in the air.

Mischief at Hamsterley St James

As a young boy, Frank was a regular attender at St James Church in Hamsterley. He would often go to Evensong on a Sunday evening, but rarely on a Sunday morning, as there were jobs to be done around the farm and the beasts to feed.

No doubt church services have always been exceedingly tedious for children, leading to boredom and restlessness. An old man named Bourne reminisced about his childhood experiences at the beginning of the 19th century, at a time when church services seemed everlasting to the children, "with not a prayer left out or a creed spared"[315]:-

> We were at church one morning and a boy named Philpotts (we called him Mugs) stuck a big shawlpin into a boy who was nodding. He jumped up into the air with pain and yelled and swore and flew at Mugs. The beadles came and turned them out.

Over a century on, in 1912 when the Rev John Holliday was vicar of Hamsterley, very little seemed to have changed. FJS recalls being in church one time with school friend Gibby Teasdale who'd brought a pipe with him. In the back pew, they started whispering and giggling to themselves, and when Gibby put the pipe in his mouth, they laughed until they laughed out loud. Much to the embarrassment of his father, a church warden, he and Gibby were thrown out of the church by one of the wardens. FJS recalled:-

> I wasn't laughing when I got out of the church, because I knew what I was going to get when my father got home! By gum I knew I was going to get tanned!

But help was at hand from cousin Frank Stothard, who had come over to Hamsterley from Carr House, Framwellgate Moor to see his grandad (Frank Sanderson of Low Harperley), and had given his uncle (FJS's father Frank) a lift home from church on his motorbike. With a visitor in the house, FJS remembered that his punishment was no more than a stern word from his father. There were also stern words for Frank and Gibby from the schoolteacher at Hamsterley School on Monday morning.

Frank also used to walk to Lynesack, about 4 miles away, at Harvest Festival time, because "there was a nice little church there". Although it was quite a walk, it would be very familiar to him because it was on the main road to Barnard Castle from Hamsterley, a road he would have travelled many times, on foot, on horseback, and by pony and trap.

A strict upbringing

Frank's parents, Frank and Edith, were very strict, particularly Edith: "My mother was very very strict. She stood no nonsense from anybody." Frank and Ella had to be in by half past nine in the winter and ten o'clock in the summer, or else the door was locked, and the same rule applied to the maids. In 1979 when Frank was at his cousin Frank Stephenson's Golden Wedding celebration at Knaresborough, they recalled the time before the First World War when the two of them were standing talking to each other late one night when Edie saw them:-

---

[315] Flora Thompson *Lark Rise to Candleford*

> My mother shouted, "If Frank Stephenson can stay out all night, that's fine for him, but you're getting in here to bed right now!" You did what you were told. There was no messing about with my mother.

After Frank's mother died in 1922, his father softened his approach and was less strict with his baby son Henry.

Another time at Hamsterley St James, in about 1910 when he was quite young, Frank was a page-boy at a wedding at Hamsterley when he witnessed enterprising villagers practising a quaint local custom. The snow was deep and a road had to be cut through the snow to the church for the carriages and horses. Some villagers put a rope across the road, barring the way, and would only remove it when money had been thrown from the carriage.

The broken knee-cap

Generally, the period of the First World War was not easy for young FJS. As described earlier, school at Wolsingham and at Barnard Castle was an ordeal. In 1915, he lost two of his grandparents, Frank Sanderson and Joseph Stephenson, both of whom he held in high regard. And in 1916, he had the misfortune to fall from a tram and break his kneecap.

The aforementioned Mr Beaver not only got him on a wood wagon and took him home but also offered to cure the broken kneecap - with iodine. "It'll mend anything", he declared. Unsurprisingly, just like the condensed milk with the piglets, the iodine didn't work, so eventually FJS was taken by his father to Matthew Simpson, a bone-setter who ran the *Shafto Arms* at Whitworth, a small village between Spennymoor and Willington and 9 miles from Hamsterley. Matthew Simpson's services were much sought after in the Bishop Auckland district.

Bone-setters enjoyed a mixed reputation until well into the 20th century. They were invariably without qualifications but there were some notably competent practitioners amongst them and they were popular with the public. However, members of the established medical profession were overwhelmingly dismissive of bone-setters and campaigned to force them out of business. An anecdote from the 1830s gives an idea of the prevailing attitudes:-

> A tradesman…took a son about ten years old to a noted bone setter; when he went into the room, the Doctor was torturing a lad, a pauper, (sent by the parish authorities) by attempting to straighten a contracted knee, with diseased bone!! When it came to the little patient's turn, the father stripped him and took him forward to the Doctor, who immediately exclaimed, without making enquiries as to the cause or situation of the injury, or taking an examination, that his left shoulder was out; and after pulling him about for five or ten minutes, told him "he had set it", placed his arm in a sling, received his fee and dismissed him. When he returned, his mother perceiving that the sling was not put upon the arm that was injured, (which by-the-by had escaped the notice of the father) sent for a medical practitioner, who found that the right clavicle was fractured., which being treated in the usual manner, soon enabled him to use his arm as before. So much for the discrimination of bone-setting Quacks![316]

[316] *North Wales Chronicle*, September 20, 1831

It was the middle of winter with snow on the ground when Frank set off with his father to visit the bone-setter. When the trap reached the bottom of Page Bank (about a mile from the *Shafto Arms*), they found an overturned steam lorry was blocking the way, and so they had to divert 4 miles to Bishop Auckland. FJS stayed overnight in Bishop Auckland with friends of the family while his father returned home. The next day, his father came back and sent a message to Mr Simpson for him to come to Bishop Auckland to attend to young Frank. But he wouldn't come because he was frightened. "They'd have me in the army", he said. Mr Simpson was clearly not persuaded by 'the old lie', "*Dulce et decorum est, pro patria mori*".

So Frank and his father had to travel to Whitworth again but there was another mishap – the shaft on the trap broke at the bottom of Page Bank, which meant that Frank, urged on by his father, had to walk up the steep hill with a broken kneecap. He was eventually treated by Mr Simpson, walked on his toe for a year afterwards and was then able to walk normally.

WHO MUST SERVE?

The Plain Facts

**Setting aside verbal niceties,
The effect of the various
Official pronouncements on
Recruiting seems to be this:-**

That the Government expect all
Eligible men, married or unmarried,
To enlist.
That, if necessary, steps will be
Taken to compel service – in the
first instance at any rate on the part of
single men.
That such necessity will arise
Should there be "any considerable
Shirkage" among the unmarried.

12-10 Notice in *The Northern Echo* in November 1915, two months before conscription was introduced.

Although there were hundreds of thousands of volunteers, there were also worldly wise men like Matt Simpson who did their very best to avoid war service after conscription was introduced on January 27, 1916. One can understand Mr Simpson's reticence as it was only a few weeks after conscription had been introduced and at a time when the British public had become acutely aware of the scale of the casualties – two years earlier, hundreds of thousands of cheerful young men had volunteered on a wave of idealism, but how different was the mood of the nation in 1916. Another understandable reason for Matthew Simpson's nervousness was that, at 40 years of age, he was just within the upper age limit of 41 for conscription,

Afternoon tea at Kinninvie

FJS could tell a good story and enjoyed playing to the gallery. There is no doubt that his tongue was often firmly in his cheek on such occasions, as evidenced by the following tale. He told of the time that he and his parents were returning to Hamsterley by pony and trap from Barnard Castle and stopped at a little pub at the cross-roads at Kinninvie on the Barnard Castle-Woodland road, about 2½ miles from Barnard Castle. They asked for afternoon tea and waited...and waited, and eventually his mother went to find out why there was a delay. The landlady told her breezily, "Oh, it won't be long. I've sent the little girl down to the village for the yeast!" The nearest village is about two miles away.

The Cowley family

The Cowley family[317] was well known in the village of Hamsterley. As well as Jack who Frank had visited at Shull, there was George who had had the friendship with Essie Wearmouth, and Charlotte. Before the First World War, FJS remembers young George (born 1900) on his bicycle[318] hanging on to his stirrup leather as he rode a horse up and down the steep hills around Hamsterley. The roads were made of compacted stones at the time. When the war came, George, who then worked at Wolsingham Steel Works, met FJS one day and said to him:-

> I want to join the Navy, you get all your cigarettes for nothing.

In this day and age, it appears hardly credible that someone would actually be willing to put his life on the line for free cigarettes. But in 1914, the nation was gripped by patriotism coupled with a widespread belief that the war would be over quickly, and hundreds of thousands of men were enthusiastic volunteers.

George Cowley did join the navy, his ship was torpedoed, and he returned home a cripple with arthritis in his feet. FJS recalled:-

> He could hardly walk. About the time that I left the north (1929), he went to Australia and died out there. His sister Charlotte married William Pearson, a jeweller in Bishop Auckland in 1920, and some years later, there was a fire and she burned to death one Sunday morning.[319]

Another brother, Bill, who was born in 1895, joined the army when the First World War broke out and served for 4 years, finishing his service in Ireland with the Black and Tans. He had many memories of Hamsterley at the turn of the century. He played cricket for the village team, hiring a pitch from one of the farmers or playing in a field at the back of the *Cross Keys* pub. He remembered the "Hamsterley Hoppings", a village games event:-

> The annual feast, or hopping, was considered one of the most notable in the county, the sports consisting of cricket, wrestling, dog-trailing, quoiting. Foot races, donkey races, &c.[320]

Bill Cowley died in the 1980s, having lived all his life in Hamsterley.

Buying and selling

From an early age, FJS had a gift for the farming business, particularly when it came to clinching a good deal:-

> My father couldn't stop me buying and selling beast! He used to be very cross with me, my poor father. He used to say, "Don't buy any, don't buy any", and I used to go

[317] Henry Cowley married Gertrude Reid in Middlesborough in 1890. They subsequently lived in nearby Bishopton before moving to Witton Park, then Bedburn.

[318] Rural isolation diminished with the introduction of the bicycle in the last years of the nineteenth century. However, in Weardale, not only were rail links good but also, the countryside was so hilly that bicycles were a mixed blessing.

[319] There is no obvious record of Charlotte's death.

[320] Hamsterley Parish, *Durham County Directory*, 1894, p 373.

> home with 20 or 30! I couldn't keep off them. But I would sell them again. When I bought them they were worth the money.

He remembered once leaving Tow Law Auction Mart and bumping into "Old Harry White", his second cousin:-

> Harry says to me, "Bye, I've got 4 cows left here and I canna sell them. I'll sell them to you cheap." I gave him £16 apiece for them. And one was a show cow.

He recalled a deal in the 1920s with "Old Joe Graham", a farmer and cattle dealer from Sedling Farm, Wearhead:

> I met Old Joe Graham at Bishop Auckland one Thursday in November, and he says to me, "Have you got a cow that could win a Christmas Show?" And I said, "Yes. She'll smother anything. She's a toff, go and have a look at her. But I want £30 for her. I'll keep it till Christmas for you." Joe said, "I'll have her". The cow won at St John's Chapel and then at Bishop Auckland.

FJS's buying and selling of livestock often involved a lot of hard work. For instance, he would buy cows in Barnard Castle and walk them to Hamsterley. Then, on a Sunday afternoon, he would take them to Tow Law - 22 miles in all - and then to Newcastle.

An Englishman and proud of it

FJS pride at being an Englishman was demonstrated by his outrageous, and, one hopes, somewhat tongue in cheek views about our Celtic cousins. In 1980, he told me of the time when he faced competition for the acquisition of Great Holland Hall from a Scotsman from Norham-on-Tweed called Chisholm. He was worried at the time but eventually prevailed. He observed of Mr Chisholm:-

> He was the only Scotsman who ever I knew that went back to Scotland to stop. The only time a Scotsman goes back to Scotland is to fetch his brothers.

The disdain he felt towards Robbie Burns and the Burns' Night celebrations at Hamsterley Club was effortlessly extended to become a generalised attack on Celts:-

> Burns was a funny old fella. Terrible keen on the women. He was all that was bloody bad and Scotsmen think he's the best man that ever walked. I'm not a Scotsman. People down here think I am. I'm an Englishman and proud of it too. Bloody Scots - I'd send all the buggers back to Scotland and give them Home Rule. There are more bloody Scotsmen in the Houses of Parliament than Englishmen. <u>And</u> Welshmen. I'd say, "There's your Home Rule. Get it! Get on with it! Bugger the lot of you!"

The Scots and Welsh thus dismissed, and warming to the subject, he aired his opinion of the Irish at a time, it must be said, when republican terrorism was at its peak:-

> I'd blow Ireland up. I'd blow the whole bloody thing into the sea and let it disappear. Did you know that every single outlaw in the Wild West was an Irishman?[321] By God, they're bad people!

[321] Billy the Kid and a few other outlaws were of Irish descent, but so were a few of the lawmen who tamed the Wild West.

Brough Hill Fair

FJS went to Brough Hill Fair in 1926 to buy some Clydesdale horses, recalling that the miners were still on strike at that time.

The Miners' Dispute

It was the year of the General Strike in support of the miners. The strike was called in May and after nine days, it was over, the TUC defeated, but the miners fought on and were still off work when FJS went to Brough Hill.

The Teesdale Board of Guardians was wrestling with the consequences of the dispute. In the October meeting, it was reported that the cost of outdoor relief over the previous six-month period had been £5,105, against an estimate of £1,586. The main overspend was in the Cockfield area where 190 miners' families were receiving relief at a total cost of £246 per week. The Guardians, who had a statutory duty to relieve destitution, were in a difficulty because they were not only Guardians of the Poor but also guardians of the ratepayers. Mr HL Fife moved for a reduction in the relief provided to families. Responding, George Lowson of Staindrop, whilst conceding that relief had prolonged the strike, argued for a continuation of the allowances:-

> For heaven's sake, let the thing continue. We should not use coercion by hungering women and children who are not responsible for the men's actions. We hope it will not be long before the strike is ended. It will fizzle out before the end of six months. Leave it to the relief committee.

Mr RW Raine argued that the sooner the miners got back to work, the better terms they would get, and that a reduction in the relief would act as leverage to get the miners back quickly. Captain Shearwood appealed to the Board to have sympathy with men like himself who struggled to find the money to pay the rate. For a "Captain", this plea sounds hollow, but Harry Shearwood, having started his working life as a plough boy and then rising through the ranks, is unlikely to have been a man of independent means.

The motion to reduce relief was carried by twenty votes to eight.[322]

The miners capitulated the following month, having achieved nothing: by the end of November most miners were back at work, forced to accept longer hours and lower wages.

The Greatest Horse and Cattle Fair

There had been an annual Fair at Brough Hill since 1330. Originally it was over 4 days, but from 1752 it was shortened and moved to September 30th and October 1st, with slight variations if one of these days was a Sunday.

Brough Hill Fair was described in 1870 as "the greatest horse and cattle fair, not just of the North, but of the whole kingdom":-

> It is… a fair of unusual interest – you may see life in all its multiformity of character. It is there that you may read a chapter from the history of nature….The fair is a monster omnium gatherum, in which every class finds a representative… There is the aristocratic brougham, from which the lordly owner gazes with condescending

[322] *Teesdale Mercury*, October 13, 1926

> curiosity on the remarkable vehicles which stand near the low arched hut of the swarthy gipsy, where the occupants perform their washing and cooking operations as if that has been their local habitation for generations. Here too, dames and damsels "on prancing palfrey borne"[323] ride side by side with the true type of "hossy man", who, conspicuous by his white neckcloth and huge breast-pin, gallops to and fro as if he were bent on annihilating every rival. Foot-passengers are there too, in infinite variety, and all seem intoxicated with either joy, or excitement, or – liquor. From innumerable booths come noisy declarations and enticing descriptions of the fantastic tricks played inside to make the unskilful laugh, whilst immediately opposite there are tents erected where the masses are invited to eat and drink, and in these the most extraordinary music is continuously discoursed, principally from reed instruments that seem to suffer from chronic bronchial affections. And amid all this bustle and noise and pleasure-seeking, the great business of the meeting – the buying, the selling, and the money-making – is being urged forward with unremitting zeal.[324]

Such a colourful event was a highlight of the year, and not only for dealers: a lot of fun was to be had by sight-seers at Brough Hill where "streets of tents and stalls may be said to form a temporary town, where every article connected with the feeding and clothing of men and the gear of horses is displayed for sale."[325]

The fair attracted thousands of visitors from far and wide, and when the railway reached nearby Warcop, travel was greatly facilitated. Amongst the dealers in 1870 were a number of purchasers on behalf of the French Government who were seeking war horses. In 1876, the multitude was so great that there were several casualties with a man and a woman having their legs broken in the crush.[326] In 1888, it was reported that many thousands of dealers from all parts of England were present, and that excursions were run from, inter alia, Liverpool, Manchester, Leeds, Bradford, Newcastle, and York. Over 2000 horses and 10,000 sheep were on sale and the best horses were purchased by the army at good prices.[327]

Brough Hill Rascality

There was to be met with on Brough Hill a larger collection of roguish and unhung humanity than could be found anywhere outside the gaols of the country.[328] The gypsies, tinkers, potters and fortune tellers added great colour to the fair, but there were real dangers for the unwary visitor. So much money changed hands, and this was a great attraction for card sharps, con men, pickpockets, and rogues of every description.

> It is a truism that horse dealing has, from the earliest times, been associated with shady tricks, and though footpads and highwaymen only exist now in old-time story and legend, yet we have still the knave with modern rascality, and the thief with dishonest dealing. Flash notes have taken the place of pistols, and cunning roguery and heartless trickery stand for the old demand of "your money or your life". Some

[323] "Prancing palfrey" - a riding horse. The phrase if from "*The Lay of the Last Minstrel*" by Walter Scott.
[324] *Northern Echo*, October 1, 1870
[325] *Teesdale Mercury*, October 7, 1891
[326] *Northern Echo*, October 2, 1876
[327] *Teesdale Mercury*, October 3, 1888
[328] *Teesdale Mercury*, October 7, 1891

> daring diddling was perpetrated at the last Brough Hill Fair, and it looks amazing that intelligent men should continue to be so easily duped. It seems to us almost incredible that a man should part with a valuable horse and accept a cheque from a perfect stranger in the hill country. To begin with there is a great want of business acumen in seriously entertaining such a proposal, for of necessity some time must elapse before the cheque can be cleared and, meanwhile, the horse and the man may be in another hemisphere. Altogether there is much looseness and criminal folly in these fair transactions…[329]

Rough Justice for Highwaymen

In the Seventeenth Century, highwaymen were an ever-present danger to visitors to Brough Hill. At that time, Hagworth Hall in Baldersdale was the residence of a man named Ambrose Appleby, and because of the threat of cattle-raiders from North of the Border, he maintained armed men to protect his cattle. A mile further up the valley was the secluded farm of Water Knott.

One year, the farmer from Water Knott took part of his stock to sell at Brough Hill Fair – a fair attended by "a motley assemblage from every county in England". Having sold the stock for a good price, he headed homewards and on the way called at the inn at Brough village, as was the custom for many buyers and sellers at the fair. He got into jovial conversation with three well-dressed strangers, rashly telling them of his successful business at the fair, showing them his purse of money, and buying them glasses of hot rum.

By midnight and somewhat the worse for drink, this "strong athletic man" took to the saddle and set off on the 14-mile journey across a moorland track to Water Knott. Soon he heard the sound of horsemen behind him, unusual on such a lonely track, and, fearing that they were highwaymen, he quickened his pace which had become a gallop by the time he reached Hunder Beck and home. With the pursuers not far behind and calling on him with oaths to stop, he rushed into the house, but in his haste he not only forgot to bolt the door but also left the key on the outside. The windows were barred preventing his escape and so he determined to resist them as best he could. But then he had an idea: he climbed cautiously up the chimney and on to the roof whilst the men entered the house and searched for him. He slid down the back of the roof and jumped deftly to the ground, before creeping to the outer door and quietly closing and locking it. At last feeling safe, he leapt on his horse and galloped down the valley to Hagworth Hall. Ambrose Appleby and his well-armed men were soon on their way to Water Knott where they found the imprisoned highwaymen who had been unable to break down the door. Soon overpowered, the would-be thieves were bound, then on the orders of Appleby, dragged to the nearest tree and despite their anguished cries for mercy, hanged. Such was Baldersdale justice in those days.

Later it was ascertained that these unfortunate men were notorious highwaymen who had long brought terror to travellers on the Great North Road, and who had committed more than one murder.

The farmer from Water Knott continued to visit Brough Hill Fair, but he was always careful to maintain sobriety and to make the journey home before nightfall.[330]

---

[329] *Teesdale Mercury*, October 14, 1908

[330] *Teesdale Mercury*, September 11, 1912

Highwaymen had disappeared by the Nineteenth Century, but many kinds of rascality continued at the fair. In 1822, several dealers in counterfeit notes attended Brough Hill but were thwarted by a bank agent who cautioned fair-goers against accepting (Scottish) banknotes from strangers. Pickpockets were active: a gentleman, "finding himself jostled, instantly put his hand on his watchpocket and rescued his watch from a thief who had seized the chain: the villain was suffered to escape with a good drubbing."[331]

Kicking Jinny

In 1842, a man was sent by his wife to Brough Hill to sell a grey pony, and to buy another of similar size and colour, but less temperamental than "Kicking Jinny". As soon as he'd sold Jinny, it was not long before the buyer had clipped her mane, cut her tail, and dressed her legs. He then went back to the seller, saying, "I think I have another pony that will please you". The man saw that the pony was of similar size and colour but was anxious to be reassured that it was 'quiet'. "Oh yes, I'll warrant her", replied the dealer, "and I only want £2 more than the one I bought from you." A bargain was struck and the man mounted his pony and set off for home. When his wife saw the new purchase, she rubbed her eyes and looked again, "I think its Jinny!" she exclaimed. "Nay", says he, "I was never better brought home in all my life". It's Jinny, I'm sure!" says she, "but take the bridle off and see if she won't go to the stable door". It soon became evident that he had bought his own pony, and for £2 more than he had sold her for. The deluded couple took the view that the husband had been brought home by Jinny without any trouble on account of the pony's increased value and importance.[332]

The Pony with One Ear

In 1849, a Westmorland Farmer who had several times been duped at Brough Hill by Yorkshire horse-dealers contrived the following scheme in retaliation. He had a handsome pony which unfortunately had lost one of its ears. He managed to acquire an ear of about the same size and colour as the one lost, and fixed it to the pony's head by the bridle. The pony was sold to a Yorkshireman at Brough Hill Fair, with the seller disappearing quickly into the crowd. The purchaser, wishing to put a halter on the pony, took off the bridle and to his surprise, the false ear fell off. He searched in vain for his deceiver who had with haste and great glee made off from the hill.[333]

A Sadder and Wiser Man

Another routine trick was played on a youth from Baldersdale in 1886. The lad had been given the responsibility of selling a horse with an estimated value of £30. As he stood by the animal, awaiting an offer, a man and a horse took up position beside him. The lad was asked the price of his animal, and another man nearby overheard the response. Affecting an air of indifference, he observed that if the lad's horse had been as good as the one stood beside it, he might well have given the money asked. Not long afterwards, the man next to him offered to swap horses, and the youth, taken in by the disparaging remark about his own horse, immediately accepted the offer. This foolish transaction resulted in the youth being

---

[331] *The Times,* October 8, 1822
[332] *Manchester Times*, October 22, 1842
[333] *North Wales Chronicle*, October 23, 1849 (originally from *Carlisle Journal*)

unable to get a reasonable price and he had to settle eventually for 30/-. The report concluded, "He departed homewards, as many had done before him, a sadder and wiser man, but only after paying dear for his experience.[334]

Horse-Dealer Disappears with Farmers' Cash

In 1887, it was reported that a young horse-dealer named Brown from North Yorkshire had disappeared with the proceeds of the sale of forty horses, conservatively valued at £300[335]. Brown was an expert with fell ponies and had been entrusted with selling the horses at Brough Hill Fair by several farmers. After selling most of the young horses at the fair, he headed homewards with the remainder and sold out *en route*. But he never arrived home. Eventually he was established that he had travelled to Liverpool and from there to New York. The report concluded, "Serious loss has thus fallen on several farmers near Hawes, and steps are likely to be taken for his arrest in the United States."[336]

Violent Robbery

By the early 1890s, the police had become more effective in dealing with disreputable elements. Detectives stopped known trouble-makers from travelling from the towns, and several of the officers on duty at Brough Hill posed as well-to-do "horsey-looking" farmers who were able to detain "card-sharpers" and hold them in a temporary lock-up. Such action served as a deterrent to other rogues.[337]

However, the police did not patrol Brough Hill overnight, thus allowing free reign in 1894 to a gang of about thirty ruffians who raided a number of innkeepers' tents:-

> About midnight a gang of about thirty roughs made a raid upon the innkeepers' tents, and attacked the persons in charge with great violence. They carried a huge hedge stake, with which they brutally maltreated all who opposed them. An innkeeper named Richardson was robbed of every farthing he had, and this after having given a drink to each man. An innkeeper named Steel had his arm broken, and a third named Clayton was so badly injured about the head and other parts of the body that he lay insensible for several hours. The police captured two of the gang and dispersed the rest. [338]

A week later, the *Teesdale Mercury* praised the police for apprehending more of the alleged robbers, and observed in an editorial that "the calibre of the miscreants may be gauged pretty accurately when we recollect that the looting was chiefly in quest of drink."[339]

At Carlisle, before Mr Justice Wills, Edward Burke (21), labourer, and John Morris Burke (19), labourer, both of Bishop Auckland, were charged with robbing John Richardson of Ravenstonedale, of six gallons of beer, while armed with sticks at Brough Hill Fair on October 2nd. Richard O'Neil (16), a hawker from Carlisle, Michael Duffy, alias Richard Lowther (23) from Lindale in Cartmel, and Edward Burke were charged with robbing Hannah Dargue, an innkeeper from Hilton, of two gallons of beer, a bottle port and a bottle

[334] *Northern Echo*, October 7 1886
[335] Purchasing power in 2011: £28,000
[336] *Northern Echo*, October 27, 1887
[337] *Teesdale Mercury*, October 7, 1891
[338] *Northern Echo,* October 3, 1894
[339] *Teesdale Mercury*, October 10, 1894

of brandy while armed with sticks at Brough Hill Fair. And Michael Duffy was charged with causing grievous bodily harm to William Steel, an innkeeper from Natby. They were found guilty as charged. Addressing Duffy, the judge said that he looked upon his case as the worst of the lot because of the "really desperate" violence he used, "You might have killed the man with your great bludgeon." He was sentenced to 12 months' hard labour.

After sentencing all the defendants to various terms of hard labour, his Lordship observed that he didn't know much about Brough Hill, but he thought that the "B" should be dropped.[340]

In Quest of Clydesdales

FJS of Hamsterley, just 22 years old in 1926, loved buying and selling stock and he was looking forward to his first visit to Brough Hill to purchase two Clydesdale horses for the farm. Early in the morning on the first day of the fair, he set off from West Auckland on one of Freddie Lockey's coaches for the hour-long journey to Brough Hill. For Freddie, a former miner who had founded Lockey's Bus Service earlier in the year, the popular fair at Brough Hill was good for business – dealers and general fair-goers from Auckland district could travel by rail to Warcop Station, about a mile from Brough Hill, but a bus which could pick up at pre-arranged locations and drop off at the destination was even more convenient.

At Brough Hill, Frank carefully viewed the available stock before striking a bargain for two unbroken three-year-old Clydesdales. He had originally decided to lead the horses to Warcop Station and transport them to Witton-le-Wear by rail, leaving a relatively short journey to Hamsterley. However, when he was on the bus in the morning, he had spoken to two strapping young lads who were on the dole. They were looking for work and persuaded FJS to let them walk the Clydesdales over the moors to Hamsterley – half the money in advance and half on completion of the task. Accordingly, in the afternoon Frank gave half the money to the youths who then set off across the moors with the Clydesdales. Meanwhile, Frank enjoyed the fun of the fair whilst waiting for Lockey's coach to make the return journey to West Auckland.

At the appointed time, the coach left Brough for Auckland with a bus-load of passengers, including not only Freddie Lockey and Frank Sanderson but also the mother of the two lads who were on the moors. The mother, who was 'half gypsy', had expected her sons to be on the coach and became agitated when she was told of their assignment, loudly exclaiming:-

> I'd like to meet the bugger who sent my sons 30 miles with them hosses!

Frank somewhat sheepishly owned up:-

> Look, missus, I sent them, but they asked me to, I didn't ask them. They wanted to, and I've paid them half the money.

But the mother was not in the least mollified, angrily declaring:-

> I don't care what you paid them. When we catch them up, they're getting on this bus and the bloody hosses can go on the moors.

This reaction called for a decisive response, and FJS persuaded Freddie Lockey to get his driver to "drive like hell" past the lads. With the lads in sight and the bus gathering speed, the mother became apoplectic and looked as though she was going to jump out of the

---

340 *Northern Echo*, October 29, 1894

window as the bus approached her sons. Fearing what might happen, Freddie ordered the driver to stop the coach. The mother got out and gave her sons a right talking to: "She didn't half rattle them", recalled FJS.

Mother and sons then got on the bus, and FJS was left with no choice but to get off and walk the horses 15 miles over the moors to Bowes.

He "walked and walked and walked," eventually reached Bowes at about 2 o'clock in the morning. At a little all-night garage, he discovered that someone in the village had a cattle lorry. After he'd got the horses up the ramp into the lorry, he was so worried that they would jump over the sides that he got in with them for the journey:-

> By gum, they pulled me about all night, thank God I was strong, but I was nearly dead. And I tell you, when we came up the hill into Barnard Castle, they were frightened by the lights and were like almost going over the sides.

He and the Clydesdales got home at 6 o'clock in the morning. "I've had some rum go's", he observed rather proudly.

Seven in a Two-Seater Car

Three years later, Freddie Lockey drove his car into a tree in Galgate, Barnard Castle on September 29, 1929, whilst ferrying passengers from Brough Hill Fair back to Bishop Auckland. He was summoned for driving a motor car in a manner dangerous to the public. Richard Gill, a cattle dealer of John Street, Barnard Castle, said he saw the defendant driving a car along Galgate and collide with the tree near the end of King Street. He saw passengers tumble out of the car and he went to help a lady who was lying on the road. PC John Smithson said he was in the Market Place when the defendant left with three people in the front and four at the back. As soon as the car started to move, one man fell off the back and then jumped on again.

12-11 Rover 9/20 hp Two-seater, 1926

Sergeant Dodds said that at 9 pm, he found a two-seater Rover car standing near the tree outside John Duffy's shop in Galgate.

It was badly damaged, and two passengers were receiving medical attention in Mr John Peat's house. Freddie Lockey was having a piece stitched on the end of his nose and one of the women was unconscious. One man had his arm in a sling; another had his leg bandaged and his arm in a sling; a woman had a bleeding foot and her arm in a sling; and two other men admitted that they were in Mr Lockey's car at the time of the accident. He understood that the three women were on the front seat with the driver when the accident occurred. It was a clear night, and the road was well illuminated. Sergeant Dodds observed that the spot where the accident happened was a parking place with a white line around it, and he had never known the tree to be bumped into at night.

Mr Lockey said he had two busloads of passengers from Brough Hill Fair, and for the purpose of seeing that all of them got home, he went in a Rover car with two friends. The busses stopped for half-an-hour at Barnard Castle for refreshments, but some of the passengers were not there when the busses left for Auckland. Two women who had missed the bus started crying because they were unable to get home. The two men who were with Mr Lockey offered to let the women have their seats in the car and to await the return of the car to Barnard Castle. But when Mr Lockey got into the car, three women got on the front seat with him, and three men jumped on the dickey seat of their own accord. It must be said that Freddie Lockey wouldn't have taken up much room in the front seat, being described by one contemporary as "five-foot nowt".

As he drove along Galgate, Mr Lockey claimed that he was dazzled by the lights of a car coming in the opposite direction, and so bumped the tree. He understood the tree had been bumped before and since, that it was an obstruction and that it should either be provided with a red light or chopped down. He argued that because the car was not insured and had become a total loss, this was sufficient punishment for him.

Archibald Brown of Witton Park said he had been on the bus and had waited at Barnard Castle with the women to eat fish and chips, with the result that the bus left without them. Mr Lockey offered to take the women in his car, and Brown and the other men jumped on behind. None of the men at the rear was seriously injured.

Hugh Iveson gave evidence that the men jumped on the back of the car while it was moving.

The bench fined Mr Lockey £1, and ordered him to pay 10s witnesses expenses in addition.[341]

Visitors and friends

Given the outgoing nature of Frank's mother Edith and the many friends she had, it is not surprising that there were always a lot of people at Pond House. Among the visitors was FJS's best friend, Arthur Wyper from Fitches Farm, near Witton Castle. Ignoring the fact that sooner or later, everyone "drops dead", FJS recalled that the whole Wyper family "dropped dead" - his father, 3 brothers, and himself, "Arthur dropped dead beside a tractor wheel - he was feeding sheep one Sunday morning, got off the tractor to open the gate and dropped dead[342]."

> Arthur was my best friend, but even then we'd only have a couple of glasses on a Saturday night. I'd have a girlfriend. I wouldn't be messing on with the men! I used to work till 4 o'clock on a Saturday afternoon. I had to run to Witton Park station - 2 ¾ miles - to catch the train to Auckland. And the last train left Bishop Auckland at 8 o'clock! It's 14 miles to Bishop Auckland and back, and I've walked it a few times. Bikes were no good. A pony and trap was okay except in frosty weather.

[341] *Teesdale Mercury*, November 6, 1929

[342] Arthur Wyper died in 1963 aged 59 years

Another visitor to Pond House was Johnny Lacey, a tailor from Wolsingham, whose father, John Noble Lacey, had been a prominent champion of a school board for Wolsingham (See p.89). Johnny used to stay for several days, sit cross-legged[343] on the kitchen table near the window and knit clothes for the family, including britches and frock coats for Frank Sanderson Snr and dresses for Eleanor and Edith.

12-12 Tailor-sitting: just like Johnny Lacey at Pond House.

Members of the family also visited the Laceys at Wolsingham; a card sent to Frank Sanderson of Shipley in 1905 and postmarked Wolsingham, read:-

> Will you please meet Mrs S tomorrow Friday night by 5 o'clock train from here as she thinks she would like to come then. Hope all are well. A M Lacey.[344]

This was Alice M Lacey, sister of Johnny Lacey and daughter of John Noble[345] and Hannah Lacey, and "Mrs S" was 73 year-old Eleanor Sanderson who had probably been on an extended visit to Wolsingham in search of a new outfit. Eleanor was known for always dressing well.

---

343 Tailors at the time would typically sit cross-legged on a table when working – known as "Tailor sitting".

344 Alice Lacey, a niece of Alice M Lacey, was at school with Freda Ellis née Gibson, just after the Great War

345 John Noble Lacey was born in Shull and was a tailor and draper (See p.90).

12-13 The white-fronted building on the left is Lacey's shop in Wolsingham

FJS's love of singing

In early April, 1980, at Vesey Farm in Essex, FJS sang some of the songs he used to sing in his youth:-

> I used to love to sing. I know a Scot's song, *My Bonnie, Bonnie Jean* that I've never heard a Scotsman sing. I've never heard it sung by anybody else.

My Bonnie, Bonnie Jean was written by famous Scotsman Sir Harry Lauder who also wrote and sang *Roamin' in the gloamin*. Harry Lauder (1870-1950), a contemporary of my grandfather Frank Sanderson, was a prominent music hall star in the early 20th Century, which means that FJS probably heard the song many times in his early life, and that he was mistaken to say that he had never heard a Scotsman sing it. It is most likely that Lauder was inspired to write the song by Robbie Burns, who himself had written about his wife, "Bonnie Jean" Armour (who apparently was anything but bonnie). That FJS should sing this song, given his apparent antipathy to Scotsmen in general and Robbie Burns in particular, has a certain irony.

After singing *Good Old Doctor Shelley* (See p.130), Frank sang another song he'd learned from his father, who used to accompany himself on the piano when he sang *Susan's Sunday In*. This is a song about a maid named Susan and her husband who managed to hide their marriage from the master of the house where Sue worked. When they had been courting, her suitor was happiest when it was her Sunday off.

They could travel to Richmond town in North Yorkshire, perhaps sampling the excellent gin served at the *Star & Garter*. But once they were married, he was just as happy to visit her when it was her 'Sunday in' – taking advantage of the master's absence at church with his family. The master, no doubt suspecting that there was a visitor during his absence, was in the habit of locking Sue in the house and taking the key with him, but her resourceful companion easily gained entry via the parlour window. This accomplished, the two of them then sat down to a good feed at the master's expense.

It was the case that for a woman marriage invariably signalled the end of paid employment. However Sue was able to continue working, even gaining promotion from scullery maid to cook by keeping their marriage secret from the master. Thus they were able to 'save their coppers' to allow them to take over the Coffee Shop, where they would live happily ever after, taking turns to stay in on Sundays!

The master of the house usually held the whip hand but Sue managed to claim some small victories for herself and her new husband. They were innocent times.

Susan's Sunday In[346]

Time used to be as well as how I used to dance and shout
And feel as merry as anything when it was Susan's Sunday Out
Oh but when it is and when it's not I dinna care a pin
As I feel just as happy when it's Susan's Sunday In
Oh, when it's Susan's Sunday In

Now my Sue has got promoted from Scullery Maid to Cook
She hasn't told them that we're spliced, too well she knows her book
On eatables and drinkables we never spend much tin
As Sue gives enough to last a week when it's her Sunday In
Oh, when it's her Sunday In

Now the Master of the House got rid with Dr Dodds' aid
He's now as sprightly as a cork, a perfect cure he's made
He takes his wife and bairns to church to wash away their sin
And I go and take care of Sue when it's her Sunday In
Oh, when it's her Sunday In

Oh, before they go they lock the door and take away the key
Which yet with all their cleverness they can't do Sue and me
I through the parlour window get and in my sleeve I grin
And crikey don't we have a feed when it's Susan's Sunday In
Oh, when it's Susan's Sunday In

Now once a fortnight regular to Richmond Town we pop
And at the Star & Garter there she always makes me stop
She says there is no other place where they sell such good gin
So when it's Susan's Sunday Out, it's not her Sunday In
Oh, it's not her Sunday In

But we're saving up our coppers now and soon the warning give

---

[346] Recorded in April, 1980 at Vesey Farm, Great Holland, Essex
"Susan's Sunday In" is a song Frank Sanderson (1904-1993) learned from his father, Frank Sanderson (1868-1955) in the early part of this century. It seems to have originated in the Northern Dales – Richmond which is referred to in the song is in North Yorkshire, about 20 miles south of Hamsterley.

As happy as two turtle doves together we will live
We mean to take the Coffee Shop when we've saved up the tin
And each in turn will take a turn to have a Sunday In
Oh, to have a Sunday In.

Leaving the North-East

To understand why FJS left the North East, it is necessary to appreciate what had been happening in agriculture over the preceding 50 years.

Following the golden age of agriculture, the great agricultural depression set in from the mid-1870s. The main cause, the repeal of the Corn Laws in 1846, thereby removing barriers to foreign grain imports, had taken 30 years to exert an impact, mainly because of deficiencies in the world transport infrastructure. At mid-century, the railway system was still underdeveloped, not least in the United States where the railroads did not yet extend beyond Chicago.

When it came, the depression was fuelled not only by cheap imports of grain and other produce but also by a succession of wet seasons from 1879-82, followed by severe droughts and frosts. A consequence was that the drift from the land accelerated and continued until well into the twentieth century. And such was the depression that many tenant farmers as well as the landless labourers left the land, particularly in the South of England where many landlords experienced great difficulty in letting the farms. From the late 1870s, desperate owners increasingly looked to find tenants from Scotland and the North of England. One landlord wrote:-

> They (north countrymen) have a notion that they know a thing or two which we don't, and that if they could get cheaper labour and cheaper rents, which are to be had in the south, they could see their way to an eventual fortune[347].

By 1891, there was a "Scotch Colony" in Essex, supplemented by many other enterprising migrants from the North of England. Driven from their regions by excessive rents and excessive competition, they brought in new methods and new ideas and were able to succeed because of their greater economy in the use of men and horses. When wheat production had become uneconomic for Essex farmers, they simply abandoned the farms – as one commentator put it, "They had always been accustomed to a certain groove and rather than move out of it they got ruined."[348] The big new idea of the incomers was to shift the focus to dairy farming, mindful that it was much less labour-intensive and that nearby London would provide a ready market for any quantity of milk they could produce.

Many of the migrants were from the Northern Dales, including William Race and family from Teesdale, whose departure from Harwood in 1905 was marked by "a pleasant little function" at the local chapel:-

> On Friday evening, February 24th, in the Primitive Methodist Chapel, Harwood, a pleasant little function took place, the occasion being to make a presentation to Mrs Wm Race (Elizabeth née Dowson), of Binks House, who has officiated as organist at

[347] Quoted in Mingay (1990) op. cit., page 63
[348] *Bristol Mercury,* March 29, 1894

> the above chapel for thirty years. Mr Robert Allinson, who was chairman, in a racy[349] speech referred to the long period Mrs Race had acted as organist, and the efficient manner in which she had performed her duties, having attended the services in all kinds of weather. The Chairman added that they were all very sorry that Mrs Race was leaving the district, and then called upon Mrs Thos Bayles to make the presentation. Mrs Bayles then rose to hand over the presents, and, in the course of a few well-chosen remarks, hoped that Mrs Race would accept them as a slight memento of her services from her many good friends she was going to leave behind in Harwood. Mrs Race very feelingly responded, and thanked them all for the kindness which they had bestowed upon her, and stated that she would ever look upon the presents and past memories of Harwood with pleasure. After the presentation supper was provided for all present, during which a few well-chosen Methodist hymns were sung with much fervour, and everyone went home highly delighted with the happy evening they had spent. The presents, which were of first-class merit, consisted of a beautiful silver teapot, suitably inscribed, a silver and gold china biscuit bowl, silver and cut-glass jelly dish, pearl inlaid workbox, and an illuminated album. All the presents were supplied by Mr Joseph Raine of Middleton. Mr Wm Race and family, who are leaving Harwood for Frinton-on-Sea to take up new duties there, will carry away with them the good wishes of everyone in the district. Mr Race was of a very clever and ingenious character, and had acted as mining manager at Lady Rake Mine for a number of years, and also held office of parish councillor and rural district councillor.

Two days later there was a similar farewell party for William Race's daughter Frances in the school-room at Harwood:-

> Miss Race, who has acted as organist at Harwood Church for a few years, was presented with a beautiful Morocco-bound church service book and a gold fountain pen. The Rev PW Francis made the presentation, and referred to Miss Race's faithful services. Miss Race suitably responded. After the presentation, a social evening was held.[350]

William's younger brother Joseph stayed in Teesdale until after the Great War, first working as a lead miner and then as a cattle and sheep farmer. In 1923, he was farming at Pennington (See p.185) when he sold up[351] and moved to Essex where William had become a partner with the Mr JW Scott,[352] also from Teesdale (Wheysyke), in the firm of Messrs Race and Scott,[353] farmers, dairymen, coal agents and livery stable proprietors.

---

[349] "Racy" in this context undoubtedly means "lively and spirited" rather than "risqué", and the pun was intended.
[350] *Teesdale Mercury*, March 8, 1905
[351] His valuable farm stock was sold by auctioneer Tom Vickers of Thornley Hall (See p.45)
[352] John William Scott collapsed and died in the Weslyan Chapel in Frinton in 1935, aged 73. His business partner William Race died in January, 1939, aged 81.
[353] William Race and John William Scott founded Messrs Race & Scott in 1909.

Joseph farmed at Dilbridge Hall with his son Percy, and in 1929, FJS left the North-East and moved to Essex to learn more about farming alongside Percy Race and under the tutelage of Joseph.[354]

FJS's explanation for the move to Essex was as follows:-

> I couldn't make a living in the north. Farms were too dear. Everybody knew where you'd bought the beasts, everybody knew what they'd cost, and everybody knew how much profit you were going to make, or if you were going to make <u>any</u>. It was useless. Where I went to Essex, there were farms derelict where I went, farms for nothing. The first farm - The Meers - I had it for less than nothing. I was being paid for having it. 180 acres and £120 rent per year. There were six cottages: 2 were let @ 12/6 pw and the others @ 7/6 pw. The Shoot was let @ £25 pa. There was £10 pa for a Wireless Relay Station, and £10 for the manure hill.

In 1932, FJS married Hilda, the daughter of William and Elizabeth Race, and they had a daughter in 1937. FJS married secondly Joan Bullough in 1952, and they had two boys.

Francis Joseph Sanderson departed this life in 1993. FJS's success as a farmer was based on hard work and hard-nosed business dealings. Like Terry Atkinson's grandfather Richard Thomas Atkinson, he could be a hard task-master who was respected by the people he came into contact with through his business. When provoked, he could display a fierce temper, but he could also be very charming and generous to a fault.

At his funeral service at All Saints, Great Holland, I felt privileged to speak about the life of such a colourful character, a person who certainly left his mark on this world and who will long be remembered.

12-14 Francis Joseph Sanderson 1904-1993

[354] Dilbridge Hall Farm was demolished in the 1960s

INDEX

Adams, James (Agent for Ransomes), 79, 80, 81, 84, 85, 86
Alderson, Ann (Bell), 22, 220
Alderson, Eleanor (Sanderson) 1832-1910, 73, 113, 116, 219, 222, 243
Alderson, Eleanor née Snowdon, 73, 220
Alderson, Jane (Nattrass), 89
Alderson, Thomas (Parish Clerk, Hurworth), 19
Alderson, William (1788-1866), 220
Allinson, Robert of Forest and Frith, 247
Anderson, Elizabeth née Watson, 193
Angus, Barbara of High Shipley, 17
Angus, George of Broomley, 38
Appleby, Ambrose of Hagworth Hall, 237
Applegarth, George (Police Constable), 173
Applegarth, Sergeant Thomas, 173
Ardincaple (Newcastle-Edinburgh Steamboat), 207, 208
Arkley, William of Broomley (Blacksmith), 82
Arnison, Dr Charles of Stanhope, 51
Asquith, Herbert (Prime Minister), 179
Atkinson, Elizabeth née Dalton, 110
Atkinson, Francis Terrence, 3, 108, 146, 149, 248
Atkinson, John George Coates, 166
Atkinson, Joseph of Kays Lea (Vestry Man), 22
Atkinson, Richard Maxwell, 146, 147, 148, 149
Atkinson, Richard Thomas of Acrum Farm, 146
Atkinson, Richard Thomas of Witton-le-Wear, 147, 248
Ayhope Shield, 17, 59, 187, 195, 197, 198, 199, 200, 204, 205, 208, 209, 210, 211, 212, 213, 214, 216
Ayton, Joseph of Thornley, 29
Backhouse, Charles J (Magistrate), 51
Bainbridge, Emerson Muschamp of Eastgate, 45
Barker, James (Ploughman for Ransomes), 78, 79, 80, 81, 82, 83, 84, 85, 86
Barnard Castle, 219, 222, 230, 232, 234, 241, 242
Barnard Castle School, 219, 222
Baron von Scheissen. See Beaver, Mr (Farm Manager)
Baty, William Thomas of Waskerley, 44
Bayles, Mary of Harwood, 247
Beadle, Jane of Ettersgill, 183
Beadle, Sarah (Race), 183
Beamont, Hubert (Liberal politician), 138
Beaver, Mr (Farm Manager), 226, 231
Bedburn, 2, 19, 24, 37, 134, 135, 141, 158, 159, 160, 164, 218, 224
Bedburn Hall Farm, 127, 154, 156, 158, 221
Bell, George (Vestry Man, Hamsterley), 22
Bell, George of Cumberland, 22, 73
Bell, John (Innkeeper), 73
Bell, Old Willy of Heathery Cleugh, 52
Bell, Rev William R (Laithkirk), 193
Bellerby, Tom (House Painter), 212
Biddick, Alexander de, 11
Bishopley, 16
Black Hall Lodge, 26, 37, 38, 55, 94
Black Ling Hole, 185, 186, 187, 189
Blackett, Mary Hannah, 176, 178
Blenkin, Wylam, 213
Bollihope, 3
Bonsor, Cosmo of Holwick Hall, 191
Bournemouth, 117, 119, 121
Bradley Hall, 37, 38, 50, 55, 56, 89
Braithwaite, Jane, 175
Broomley, 17, 38, 39, 43, 54, 58, 59, 211
Broomley Villa, Hexham, 50
Brough Hill Fair, 235, 237, 238, 239, 241, 242
Brown Humes, John Edward (Coroner), 107, 111, 164
Brown, Albert Ernest (Policeman), 125
Brown, Archibald of Witton Park, 242
Brown, Joseph of Greenhead, 18
Brunskill, John of East Fold Garth Farm, 211
Burke, Edward (Brough Hill Robber), 239
Burke, John Morris (Brough Hill Robber), 239
Burnigill Farm, 29, 97, 99, 104, 107
Burns, Jean née Armour, 244
Burns, Robert (Poet), 33, 39, 185, 193, 195, 225, 234, 244
Butler, Joseph (Rector of Stanhope), 13
Butsfield Burn Farm, 100, 108, 117
Caile, John of Etherley, 184
Carmichael, Dougal of Neighbour Moor, 189, 191
Chapman, Moses of St Helens Auckland, 213

Charge of the Light Brigade, 220
Chaytor, Dr Henry LLD (Canon of the Third Prebend), 200, 206
Chisholm, Robert of Norham-on-Tweed, 234
Churchill, Winston (Home Secretary), 133
Coates, Harry (Farmer and colliery owner), 112
Coatsworth, Joseph Walton of Bedburn Lane, 9, 223, 225, 228
Coatsworth, William of Hamsterley, 173, 187
Cockfield, 165, 178, 180, 187, 235
Corn Laws, Repeal of, 1846, 246
Cousins, Jackie of West Auckland, 10, 123, 146, 147, 148, 150
Cowley, Charlotte A (Pearson), 233
Cowley, George of Shull, 144, 233
Cowley, Henry of Shull, 233
Cowley, Jack of Shull, 224, 233
Cowley, William of Hamsterley, 233
Crimean War, 220
Criminal Appeal Act, 179
Crook's Altar, 58, 97, 98, 99, 109, 112
Cross Keys, Hamsterley, 65, 94, 162, 175, 187, 228, 233
Crossling, Ralph of Wolsingham, 90
Cruikshanks, Alexander (Police Sergeant), 169
Cruikshanks, William (Police Constable), 169
Dalton, Ann née Emerson, 110
Dalton, John William (Johnny) of Snowhope Close, 109
Dalton, John William (Willie) of Crook's Altar, 110
Dalton, Walter of Westgate, 112
Dalton, William of Snowhope Close, 110
Dawson, John of Brignall, 209
Dawson, Joseph of Ireshopeburn, 51, 52
Dawson, Mary ('wife' of John Hankey Snr), 200
Dawson, Watson of Brignall, 209
Dean, Thomas (Coroner), 173
Denby, John, 159, 214
Dickman, John Alexander (hung for murder on train), 133
Dickman, John Alexander (Murderer), 132
Diddridge Farm, 129, 184
Disraeli, Benjamin (English Statesman), 113
Dix, Charles (Solicitor), 51, 52
Dodd, Jessie (Sanderson), 57
Dodds, John of Bedburn, 169
Dodds, Matthew (Edge Tool Manufacturer), 167
Dodds, Matthew James (Joiner), 167, 174, 175, 176, 177, 178, 179, 181
Dodds, Michael John (Timber Merchant), 167, 181
Dodds, Nancy (Stephenson), 157, 167
Dodds, Philliip W (Coroner), 57
Dodds, Sergeant (Policeman), 241
Dolphin, John (Wolsingham Solicitor), 91
Douglas, Rose Ellen of Thornley, 10, 126, 141, 162
Dove, Jane (Lamb), 169
Dove, John George of Cockfield, 169, 170
Dove, Thomas of Gilling, 169
Duffy, John (Grocer), 241
Dunn, Mary Elizabeth (Blenkin/Chapman), 150
East Rackwood Hill, 143, 196
Eden, Sir Anthony, 107
Education Act, (1870), 89, 92
Egdell, Mary Ann (Noble/Taylorson), 172
Egglestone, John (Game-watcher), 172
Egglestone, William Morley of Stanhope (Inspector of Nuisances), 194, 195
Elliot, Mary Annie (Dalton), 110
Elliot, Mary Elizabeth née Craig, 110, 111
Ellis, Freda née Gibson, 134, 135, 223, 243
Ellis, Ted of Crook, 134
Elm Park, Tow Law, 47, 48
Emerson, Elizabeth (Sanderson), 14
Emerson, Henry of Hamsterley, 18
Emmerson, John of Tow Law, 91
Farrage, Minnie née Vickers, 2, 43
Fatkin, Elizabeth née Hodgson, 168, 173
Fatkin, Mary Jane (Marquis/Dodds), 168, 170, 171, 173, 174, 175, 176, 177, 178, 179, 181
Fatkin, William (Coke Drawer), 168
Featherstone, Mary (Sanderson), 209
Fife, Mr Herbert Legard of Cleatlam (Teesdale Guardian), 235
FJS. *See* Sanderson, Francis Joseph of Hamsterley (1904-1993)
Fogg-Elliot, Charles T (Private Secretary to Lord Barnard), 174
Fogg-Elliot, John Walton (Land Agent), 158, 163
Follansby, Alyce (Sanderson), 12
Foster, Mary (Simpson), 196
Fowler, Chief Inspector Thomas of Stanhope, 111
Fulforth Farm, 199
General Strike of 1926, 235

Gibbon, Thomas (Rent Collector for Dean &Chapter), 206
Gibson, George of Wolsingham Park, 19
Gibson, Joseph of Howden-le-Wear, 135
Gibson, Rev Thomas of Hamsterley, 66
Gibson, William (Excise Officer), 188
Gill, George (Farmer from Woodland), 100
Gilmore, Rev Hugh (Primitive Methodist Minister), 90
Gipps, Harry (Innkeeper and Farmer), 57
Gladstone, William (Engish Statesman), 161
Glass, Alison (Millie), 204, 206
Glass, Ann née Taylor, 203
Glass, Ann of Wemyss, 206
Glass, Emma Wemyss of Wemyss, 207, 208
Glass, Isabella of Wemyss, 208
Glass, Jane (Webster), 204, 206
Glass, Mary (Leitch), 208
Glass, Richard of Wemyss (Shepherd), 203, 204, 205, 207
Glass, William (Shepherd at Wemyss Castle), 204
Graham, Joseph of Wearhead (Cattle Dealer), 234
Graham-Barton, Rev Alexander, 170
Grantham, Sir William (Judge, Queen's Bench), 175, 178, 179
Gray, Lizzie née Walton, 129
Gregory, John of South Shields (Agricultural Implement Maker), 83, 84, 85
Grey, Hannah (Sanderson) 1754-1839, 16, 73
Grey, John, 16
Grove, The, 154, 172, 183, 205
Guy's Close, 18, 200, 203
Hagworth Hall in Baldersdale, 237
Hall, Jane (Sanderson), 53
Hall, Joseph Jnr, 29
Hall, Joseph of Monkfield, 23, 73
Hall, Norman (Farmer from Woodland), 112
Hall, Thomas of Tow Law, 53
Hamilton, Joseph of Wolsingham (Tailor), 44
Hamilton, Mary Elizabeth (Vickers), 44, 45, 46, 47
Hamsterley, 123, 124, 126, 127, 131, 134, 168, 171, 173, 174, 175, 176, 181, 198, 199, 205, 213, 214, 216, 219, 220, 221, 222, 224, 230, 231, 232, 233, 234, 240, 244, 245
Hamsterley Hoppings, 131, 233
Hankey, Alice Ann née Angus, 17, 210
Hankey, Charles of Evenwood Gate, 129
Hankey, George II of Ayhope Shield, 210
Hankey, George of Ayhope Shield, 199, 200
Hankey, Jane (Sanderson), 200
Hankey, John Jnr of Ayhope Shield, 186, 200, 210
Hankey, John Joseph of Ayhope Shield, 210
Hankey, John Snr of Ayhope Shield, 200, 203, 204, 205, 208
Hankey, Mary (Simpson), 195, 210
Hardcastle, William (Medical Practioner), 133
Harle, Martha (Wall), 156
Harle, Martha (wife of William), 156
Harle, Mary (Stott), 156
Harle, William of Corsenside, 154, 156
Harle, William of Witton Gilbert, 156
Harperley, 25, 34, 35, 58, 72, 73, 78, 113
Harperley and Helme Park Ploughing Match, (1856), 77
Harrison, Jasper of Wolsingham, 199
Harrowbank, 200, 203
Hauxwell, Hannah, 35
Hay, Lady Emma (Wemyss), 206
Hay, William, 17th Earl of Erroll, 206
Heads, John George (Colliery Blacksmith), 180
Henderson, Arthur (MP for Barnard Castle), 5, 138, 139
Henderson, John of Hamsterley (Blacksmith), 19
Henderson, Margaret of Blazon Hill, 154
Henderson, Michael of Hamsterley (Blacksmith), 172
Henderson, William of Blazon Hill, 154
Henderson, William of Hamsterley (Blacksmith), 177
Hewitson, Constance Mary, née Smith, 109
Hewitson, Henry of Walworth, 103, 108, 109
Hewitson, Henry Scoror of Heighington, 107
High Moor Hill Farm, 19
High Shipley, 24, 25, 34, 63, 64, 65, 72, 73, 94, 219
Hill House Farm, Brandon, 93, 97
Hodgson, Dorothy (Housekeeper for Dodds family), 174
Hodgson, Elizabeth (Fatkin), 168
Hodgson, Thomas (Vestry Man, Hamsterley), 22
Holland, Rev WH (Prison Reformer), 90
Holliday, Rev John (Vicar of Hamsterley), 9, 176, 224, 230
Honeybee, 59, 214, 216

Hooppell, Rev Dr Robert E (Rector of Byers Green), 22
Hoppyland, 156, 167, 187, 217, 218
Howl John Farm, 18
Hudson, William (Nature Writer), 67
Hutchinson, William (Police Constable), 169
Iveson, Hugh, 242
Jewitt, Arnold (Butcher), 143
Jewitt, Edger of Hamsterley, 143
Jewitt, James of Hamsterley, 143, 196
Jewitt, Josiah of Hamsterley, 143, 196
Jolby Farm, 19
Jones, Rachel of Hunwick, 123
Kinninvie, 232
Kipling, Joseph of Stackholme, 35
Kipling, Mary of Stackholme, 71
Kipling, Sarah (Sanderson), 24, 35, 39, 41, 71, 72
Kirton, Hugh of Hill House, Brandon, 89
Knavesmire, 78
Lacey, Alice Mary (Hawdon), 243
Lacey, Hannah née Gardiner, 243
Lacey, John Noble (Wolsingham Tailor and Draper), 90, 92, 243
Lacey, Johnny (Wolsingham Tailor and Draper), 243
Lamb, Samuel of Dixon Carr (Farmer), 169
Langstaff, Mary Margaret née Gibson, 24
Larch Hill, 153
Lasses, The (Ann, Margaret, Mary, and Elizabeth Jane Stephenson), 26
Lauder, Harry (Music Hall Star), 244
Lawson, Mary (Dodds), 167
Lightfoot, Joseph Barber (Bishop of Durham), 120, 121
Lincoln, Abraham, 25
Little Titch, 225, 226, 227, 228, 229
Littlefair, George of South Bedburn, 184, 187
Littlefair, Hannah (Dodds), 167, 181
Littlefair, Martha née Watson, 193
Lloyd George, David (Statesman), 129
Lockey, Freddie (Lockey's Bus Service), 240, 241, 242
Longstaff, Thomas of Bedburn, 155
Lovejoy, Rev Henry Taylor of Hamsterley, 126, 161
Low Harperley, 72, 90
Low Shipley, 227
Lowe, Thomas (Police Constable), 176
Lowson, Elizabeth Jane, 124
Lowson, Eveline (Brown), 10, 125
Lowson, George (Teesdale Guardian), 235
Lumley, Maud (Sanderson), 54
Lumsdon, Florence (Sanderson), 54
Lyle, Professor Robert Patton Ranken (Obstetrician), 145
Maher, Henrietta Maggie (Stephenson), 158
Manners, George of Westerton, 29
Marquis, Elizabeth Ann, 175, 176
Marquis, John of Hamsterley, 168, 169, 170, 171, 173, 174, 188
Marquis, John Snr of Hamsterley, 153
Marquis, Joseph of Hamsterley, 168
Marr, George of Lynesack, 175, 176, 178
Marshall Green, 27, 37, 42, 53, 72, 94
Mason, Nora (Sanderson), 107
McEleavey, John of Etherley, 169
McEleavey, Michael of Etherley, 169
McLeod, Capt (Master of *Ardincaple*), 208
Meeting of the Grains, 198, 213, 214
Metcalfe's House, 214, 216
Milner, Rev James George of Hamsterley, 21, 66, 126
Milner, Rev John (Middleton-in-Teesdale), 193
Milner, Rev William Kirkbank, 23, 73
Monkfield, 23, 73
Moore KB, General Sir John, 222
Moore, Mary (Stephenson), 27
Moralee, Thomas of Newlandside, 16
Nafferton, 55, 56, 57, 131, 146
Nafferton Lad, 56
Nattrass, Hugh Kirton, 89
Nattrass, John Kirton, 73, 89, 220
Nattrass, Mary, 88
Nattress, Willie, 107
Nesbit, John (Colliery Book-keeper), 131, 132
Nicholson, John of Broomshiels, 38
Nickels, Mary (Stephenson), 153
O'Hara, Dr John of Stanhope, 111
O'Neil, Richard (Brough Hill Robber), 239
Palletstone House, Langleydale, 183
Pallister, Annie née Williamson, 135
Pallister, Elizabeth Anne (Gibson), 20, 135
Pallister, John of Bedburn, 136
Pallister, Joseph of Hamsterley, 136
Pallister, Mary of Bedburn, 136
Pallister, William of Cockfield, 153
Parker, Norman (Farm hand at Crook's Altar), 111
Parsons, Charles (*Cleveland Arms*, Middleton), 193
Patterson, Dr Browning of Butterknowle, 171

Pattison, Alfred Stephenson of Witton-le-Wear, 108
Pattison, Margaret Jane née Gittins, 177
Pattison, Richard of Witton-le-Wear, 29, 98
Pearson, John of Stanhope, 203
Pearson, William (Jeweller, Bishop Auckland), 233
Pease Myers Farm, 18, 63
Peat, John of Barnard Castle, 241
Pennington Farm, 183, 184, 185, 187, 188, 189, 191, 196, 210, 227
Perkins, Eileen née Hankey, 198, 199, 205, 208, 210, 211, 212
Pettitt, Alice Mary (died of burns), 66
Philipson, John of Weardale (Mayor of South Melbourne), 158
Pierrepoint, Henry (Hangman), 180
Pierrepoint, Thomas (Hangman), 180
Piper, Barbara of Hexham, 66
Pond House, Hamsterley, 94, 123, 124, 135, 137, 145, 160, 212, 221, 242, 243
Pooltree, 209
Powell, Benezer of Shield Ash, 14
Pratt, Fleetham Watson of South Shields, 60
Price, Rev Dr Robert (Canon of the Third Prebend), 206
Price, Thomas, 206
Primitive Methodism, 90
Proud, Charles of Pennington, 29, 196, 227
Proud, Elizabeth (Gardener/Stephenson), 156
Proud, Hannah née Hall, 29, 227
Proud, John (Butcher Proud), 227
Proud, John Thomas (Solicitor and Coroner), 52, 175, 227
Proud, William (Farmer), 227
Race, Elizabeth, née Dowson, 246
Race, Frances Elizabeth, 247
Race, Hilda (Sanderson), 248
Race, John Percy of Dilbridge Hall, 248
Race, Joseph of Pennington, 247
Race, Thomas of Hamsterley, 184
Race, William Watson of Bink's House, Teesdale, 246
Railways, 5, 31, 32, 34, 160
Raine, Annie Eliza, 29, 109, 112
Raine, Cissie, 148
Raine, John Hall, 97, 112
Raine, Joseph of Middleton-in-Teesdale, 247
Raine, Mr RW (Teesdale Guardian), 235
Ravensford Farm, 19, 23, 102, 103, 157
Reade, Rev Richard (Vicar, Romaldkirk), 35
Redgate Shield, 205, 206
Reid, Gertrude (Cowley), 233
Relph, Harry (Little Titch), 227
Rhodes, Cecil, 86
Richards, Mr Tantobie (Egg Collector), 61
Richardson, George of Stotley, 189, 190
Richardson, John (Brough Hill Victim), 239
Richmond, North Yorks, 227, 244, 245
Riding of the Bounds, 199
Robey, Sir George (Music Hall Star), 228
Robinson, Maurice of Westgate (Quarryman), 111
Robinson, Sid of West Auckland, 228
Robson, Elizabeth (Sanderson), 200
Robson, John of Hamsterley (Grocer), 174
Rodmell, Frances Muriel, 166
Rolls, Charles (Motor-car pioneer), 219
Ross, John Rueben of Castle Hill, 50
Royce, Henry (Motor-car pioneer), 219
Ruddy Carr, 17, 59, 198, 211, 222
Rushy Lea, 17
Sacriston Heugh, 199
Samplers in the Sanderson Family, 69
Samson, The Strongest Man on Earth, 52
Sanderson, Agnes, 12
Sanderson, Steven of Hamsterley, 12
Sanderson, Alfred Stephenson of Butsfield Burn, 108, 109, 110, 112
Sanderson, Alice (Hewitson), 107
Sanderson, Allison of Hamsterley by Bishop Auckland, 12
Sanderson, Ann (Watson), 14
Sanderson, Bertha Isabella (Hall), 112
Sanderson, Caroline of Bradley Hall, 37
Sanderson, Dinah (Dunn), 19
Sanderson, Edgar of Butsfield Burn, 104, 117, 213
Sanderson, Eleanor Eliza (Atkinson), 3, 95, 117, 129, 134, 135, 136, 137, 145, 147, 152, 161, 166, 212, 213, 219, 223, 230
Sanderson, Eleanor Margaret (Coates), 112
Sanderson, Elizabeth (Stobbs), 14
Sanderson, Elizabeth Eleanor (Stothard), 87, 89, 113, 115, 116, 151, 222
Sanderson, Elizabeth Jane of Burnigill, 103
Sanderson, Elizabeth of Harrowbank, 200, 203
Sanderson, Elizabeth of High Shipley, 24, 35, 69, 72
Sanderson, Ellen Ann (1888-1917), 104, 105
Sanderson, Elsie (Tipler), 104, 109
Sanderson, Elsie Mary (Gill), 100
Sanderson, Evelyn (Pratt), 59

Sanderson, Francis (1866), 89
Sanderson, Francis Joseph of Hamsterley (1904-1993), 2, 4, 5, 67, 87, 95, 96, 114, 115, 117, 122, 127, 128, 134, 151, 152, 198, 213, 219, 220, 222, 223, 226, 230, 232, 233, 234, 240, 242, 244, 246, 248
Sanderson, Francis William of Acomb, 146
Sanderson, Frank junior of Nafferton, 56, 130
Sanderson, Frank of Burnigill, 2, 96, 106, 144
Sanderson, Frank of Hamsterley (1868-1955), 1, 9, 60, 87, 96, 103, 113, 121, 123, 131, 145, 213, 244
Sanderson, Frank of Low Harperley (1828-1915), 24, 26, 35, 63, 89, 90, 93, 100, 103, 112, 113, 120, 219, 231
Sanderson, Frank of Nafferton (1852-1935), 5, 37, 45, 49, 53, 54, 131
Sanderson, Gordon, 57
Sanderson, Hannah (1818-1839), 24
Sanderson, Hannah Richardson (White), 59
Sanderson, Henry of Hamsterley, 1, 3, 108, 117, 147, 148, 213, 231
Sanderson, Jack of Stocksfield, 2, 56
Sanderson, Jackie (1923-44), 107, 213
Sanderson, Jane (Vickers) of Elm Park, 37, 39, 42, 46, 57
Sanderson, Jane (Vickers) of Guy's Close, 18, 200, 202
Sanderson, Jane of Harrowbank, 200, 203
Sanderson, Jane of High Shipley (1826-1834), 24, 42, 64
Sanderson, Jean (1924-1941), 107
Sanderson, Jenny (Thompson), 49, 56
Sanderson, Joan née Bullough, 248
Sanderson, John George of Saskatchewan, 4
Sanderson, John Jnr of Burnigill, 107
Sanderson, John of Bishopley (1782-1865), 9, 16, 18, 22, 25, 26, 65
Sanderson, John of Broomley (1821-1897), 9, 17, 24, 26, 29, 31, 38, 41, 43, 72
Sanderson, John of Burnigill (1862-1939), 4, 87, 89, 97, 113, 114, 122
Sanderson, John of Hamsterley by Bishop Auckland, 12
Sanderson, John of Harrowbank, 200, 203, 209
Sanderson, John of Low Bishopley (1725-1775), 13, 14
Sanderson, John of Milnhouses (1752-1835), 14, 15
Sanderson, John Taylor, 2, 10
Sanderson, John Thomas of Broomley, 59
Sanderson, John Thomas of Nafferton, 49, 56, 130
Sanderson, Joseph of Stackholme, 37, 39
Sanderson, Lawrence of Nafferton, 57
Sanderson, Margaret (Hall/Toward), 23, 26, 73
Sanderson, Margaret (Nicholson), 39
Sanderson, Mary (Moralee), 14
Sanderson, Mary (Stephenson), 24, 72
Sanderson, Mary Ann (1860-63), 89
Sanderson, Mary Eleanor née Raine, 29, 97, 117
Sanderson, Mary Hannah (Murray) of Saskatchewan, 4
Sanderson, Mary Isabella, 37
Sanderson, Matthew of Harrowbank, 200
Sanderson, Mavis (MacLean), 109
Sanderson, Nancy née Rogerson, 57, 146
Sanderson, Patricia née Cummings, 213
Sanderson, Ralph of Whelpshillend, 14
Sanderson, Ruth Kipling (Watson), 37, 38, 50, 52, 53
Sanderson, Sarah Ann (Baty), 37, 39, 45
Sanderson, Sarah Elizabeth (Whitfield), 53, 57
Sanderson, Susannah (Dawson), 200, 203, 204, 206, 207, 209
Sanderson, Thomas (1864-1865), 89
Sanderson, Thomas of Broomley (1853-1941), 17, 37, 38, 49, 58, 130, 198
Sanderson, Thomas of Snapegate, 200
Sanderson, William Henry of Butsfield Burn, 104, 117
Sanderson, William Henry of Harperley (1871-75), 5, 113, 114, 115
Sanderson, William of Milnhouses (1778-1859), 15, 23, 73
Sandow, Eugen, 52
Scott, Jane (Servant at The Grove), 205
Scott, John William of Teesdale, 247
Scottish Admiral (ship), 27, 28
Seavers, John of Thirsk, 29
Sedgewick, Tom of Marshall Green, 93
Seers, Jane, née Jewitt, 143
Shaw, Crosyer Surtees of Pennington, 183
Shaw, George Surtees of Pennington, 183
Shaw, Jane (Farm Lass), 183
Shaw, Robert Surtees of Pennington, 183
Shearwood, Capt Harry (Teesdale Guardian), 235
Shull, 222, 224, 233, 243
Siddle, Annie (Vickers), 45

Siddle, Jane, née Vickers, 4
Simpson, Ann née Beadle, 183, 186, 187, 189, 196
Simpson, Edward of Langleydale, 183
Simpson, Elizabeth (Swinbank), 184
Simpson, Emma (Littlefair), 184
Simpson, Joannah née Welsh, 208, 209
Simpson, John of Pennington, 196
Simpson, Matthew (Bone-setter of Whitworth), 231
Simpson, Sarah née Talentire, 183
Simpson, William of Langleydale, 183, 184, 185
Simpson, William of Monkwearmouth Shore, 208
Simpson, William of Pennington, 186, 196, 227
Smailes, George Southern (Schoolmaster), 123
Smart, Agnes (Glass), 204
Smith, William of Low Fotherley, 82, 83, 84, 85
Smithson, John (Police Constable), 241
Snaith, Elizabeth (Sanderson), 209
Snowdon, Florrie (Vickers), 48
Snowdon, John, 50
Spark, Henry King (Colliery Owner), 192, 193
Sparks, John (aka Etherington), 169
Spence, Hugh of Hamsterley, 158
Spence, Margaret née Anderson, 172
Spence, Mark of Hamsterley, 172
Spence, Mary Ann née Gipps, 57
Spinning Wheel, Hamsterley, 135
Spratt, Peter (Police Constable), 38
Stackholme, 35
Stanhope St Thomas, 13
Stanhope Town Hall, 51
Steel, William (Innkeeper), 240
Stephenson, Alice Dowson née Kirkup, 176, 178
Stephenson, Ann (Marquis), 153, 168
Stephenson, Doris née Lockerbie, 137
Stephenson, Edith (Sanderson) 1883-1922, 1, 10, 124, 126, 129, 135, 137, 141, 160, 161, 219, 221, 224, 227, 242, 243
Stephenson, Edward of Hamsterley, 162, 165
Stephenson, Eliza née Beadle, 183, 184, 196, 197, 223
Stephenson, Elizabeth Jane (Seavers), 29
Stephenson, Ena (Gowland), 163
Stephenson, Francis Simpson, 230
Stephenson, Frank of Harperley, 26, 136
Stephenson, George Norman of Hamsterley, 228
Stephenson, George of Bedburn, 126, 160, 161
Stephenson, Gladys (Wilkinson), 147, 162, 166, 167
Stephenson, Hannah née Beaston, 153
Stephenson, Henry of West Hoppyland, 153, 156, 160
Stephenson, John of Brancepeth, 24, 26, 72
Stephenson, John of Eastgate, 153
Stephenson, John of Hamsterley, 153
Stephenson, John of Harperley, 24, 27
Stephenson, Joseph Hamsterley of Victoria, 157
Stephenson, Joseph Jnr of Bedburn, 4
Stephenson, Joseph of Bedburn (1829-1915), 124, 155, 156, 167, 231
Stephenson, Joseph of Hamsterley (shoemaker), 172
Stephenson, Joseph of Weardale (1781-1870), 153, 156
Stephenson, Lawrence Kirkup of Hamsterley, 162, 164
Stephenson, Margaret (Ayton), 29
Stephenson, Marjorie (Cooper), 163
Stephenson, Mary (Pallister), 135, 153
Stephenson, Mary (Pattison), 24, 29
Stephenson, Mary Ann (Spence), 157, 160
Stephenson, Samuel of Bedburn, 160
Stephenson, Sarah née Spence, 172
Stephenson, Thomas of Bedburn, 159, 160, 164, 176
Stephenson, Thomas of Low Redford, 153
Stephenson, William of Bedburn, 160
Stephenson, William of Black Hill Top, 163
Story, Jane (Sanderson), 56
Stothard, Francis Sanderson Jnr, 3
Stothard, Frank Sanderson of Framwellgate, 87, 96, 230
Stothard, John of Pickering, 88
Stothard, Ralph Edward of Framwellgate, 87, 213
Stothard, Ralph of Carr House (Champion Ploughman), 82, 83, 84, 85, 86, 87, 96, 129
Stothard, William Henry of Framwellgate, 87, 116
Surtees, Crosyer of Redford Grove, 183
Surtees, Henry Edward of The Grove, 185, 210
Surtees, Jane née Surtees, 183

Surtees, Robert of The Grove, 154, 205
Swinbank, Bill of Carabooda, 184
Swinbank, Joseph of Woodland, 184
Swinbank, Mary Jane (Jennie), 125
Swinney, Neil (itinerant sailor), 19
Taylorson, John of Chester-le-Street, 172
Teasdale, Gibson (Gibby) of Hamsterley, 230
Teasdale, Gibson Snr (Innkeeper), 228
Teesdale Board of Guardians, 235
Thompson, James (Police Constable), 170, 171, 172, 187
Tipler, Thomas of Brandon, 109
Tow Law, 90, 91, 93, 234
Tow Law Auction Mart, 43, 44, 47, 52
Trotter, Thomas of Stocksfield, 80
Trotter, William of Bishop Auckland (Coroner), 155
Tunstall House, 43
Vasey, Catherine, 19
Vesey Farm, Great Holland, 2, 152
Vickers, Arthur of Howl John, 45
Vickers, Esther of Snowfield (Whitfield), 18
Vickers, Francis (1749-1822), 19, 63
Vickers, Francis (1782-1877), 2
Vickers, Francis Edwin, 47
Vickers, Francis of Belle Vue, 47, 210
Vickers, Francis of Pease Mires, 144
Vickers, George of Ontario, 4
Vickers, James of Guy's Close, 18, 200
Vickers, Jennie Hamilton, 43, 47, 48, 49
Vickers, John of Mown Meadows, 210
Vickers, Joseph of Howl John 1790-1885, 2, 210
Vickers, Joseph of Tow Law (1851-1909), 44, 49
Vickers, Joseph of Victoria, Australia, 4
Vickers, Lawrence William of Belle Vue, 45, 48
Vickers, Margaret (Sanderson), 2, 18, 26, 65
Vickers, Mary (née Raine, 1753-1833), 19
Vickers, Mary Annie of Pease Myers, 43
Vickers, Mary née Bowman, 2, 47
Vickers, Sarah née Petty, 43
Vickers, Thomas Herbert of Thornley Hall, 45, 46, 47, 48
Vickers, Thomas of Ontario, 4
Vickers, William of Howl John, 210
Vickers, William of Pease Myers, 43, 52
Wade, George Appleton (Farmer), 174
Wade, Sarah Jane née Wild, 174, 176, 178
Waistell, William of Podge Hole, 175
Walker, Ned (Hay and Straw Dealer), 107
Wall, James of Frosterley, 203
Wandlis, Hannah of Fulwell (Emerson), 18
Wandlis, Sanderson, 18
Water Knott, 237
Watson, Ann (Hunt), 193
Watson, Ann (Sanderson), 19
Watson, Anthony of Ayhope Shield, 198, 199
Watson, Anthony of Castle Hill, 50
Watson, Jane (Hankey), 199, 200
Watson, John of Ayhope Shield, 198, 199
Watson, John Walton of Castle Hill, 50, 51, 52
Watson, Matthew Jnr of Ayhope Shield, 198
Watson, Matthew Snr of Ayhope Shield, 198
Watson, Richard (The Teesdale Bard), 185, 187, 189, 190, 191, 192, 193, 194
Wearmouth, Charlotte Violet, 143
Wearmouth, Florence Esther (Jewitt/Sanderson), 2, 96, 106, 143, 233
Wedding, The Double (1855), 73
Weir, George Ridley of Hamsterley, 137
Weir, Mary, née Adkin (Land-Girl), 137
Wemyss Castle, 204, 206, 207, 208
Wemyss, Frances Harriet, 206
Wemyss, James Erskine of Wemyss Castle, 206, 207
West Shipley, 211
White, Harry of Fotherley, 60, 234
White, Mary Kathleen (Douglas), 61
White, Thomas of Fotherley, 60, 62
White, Thomas of Whittonstall, 60
Whitfield, Fred, 57
Wier, Elizabeth née Watson, 201, 202
Wier, William of Newlandside, 201
Wilburn, Raphe of Hamsterley, 12
Wilkinson, Garthwaite, 176
Wilkinson, Harold of Evenwood, 167
Wilkinson, Joseph of Knavesmire, 78
Wilkinson, Ken, 147, 159
Wilkinson, Margaret (Wilkinson), 78
Wilkinson, Matthew of Knavesmire, 78
Wilkinson, Rev George P, JP (Vicar of Thornley), 169
Williamson, Dr of Witton Park, 170
Wilson, Andrew of Wilson's Forge, 226
Wilson, Jacob of Morpeth, 81
Wilson, Mary (Hankey), 210
Wilson, Rev William of Wolsingham, 199
Witton Park, 233, 242
Wolfe, Charles (Poet), 222
Wolsingham, 89, 90, 91, 92, 93

Wolsingham Grammar School, 92, 128, 219, 222, 223
Wyper, Arthur of Fitches Farm, 242

Frank Sanderson was born in 1946 in Barnard Castle and was brought up in St Helens Auckland. He attended King James 1 Grammar School, Bishop Auckland before graduating as a teacher in the 1960s. After a brief school-teaching career, Frank returned to the University of Leeds to complete a Masters degree, followed by a Doctorate in 1974. In 1975, he and colleagues at Liverpool Polytechnic launched the first single-honours Sports Science degree in Western Europe. He was awarded a professorship in Health Sciences at Liverpool John Moores University in 1992.

A former county squash player, Frank is an experienced skier, an improving golfer and an enthusiastic gardener.

He has been an active family and local history researcher since the 1970s and has now written three books since retiring in 2011.

The first book, *Life and Times in Victorian Weardale: The Letters of Francis Vickers* (2012) has received consistently excellent reviews on Amazon.co.uk and Amazon.com. This book was updated in 2014.
The second book resulted from an eye-opening visit to Cuba in December, 2015 at a time when relations with the US are dramatically changing.

Queries, comments, corrections and additional information would be welcome – contact by email: fhsand35@yahoo.co.uk

27665111R00149

Printed in Great Britain
by Amazon